HOUSE OF COMMONS LIBRARY

D0120465

DISPOSED OF
BY AUTHORITY

DEPORTATION IS FREEDOM!

House of Commons Library

54056000833753

by the same author

Immigration Controls, the Family and the Welfare State
A Handbook of Law, Theory, Politics and Practice for Local Authority,
Voluntary Sector and Welfare State Workers and Legal Advisors
Steve Cohen
ISBN 1 85302 723 5

of related interest

Social Work, Immigration and Asylum
Debates, Dilemmas and Ethical Issues for Social Work and Social Care
Practice
Edited by Debra Hayes and Beth Humphries
Foreword by Steve Cohen
ISBN 1 84310 194 7

Welfare and Culture in Europe
Towards a New Paradigm in Social Policy
Edited by Prue Chamberlayne, Andrew Cooper and Richard Freeman
ISBN 1 85302 700 6

Social Work and Evidence-Based Practice
Edited by David Smith
ISBN 1 84310 156 4
Research Highlights in Social Work 45

Community Care Practice and the Law
Third Edition
Michael Mandelstam
ISBN 1 84310 233 1

Research in Social Care and Social Welfare
Issues and Debates for Practice
Edited by Beth Humphries
ISBN 1 85302 900 9

Counselling and Psychotherapy with Refugees
Dick Blackwell
ISBN1 84310 316 8

DEPORTATION IS FREEDOM!

THE ORWELLIAN WORLD OF IMMIGRATION CONTROLS

Steve Cohen

Jessica Kingsley Publishers
London and Philadelphia

First published in 2006
by Jessica Kingsley Publishers
116 Pentonville Road
London N1 9JB, UK
and
400 Market Street, Suite 400
Philadelphia, PA 19106, USA

www.jkp.com

Copyright © Steve Cohen 2006

All rights reserved. No part of this publication may be reproduced in any material form
(including photocopying or storing it in any medium by electronic means and whether or not
transiently or incidentally to some other use of this publication) without the written
permission of the copyright owner except in accordance with the provisions of the
Copyright, Designs and Patents Act 1988 or under the terms of a licence issued by the
Copyright Licensing Agency Ltd, 90 Tottenham Court Road, London, England W1T 4LP.
Applications for the copyright owner's written permission to reproduce any part of this
publication should be addressed to the publisher.
Warning: The doing of an unauthorised act in relation to a copyright work may result in both
a civil claim for damages and criminal prosecution.

The right of Steve Cohen to be identified as author of this work has been asserted by him in
accordance with the Copyright, Designs and Patents Act 1988.

Library of Congress Cataloging in Publication Data
Cohen, Steve, 1945-
Deportation is freedom! : the Orwellian world of immigration controls / Steve Co-
hen.-- 1st American pbk. ed.
p. cm.
Includes bibliographical references and index.
ISBN-13: 978-1-84310-294-6 (pbk. : alk. paper)
ISBN-10: 1-84310-294-3 (pbk. : alk. paper) 1. Immigration--Government policy. 2.
Immigration--Government policy--Great Britain. 3. Orwell, George, 1903-1950. Nineteen
eighty-four. I. Title.
JV6038.C64 2005
325.1'09'051--dc22

2005015767

British Library Cataloguing in Publication Data
A CIP catalogue record for this book is available from the British Library

ISBN-13: 978 1 84310 294 6
ISBN-10: 1 84310 294 3

Printed and Bound in Great Britain by
Athenaeum Press, Gateshead, Tyne and Wear

This book is lovingly dedicated to the memory of
Maire O'Shea who spent a lifetime defying borders
and boundaries of all kind. I hope Tom, Rachel,
Fintan and Ellen go down the same road.

Thanks are due to Frank Corrigan and the
indispensable website www.asylumpolicy.info for
providing contemporary information.

CONTENTS

CONTENTS

PREFACE
THE IRRATIONALITY OF IMMIGRATION CONTROLS

This is absurd, they really do everything they can to devalue you.

– Algerian refugee seeking asylum in Canada[1]

I agree with your opposition to immigration controls, but it is not practical. It is a good idea, but there are too many people here already. In principle you are right, but there are not enough jobs. It sounds OK, but the welfare system could not cope. It would be fine, but there are not enough houses. I support your idealism, but the country is already overpopulated. What you say might make sense, but how will we preserve British culture? I am on your side, but all other countries have controls. In theory I see eye to eye with you, but how will you stop terrorists getting in? I'm not a racist, but…

The first quotation provides a one-sentence summary of the political and psychological consequences of immigration controls as experienced by someone on the receiving end. The second passage is a concocted monologue by an onlooker of controls. I have repeatedly heard similar monologues expressed in response to the case for the abolition or destruction of immigration controls – that is, the case for a world with no borders. The mantra of the 'but' has achieved near-Zen status.

Positing the complete abolition of controls seems to be one of the last few remaining areas of human discourse that is, intellectually, forbidden territory. It has been caricatured as being so extreme as to rank alongside support for child abuse as a politically unsustainable position. Ironically, the assertion that controls have to be maintained as other countries possess them would appear to place abolition of immigration restrictions alongside unilateral nuclear disarmament as a political project, as if the free movement of people is on some level equated with nuclear military annihilation.

Even on the Left–liberal continuum – the presumed natural constituency of opposition to all controls, there is the culture of the 'but':

> You are correct in principle. I personally agree with you, but you will frighten people away with your extreme views. I appreciate what you are saying, my organisation agrees with you – but it is too premature. As progressive people we all agree with you, but ordinary people are not ready for it.

So keep silent. Or water down your beliefs. Or just confine your criticisms to 'unfair' or 'unreasonable' controls. Or say anything that does not imply the outrage of *no* controls. The view that it is 'premature' to argue for the abolition of controls raises the question as to when exactly it will be correct or opportune to raise such an apparently heretical demand. It raises the question as to when so-called 'ordinary' people will be allowed to possess the ideas of the elite. The reality is that opposition to controls in principle has become the programme that dare not speak its name.

The suppression of debate, the use of language to conceal real meaning and the real political agenda, the constant repetition of the irrational – this is all part of the daily experience of people subject to controls. I have spent nearly thirty years as an immigration lawyer and political activist against controls – (the first identity in my view being inseparable from the second). In opposition to government attempts to define and redefine sections of humanity as illegal, I have been motivated by the slogan 'No One Is Illegal'. This slogan not only challenges the designation 'illegals' as used in immigration control discourse. It also confronts increasing state authoritarianism – such as the proposed introduction of identity cards – in which the government appears to have its own neo-Orwellian slogan of 'Everyone Is Illegal'. During this thirty-year period I have met many resilient and wonderful people and have been sustained by their resistance to detentions, deportation and denial of entry. Throughout this time I have been repeatedly aware of three types of response from those resisting.

First, where cases have been successful and a victory won then I am often told that this has been the result of prayer or divine intervention in some way. I usually challenge this by pointing to the years – exhausting years – we shared together of legal preparation alongside maybe the demonstrations, the pickets and the marches. I didn't see God on any of these.

Second, I have heard screaming, literally screaming out for *fairness* those who were struggling to remain here or to be reunited with family here, as though fairness was a legitimate expectation that was going unmet. My reply has always been, and remains, that immigration controls are intrinsically unfair: racist, unjust and inequitable. They are racist because they emanate from the basest nationalism. They are unjust and inequitable because, however controls are constructed or reconstructed, some applicants will be excluded.

Given the centrality of controls to the British state – which essentially now defines itself in terms of who can come and who can remain – it would probably require a revolution to get rid of them. However, to implement *fair* controls would require a miracle – and God really is absent from the struggle. A central feature of this book is to show that the only equitable controls are no controls. There cannot be equal-opportunity immigration restrictions.

The third type of response I have seen from the resistors brings the irrational nature of immigration restrictions to centre stage. It is a response that exists on the level of political analysis – or rather what initially appears to be a lack of it.

Most people fighting immigration controls don't normally articulate, or spontaneously articulate, any great political or economic analysis of the monster they are confronting. Their spontaneous reaction is simply that the immigration laws are mad, insane, irrational. The refugee at the start of this preface used the word 'absurd'. I used to try to challenge this analysis and this vocabulary by coming out with what I saw (and see) as the full Marxist programme – that is, a materialist explanation of racism based on the development of class society. I used to (and still do) try to show that although immigration controls might be experienced as being utterly bizarre, they served a function and only became universalized in a period of imperialism. They are a product of imperialism. They were an effort literally to control the global movement of labour by the newly industrialized countries just at the point where labour acquired the technical mobility to move around the world in search of work or safety or both.

However, I have learned a lesson from the resistors. My explanation is inadequate because it constitutes only half the story. Or rather, for the story to make sense then there has to be incorporated into it another equally important part of material reality – namely the mad world in which those caught up in immigration controls find themselves. It is a crazy world that can drive its inhabitants crazy, and often does to the point of suicide. It is a weird world where the real meets the surreal. It is a world with no apparent answers, only questions. It is a world where everything is denied by the authorities: refugees are bogus, marriages are ones of convenience, children are not related to their parents as claimed. It is a world not simply *perceived* as mad, it is a world which actually *is* mad in its project of denying the free movement of people. And this is a project which literally encompasses the world.

The main title of the present book – *Deportation is Freedom!* – is intended as an illustration of the profound illogicality of controls. Yet, it will be seen, this is constantly presented as an argument by the Home Office. For instance, the House of Lords has declared detention of alleged terrorists under Part 4 of the Anti-terrorism, Crime and Security Act 2001 to be unlawful, on the grounds that the legislation was confined to non-British citizens. The response to this by the government and its lawyers was to argue that detention could be avoided by agreeing to deportation![2]

There is often confusion between the terms 'refugee' and 'asylum seeker'. In this book the terms are usually used interchangeably, though *refugee* technically denotes a person granted asylum status. The only reason for the technical distinction is a political one – that the British government, like all others, operate a culture of disbelief whereby those fleeing persecution (refugees) have to justify their need for asylum.

The quotation at the start of this preface is the voice of Nacera Kellou, an Algerian asylum-seeker in Canada – a voice that was resisting deportation and which was articulated in a round-table discussion with other asylum-seekers and their allies. The voice of Nacera Kellou is important. The ferocity of controls in this country makes it all too easy, even for those of us who find immigration restrictions problematic, to view them as a purely British phenomenon. Instead, globally there exists a huge apparatus of human resources devoted to this project of control – an apparatus of entry clearance officers constructed to refuse entry clearance, of immigration officers designed to deny immigration status, of welfare workers whose role is to withhold welfare from those without immigration status, all alongside the police, the judges and other state functionaries. The legal framework of immigration controls is ever-expanding, with the demand for more and more controls being insatiable.

Throughout the world there is a huge number of people under the control of immigration regulations. Most of them remain anonymous, unknown to each other and separated not just by border guards but also by oceans and continents. So Nacera Kellou has never met Sikandar Ali, and has probably never heard of him. However, whilst working at Manchester Law Centre, I did meet Sikandar in the early 1980s. He arrived in this country from Bangladesh in 1963 to spend the rest of his working life in the mills of Bradford and Oldham. Eventually his wife and one daughter were allowed to join him, but his eldest daughter Shahida was denied entry. Without a birth certificate – no one in Bangladesh having birth certificates – she was reduced to the status of 'not being genuine'. Sikandar describes this world, his world, in this way:

> The immigration officers won't believe that she is our daughter. I have so much evidence but they won't believe me. They ask all sorts of irrelevant questions, making crazy accusations. They say how come you are 48 and your brother is 23; it is not possible. You are a liar and you are lying about Shahida. We appealed against the decision and in court they told us we were too poor. They said 'Where will you keep your daughter; what will she eat?' That is how kind this government is! As though we parents will push our babies out of door and let them starve.[3]

Sikandar Ali's story was recorded by Amrit Wilson and Sushma Lal in their 1985 pamphlet *But My Cows Aren't Going to England*, the title itself being a reference back to the bizarre nature of the questions asked of applicants wishing to come to the UK in order to undermine their credibility, their truthfulness and their genuineness. How many cows do you have? Where do you keep your string beds?[4] This is the fantastic, unfathomable world of immigration control. It is a world of endless circles and dead-ends, a world which appears to have put its entire energy and deviousness into preventing a young daughter entering the UK. Eventually Shahida's parents ask 'Why? Why? Why?'

Ultimately this is a world where the only hope for sanity is through resistance, though even resistance does not guarantee success. So in Oldham, England, Sikandar Ali and his wife join the Bangladeshi Divided Families Campaign, the purpose of which is to unite families from Bangladesh split by immigration controls. And several thousand miles away and an ocean apart in Quebec, Canada, Nacera Kellou becomes a member of the Action Committee for Non-Status Algerians, which fights collectively for the regularization of the position of Algerians.

Why? Why? Why? These are crucial questions born out of a world turned upside down. They are deserving of proper and political responses. They are also a desperate cry from the heart. They are a desperate cry from those subject to controls whose own world appears to be out of control. The aim of this book is to understand what provokes the desperate cry and to provide an appropriate political response. It is to enrich the objective political analysis of the racism of controls by looking at the subjective feelings of those to whom the world seems irrational. It is to enter, as much as this is possible, into the experience of this irrationality – and to politicize it.

The book will provide a political and historical analysis of immigration restrictions. However, the use of literary metaphor helps develop the focus on controls from simply being an analytical exercise to one where the perceptions of those subject to control – perceptions of a reality that appears dictatorial and crazy – are given proper credence. Literary metaphor is important because it does require a feat of imagination to appreciate the almost unimaginable cruelty of immigration controls. I have thought for a while that perhaps the best way to achieve this aim is not through formal political analysis at all. After all, the politics of this book is opposition to all controls on principle; and I am sceptical, given the huge ideological strength of controls, that many minds can be won over to the principle simply by formal reasoning. I consider that the best way forward is through the creative fictionalization of controls, a fictionalization that will allow for an appropriate exploration of the mad alongside the bad.

Certainly it requires a highly creative mind to best express the mad. In my view it is, in contemporary society, the mind of George Orwell that can most obviously fulfil this task. Why bother fictionalizing immigration controls when the novel *Nineteen Eighty-Four* so well describes the world constructed through controls: a world of totalitarianism, of Big Brother, of the Thought Police, of Newspeak, of memory holes, of perpetual war. Orwell is not the only author to provide symbolic representations of the deep-rooted lunacy of controls. The present study will, in passing, also look at some of the fictional and non-fictional writings of Franz Kafka, Arthur Miller and others as containing metaphors and allegories for, or direct allusions to, the politics of immigration restrictions. But ultimately it is *Nineteen Eighty-Four* that is the metaphor *par excellence* for immigration controls. So why not explore the mad by exploring the metaphor? That is what this book seeks to do.

1. ORWELL, *NINETEEN EIGHTY-FOUR* AND IMMIGRATION CONTROLS

AN OVERVIEW OF LANGUAGE AND POLITICS

> You wake up early in the morning to see other people's fears. You wake up: several people's faces don't exist any more.
>
> *— Ugandan refugee speaking of detention and deportation in the UK*[1]

On 6 December 2004, *The Guardian* contained an interesting article, though one that in the normal course of events would have been forgotten by now. It is an article worth remembering and reflecting on, because it starts to illuminate some of the Orwellian aspects of immigration controls (and in particular some of the hidden analogies with *Nineteen Eighty-Four* that are explored and developed in detail throughout this study).

The *Guardian* article concerned the threatened deportation of Farhat Khan to Pakistan and her militant campaign based in Manchester to stay here. She was a failed asylum-seeker. The central feature of Farhat's story was the revelation that, though the Home Office was intent on removing her, the Queen had invited her to a reception at Buckingham Palace in order to thank her for her socially useful work within migrant communities in Manchester! The article alluded to the fact that Farhat had the support of her local member of parliament, Graham Stringer, who was quoted as saying: 'Twenty years ago a person with Farhat's record of work in the community and with the kind of support that she has in the community would not have been under threat of deportation… humanity and justice have been taken out of the system.'

DOWN THE MEMORY HOLE

Nineteen Eighty-Four is itself a victim of its own philosophy. Central to this philosophy is the idea of the 'memory hole' – that is, the hole in which the past can be altered by the ruling party in order to make it conform to the political needs of the moment. For instance, Orwell writes of the fabrication of the past that 'you could prove nothing. There was never any evidence'[2] – just as the detained Ugandan asylum-seeker in the quotation at the start of this chapter had no evidence of the deportation of fellow detainees. Orwell writes that although the ruling party said that the state of Oceania had never been in alliance with Eurasia, Winston Smith (the book's anti-hero) knew the opposite was the case and that Oceania had been in alliance with Eurasia as short a time as four years ago. The question the book asks is where that knowledge existed. The answer given is: 'Only in his own consciousness'[3] – a consciousness which in any case must soon be obliterated.

Ironically *Nineteen Eighty-Four* has, as a novel, gone down its own memory hole. It enjoyed great popularity in the Cold War period, understandably so as it depicted a world dominated by perpetual conflict between the superpowers of Oceania, Eastasia and Eurasia (as seen from the perspective of Oceania). Today, though various images and phrases from the book are still well known and remain popular currency, their source is often forgotten. Farhat Khan's story helps us remember this source. For instance, politician Graham Stringer's observation that two decades ago there were 'humanity' and 'justice' within controls is itself a rewriting of the past – it is dropping history down the memory hole. Twenty years ago, families from the Indian subcontinent were the main victims of immigration restrictions and were being split up by them. Children were being denied entry to join parents, parents were being denied entry to join children, and husbands and wives were being kept apart. Twenty years ago the Home Office showed its intent by employing one hundred police officers to break into the Church of the Ascension in Manchester and deport Viraj Mendis, who had been given sanctuary there (this was at a time when Graham Stringer was leader of the city council and supported Viraj).

The myth of a 'golden age' of immigration is a dangerous one. It constantly resurfaces under the guise that the UK has historically had a generous and open-door policy towards asylum-seekers. The truth is that this country's first immigration control – the 1905 Aliens Act – was directed at Jewish refugees and (as will be seen in Chapter 9) was re-employed against their descendants in the 1930s.

DOUBLETHINK

The operation of the memory hole, the annihilation of consciousness, in *Nineteen Eighty-Four* is the job of Winston Smith. This falsification of history takes place in the Ministry of Truth. In the novel there is a word, a political construct, central to the rule of the party, which describes the incongruity whereby falsehoods are manufactured in the truth ministry. The construct is *doublethink*. This is described as the ability to 'tell deliberate lies while genuinely believing in them'.[4] The memory hole is itself doublethink as its purpose is not to restore but to destroy memory.

Immigration control and the ideology used to justify controls is premised on its own doublethink. Indeed to describe, as Graham Stringer does, even the possibility of controls being just or humane (or alternatively compassionate or fair) is itself doublethink. Immigration restrictions can never possess these qualities for those who are subject to them – for those denied entry, detained or deported.

Doublethink thrives within the debates over immigration into and within the European Union (EU). The EU is a political construction where, for most purposes, immigration control has ceased to exist and free movement is available for millions of people. Those who regard open borders as utopic live in denial of the reality of the open borders of the EU. This is doublethink. Furthermore it is doublethink within doublethink, because the EU does not mean open borders for everyone – it exists only for nationals of EU countries. For everyone else Europe is a fortress.

Doublethink runs rampant amongst the apologists for control. Examples can be taken at random from the February 2005 Labour government white paper on restrictions – *Controlling Our Borders: Making Migration Work for Britain.*[5] The title is itself quite ominous and Orwellian. What is at stake here is manifestly not the best interests of the migrant but of Britain, a position which presents itself as commonsensical but is in fact politically value-laden.

There are two forewords to this document. One is by the Home Secretary, Charles Clarke, in which he writes in the same paragraph of his intention to 'abolish the right of appeal' against various immigration decisions (for instance the refusal of leave to enter here for work or study purposes) whilst at the same time describing these restrictions as helping 'to improve access to justice'. The other foreword is by Tony Blair, the Prime Minister. He writes of Britain's 'traditional tolerance' towards those coming here, an assertion which itself dumps more of the past down the memory hole and is negated by the entire history of immigration controls. He also claims that this 'tolerance' is 'under threat from those…abusing our hospitality'. This is classic doublethink. Intolerance (racism) is no longer the product of the racists but of their victims who misuse 'our' hospitality simply by their presence here.

PROLES AND ILLEGALS

The *Guardian* article about Farhat Khan contains other analogies to *Nineteen Eighty-Four*. In particular there is the political situation in which Farhat finds herself – namely outside of the rest of civil society and at the mercy of some anonymous authority. This is similar to the position of the 'proles' in Orwell's book. The proles constitute the mass of Oceania's population but are completely disconnected from the rest of society. Likewise all those subject to immigration law exist outside of the state's juridical and welfare systems. Since the 1981 British Nationality Act those subject to controls have in essence been defined as those without British citizenship, a status that the Act was designed to make difficult to acquire. These non-citizens are subject to their own legal systems – immigration controls – and have somehow to survive within their own poor law. In this sense all those subject to controls, whatever their precise status, are 'illegals' (literally 'outlaws').

Just as racism is fundamental to understanding immigration restrictions and the plight of Farhat Khan, so racism is a fundamental feature of life in Oceania. In the novel, proles and 'foreigners' are nominally distinct; in fact the latter are supposed to be the enemy of everyone within Oceania and are the object of organized hate. However, in practice both groups share a common identity of having no material or any stake in society. So we read both that the proles are 'not human beings'[6] and that foreigners are a 'kind of strange animal'[7] who are never seen except as prisoners. With the proliferation of detention and removal centres in modern Britain, an increasing number of those subject to immigration controls (including children) exist only as prisoners. Lack of immigration status and absence of freedom are becoming synonymous.

BIG BROTHER

The immediate enemy with which Farhat Khan finds herself confronted is the Home Office, the government department responsible for immigration. It is emphasized throughout the present book (in particular in Chapter 8) that in fact the machinery of immigration restriction extends well outside the Home Office and that we are all immigration officers now. The role increasingly played by the Home Office is that of coordinating the many other agencies of control. At the same time the Home Office, because of the dominant all-pervasive nature of controls, has assumed a dominant all-pervasive role within government and society as a whole. In this respect it resembles the infamous Big Brother of *Nineteen Eighty-Four.*

Big Brother dominates the party, which exercises totalitarian power over Oceania. In describing Oceanic society, Orwell says that Big Brother is not only infallible and all-powerful but also is 'the guise in which the Party chooses to exhibit itself to the world' and as such his role is to be the 'focusing point for…fear'.[8]

Of course, the Home Office would not normally consciously claim this hyperbolic omnipotence for itself. However, the plethora of immigration legislation, the constant media appearances announcing decreases in the number of entrants and increases in the number of detainees, the fear induced by the immigration service and its acolytes – all this is Big Brother incarnate.

INGSOC AND THE LABOUR PARTY

There is another way in which *Nineteen Eighty-Four* is a metaphor for immigration control and which appears obliquely in the *Guardian* article about Farhat Khan. Farhat would be at risk of deportation as a failed asylum-seeker whichever government was in power, but there is perhaps something doubly depressing in the fact that it is a Labour government that has put her under threat.

There was one moment when Labour adopted a principled position against controls. This was in 1961 when the Tories enacted the Commonwealth Immigrants Act – the first legislation explicitly against the movement of black people. Hugh Gaitskill, the then otherwise right-wing leader of the party, said in parliament:

It has been said that the test of a civilized country is how it treats its Jews. I would extend that and say that the test of a civilized country is how it behaves to all its citizens of a different race, religion and colour.[9]

Gaitskill and his objection to controls were quickly assigned to the memory hole. The Labour government under Harold Wilson was responsible for the notorious Commonwealth Immigrants Act of 1968, which was designed to exclude from the UK East African Asians who had retained UK citizenship.

Labour's championing of controls (which actually predates Gaitskill[10]) relates to a political construct found within Orwell's book which deserves to be better known, namely the ideology of so-called 'Ingsoc' – the Oceanic word for English socialism.[11] It is quite clear that Orwell regarded Oceania alongside the then existing USSR as a perversion of what he saw as the socialist ideal. He writes that the party 'vilifies every principle for which the Socialist movement originally stood'.[12] Furthermore, with classic doublethink, it does this in the name of socialism.

Orwell is in every respect differentiating between democratic socialism from beneath and state control of the individual from above. In using the vocabulary of Ingsoc he is also seeking to make a clear distinction between the politics of the English Labour Party and socialism. This has a relevance for immigration controls. Throughout the whole period when Labour consciously advocated socialism, it always defined the latter simply as the state owning or managing all resources.[13] So support for immigration controls could be justified as just another form of state planning – as the state managing the movement of people. In this way the racism of controls is masked.

At a Leyton by-election meeting in January 1965, Lord Sorenson said: 'We need planned growth of the economy and planned control of immigration'.[14] Similarly, even today the Labour Party has adopted the catch-phrase 'managed migration' to justify immigration controls.[15] This is echoed by George Galloway, formerly a Labour member of parliament until he was expelled, who defines himself as a socialist. Galloway supports immigration controls which, he claimed in a newspaper article, should be based on an 'economic–social–demographic plan for population growth based on a points system and our own needs'.[16] One might ask what is meant by 'our own needs', as controls certainly do not meet the needs of the undocumented. Galloway's apologia for controls could come straight out of the 2005 Labour White Paper *Controlling Our Borders: Making Migration Work for Britain* – in its title, its faith in 'managed migration' and its advocacy of a points system as a method of exclusion. In any event, all the above are clear examples of nationalism and English socialism (or 'statism' as some people call it) – as opposed to the internationalism that supports the free movement of peoples globally.

Ingsoc is a deviation not just within the Labour Party. It extends into the wider reaches of self-professed socialist organisations. Galloway is no longer a member of Labour, and in fact his article appeared in the *Morning Star,* the paper of the Communist Party. However, Galloway has added a new 'socialist' gloss to Ingsoc in his justification of controls. He asserts that 'urging all the most accomplished and determined people to leave the poor countries of the world and come to the richest [makes] the poor countries even poorer and the rich countries richer'. This really is doublethink. Immigration controls are not necessarily about total exclusion. They are, literally, about control – about separating out the *wanted* from the *unwanted.* The situation today is precisely that the 'accomplished' are welcome here (or at least their labour is). The poor, the landless, the disposessed and the persecuted constitute the unwanted. The idea that the unwanted will be helped by being excluded is ludicrous.

A socialist understanding of the fight against poverty necessitates not only free movement but also support for struggles by the dispossessed in their countries of origin – not forced imprisonment in these countries (because they are not allowed elsewhere) to be matched by forced detention in the UK for those who do make it here. Likewise support for those who do make it here requires that they be protected by labour and welfare legislation – as opposed to their present exclusion or partial exclusion from such laws. Global free movement is not a panacea for the elimination of poverty and exploitation. But it is a major step on the road to human liberation and workers' solidarity. The old slogan *Workers of the world unite* does not say or mean *Only workers with the correct immigration status unite.*

NEWSPEAK

There is another analogy between immigration controls and *Nineteen Eighty-Four* which is so fundamental, so central to understanding immigration restrictions and the ideology behind them, that it is developed throughout this book. It is the corruption of language itself as a means of justifying and enforcing immigration laws.

A prime example of this has already been given, namely the reduction of those unwanted here to the status of 'illegals' – that is, of non-beings, of people (in the words of the refugee quoted at the start of this chapter) whose 'faces don't exist any more'. The use of 'just' and 'humane' (as found in the Farhat Khan article) to describe controls historically is another example of such corruption.

In *Nineteen Eighty-Four*, this perversity of language is developed into an entirely new language form known as *Newspeak*. Within Orwell's novel, Newspeak takes several forms, the most significant of which is the 'B vocabulary' consisting of words that have been 'deliberately constructed for political purposes'.[17] It is the construction of such a language and vocabulary, and the consequent destruction of rational thought, that offers a specious ideological support to immigration controls.

MORAL PANIC

The abuse of language in *Nineteen Eighty-Four* and in the operation of immigration controls is insidious, but it is politically explicable. Big Brother exercises ultimate power by castigating and intimidating those he wishes to destroy as 'outlaws' and 'untouchables'[18] and as 'enemies of the state' and, 'foreigners, traitors, saboteurs, thought-criminals'.[19] Likewise, as part of the justification for immigration controls, the Home Office constantly conflates and portrays as synonymous 'illegal immigration, international crime and terrorism'.[20] In this way, all those controlled by Big Brother and all those regulated by immigration controls become undistinguished, indistinguishable foes of the state. They become folk devils.

Farhat Khan, then, is the archetypal folk devil engendering popular panic. As a folk devil she is *the other*, she is *alien*, she is *abnormal*. She is the modern representation of the medieval witch. She is the cannon fodder of media and politician hate propaganda. She shares this with everyone else immigration controls are designed to exclude.

The concept of *moral panic* has entered political discourse through Stanley Cohen's pioneering work *Folk Devils and Moral Panics*.[21] Cohen describes the concept in this way:

> Societies appear to be subject, every now and then, to periods of
> moral panic. A condition, episode, person or group of persons

emerge to become defined as a threat to societal values and interests; its nature is presented in a stylized and stereotypical fashion by the mass media; the moral barricades are manned by editors, bishops, politicians, and other right-thinking people; socially accredited experts pronounce their diagnoses and solutions; ways of coping are evolved or (more often) resorted to; the condition then disappears, submerges or deteriorates and becomes more visible'.[22]

Cohen's book was first published in 1972 as a contribution to radical criminology. It did have, or should have had, a particular relevance to the perception of the alien (particularly the black alien), because its publication followed rapidly on the heels of the Commonwealth Immigrants Acts of 1962 and 1968 and the Immigration Act 1971. These pieces of legislation both defined those subject to controls (black people) and criminalized them through sanctioning deportation without charge or trial. The legislation popularized the construct of alien as *deviant*.

However, it is indicative of how unimportant this racist leap was perceived as, even in otherwise politically progressive circles, that it went unmentioned in Cohen's original book. The issue of controls only appeared in 2002 in the introduction to the third edition. That edition firmly situates asylum-seekers among the moral devils – along with single mothers, paedophiles, drug-takers and welfare cheats. In fact, though Cohen doesn't say so, it is in many ways the accumulative image of these 'deviants' that constructs the popular image of the asylum-seeker, and indeed of everyone else subject to immigration controls.

SIKANDAR ALI AND THE *UNDOCUMENTED*

The implications of Newspeak, of a politically contrived language creating moral panic, within immigration control are enormous. As an introduction to this enormity let us leave the case of Farhat Khan and return to that of Sikandar Ali and his family. We saw in the preface how Sikandar's daughter was refused admission to the UK to join her parents on the grounds she was not related as claimed, that she was not 'genuine' (itself an Orwellian concept).

Sikandar Ali came to this country looking for work. He was fleeing a poverty ultimately created through the devastation of his country by British imperialism. As the Asian Youth Movement used to proclaim: 'We are here because you were there.' In the Orwellian Newspeak of New Labour, he would now be described – or disparaged – as a 'bogus refugee' or a 'bogus migrant' or a 'bogus immigrant' or an 'economic refugee' or an 'economic migrant' or an 'economic immigrant' or as any combination of these. All of this Newspeak suggests that the otherwise acceptable language of 'refugee'[23] (those coming for asylum), 'migrant' (those coming for work) and 'immigrant' (those coming for settlement) has become so politically loaded, so politically devalued, so deviously constructed, so divisive, that it itself needs to be reassessed and replaced where the context requires it by the more politically appropriate *undocumented* – the vocabulary of the French *sans-papiers*.

In particular, the category of 'refugee' or 'asylum-seeker' has today lost its original meaning – those fleeing persecution. It has become a code to categorise all those unwanted here. The use, in the interest of reclaiming truth and accuracy, of the term 'undocumented' is based on another political reality. This is a reality whereby even the existence of immigration documents may lead to a situation of insecurity and precariousness – such as imposing limits and conditions on stay, or on employment, or on access to welfare, or ultimately on freedom from deportation. At the same time these so-called documents can result in a virtual hierarchy, and therefore division, amongst those in receipt of them, with different conditions being imposed on different applicants as a matter of law and of whim. In this political sense all those subject to the reign of controls can be perceived as undocumented as their papers may be without use or merit. To be seen as undocumented whilst formally being possessed of documents is itself classic doublethink.

THE RANGE OF DEMONS

Sikander Ali was not a refugee – and never claimed such status – in the sense of having suffered any immediate political persecution. This is an important point because today both the proponents and opponents of immigration controls tend to reduce the issue to one of asylum-seekers, or of asylum-seekers as disguised workers. Both sides in the political debate either encourage or accept the Newspeak language of 'refugee' to describe anyone wanting to come here. In spite of the numbers of refugees this is not the case. Workers, students, visitors and those coming for family reunion – these remain subject to controls. Refugees are just the latest demons, the latest objects of moral panic. It is a panic which is also both ever-constant (being always present against all those subject to controls) and ever-changing (constantly redefining and increasing those subject to controls).

Supporters of immigration controls themselves face contradictions in implementing immigration policy universally against everyone at the same time. In practice, certain groups have at any one time been given privileged entry, with other groups being selectively denied entry. Before asylum-seekers were denied this entry it was spouses of arranged marriages in Pakistan.[24] Before them it was 'bogus' children from Bangladesh.[25] Before them it was Asian asylum-seekers from East Africa.[26] Before them it was any black worker from the Commonwealth.[27] In the 1930s it was Jewish refugees from Nazi Germany.[28] In the 1920s it was Jewish communists from Russia.[29] In the early 1900s it was Jewish refugees from Russia.[30] In the future new target groups will be chosen or old ones will re-emerge. Thus, the Labour government's white paper *Controlling Our Borders: Making Migration Work for Britain* is envisaging a renewed attack (last seen in the 1970s and 1980s) on those seeking entry for the purposes of family unity. The Executive Summary of this document commits the government to 'end chain migration – no immediate or automatic right for relatives to bring in more relatives'.[31]

Whichever group is excluded at any time, what remains is the fundamental racism of controls, a racism directed against the undocumented of any description. As Orwell writes in *Nineteen Eighty-Four*, in describing the constant shift in alliances between Oceania, Eastasia and Eurasia, the Hate continued as previously, 'except that the target had been changed'.[32]

UNITING THE UNDOCUMENTED

All the time, divide and rule is the name of the game. In *Nineteen Eighty-Four*, the book's anti-hero, Winston Smith, resists the system by keeping a secret diary and making love. After his inevitable arrest he notes that the ordinary criminals ignored the Party prisoners: '"The Polits" they called them with…contempt'.[33]

I've been in many detention centres where the imprisoned refugees sought to distinguish themselves from the imprisoned migrants/immigrants on the grounds that the latter were in the country illegally; and the imprisoned migrants/immigrants sought to distinguish themselves from the imprisoned refugees on the grounds that the latter were in some way political terrorists. The language and categories of the *illegal* and the *political terrorist* are simply more Newspeak for the *unwanted*, and they are here being used by the unwanted themselves. As such it weakens opposition to immigration controls through allowing divide and rule by the Home Office. Obviously (and objectively) what is being denied, but what really exists here, is a communality of political interests between all three groups, migrants, immigrants and refugees. This shared political interest exists quite irrespective of the reason for coming here and consists of opposition to detention, deportation and controls. The use of the word 'undocumented' in defining all the three groups helps politically to stand Newspeak on its head. It describes rather than derides, and unites rather than divides.

We saw in the preface how Stanley Cohen's concept of moral panic helps illuminate the politics of immigration controls. However, even he seems to have become a victim of the moral panic he describes in that he seeks to draw a political distinction between immigrants and refugees. He writes: 'In media, public and political discourse in Britain the distinction between immigrants...and asylum seekers [has] become hopelessly blurred'.[34]

Cohen as a liberal critic of controls is not alone in making or preserving such distinctions. For instance, on 23 February 2005 Refugee Action circulated an email in response to an invitation by the BBC to make an audience participation programme on issues of immigration controls. The email stated: 'Refugee Action has stressed to the researchers that they must make a clear distinction between the issues of asylum, economic migrancy and illegal immigration during the debate.' This insistence on making or preserving such distinctions seems to be based on challenging the moral panic against asylum-seekers. However, all it does is reinforce the moral panic against all *other* entrants. It seems to suggest that 'asylum-seekers' should have unfettered rights of entry but not 'immigrants' or 'migrants', or in other words, *asylum seekers good – immigrants bad*, or even *genuine asylum seekers good – illegal immigrants bad*.

Again, this is why the category of the undocumented or *sans papiers* is preferable as a way of claiming and reclaiming the right of entry for all, irrespective of their reasons for entry. It is a unifying category.

The unifying category of 'undocumented' allows discussion of a reality that has been a matter of taboo on all sides of the polemics around immigration controls – namely that vast numbers of those seeking entry here (mainly from Russia and eastern Europe) are white, whereas much of the discourse on immigration still proceeds on the assumption that those subject to controls are *black.*

This is important as it shows that ultimately racism is a political issue, not one of colour. It reinforces the central political point at issue here – namely, the shared interest in resisting controls owned by anyone who wishes to come here and for whatever reason they wish to come.

The history of immigration controls, which is very much the history of the twentieth century, can be divided into three. The first half was controls against Jews; this extended from the Aliens Act 1905 to the closing of the doors against Jewish refugees fleeing Nazism. The second was controls against black people, commencing legislatively with the Commonwealth Immigrants Act 1962. The third was controls against anyone fleeing war, poverty or mayhem. This can be dated from three pieces of 1990s legislation whose profoundly unimaginative titles themselves reflect an Orwellian use of language: the Asylum and Immigration Appeals Act 1993, the Asylum and Immigration Act 1996 and the Immigration and Asylum Act 1999. These were all subsequently followed by the Nationality, Immigration and Asylum Act 2002 and the Asylum and Immigration (Treatment of Claimants) Act 2004. We are now awaiting the 2005 Immigration, Asylum and Nationality Act. Throughout this history, moral panic has been exhibited politically and equally towards whatever sociological category has been excluded.

The fact that certain categories happen to be white does not diminish or detract from the fundamental racism of controls. No-one would deny that the anti-semitism used to justify Jewish exclusion was a virulent form of racism, and the vast majority of European (but not non-European) Jews are white. However, what ultimately defines the racism of controls is the profound nationalism on which are premised all immigration restrictions – a nationalism which assumes that only certain categories have a right to reside within borders.

BORDERS AND THEIR HISTORICAL CONTEXT

There is an historical specificity to both controls and their development. In particular, as is emphasized throughout the present book, controls are linked to the age of imperialism and the imperialist enterprise.

There is nothing natural about state borders, which are normally the product of war or diplomacy (war by another means). Likewise there is nothing natural about controls; everything is political. For example, in the USA the first restrictions were contained in the self-explanatory Chinese Exclusion Act 1882, and in the UK controls were first generalized in the Aliens Act 1905. Prior to this period national borders undoubtedly had a significance, but it is the shift in this significance that is important for our modern world.

Prior to the age of controls, national borders represented the limits of state sovereignty. Those of whatever citizenship within the borders were subject to the power of the state executive. This is still the case today. However, the difference now is that since the imposition of immigration restrictions, borders, along with all the accoutrements of control, have themselves become a physical block to the free movement of people without the appropriate citizenship status. This has reached the point where there has emerged the vocabulary of the 'fortress', as in Fortress Britain or Fortress Europe, or even Fortress World.

One of the many remarkable aspects of the irrational nature of controls is the way in which advocates of control posit their arguments. This is done in the classic Orwellian manner whereby the same arguments are presented, irrespective of the circumstances, as natural God-given truths. While the historical transformation on the role of borders is obviously very real, it has now existed for over a century. What has every appearance of unreality is that controls are presented by their supporters as being timeless – as having no context, as having existed for ever, and as being literally a-historical. This is clearly seen over the last century where every argument for the further development of controls has simply repeated *ad nauseam* what we are apparently being asked to accept as pre-ordained truths. Recall the propositions articulated at the start of the preface to this book, namely that 'foreigners' are taking 'our' jobs, 'our' housing, 'our' welfare and that essentially 'our country' is overcrowded. These concepts – in particular the 'our' and the 'foreigner' – are not neutral but are value-loaded. They simply assume that only certain people have the right to be here. As such they are fundamentally irrational.

The notion of 'overcrowded' is itself patently irrational. If the country was overcrowded in 1905 then it would have literally sunk without trace by now. But none of this has anything to do with the literal any more than it has to do with the logical. Instead it has everything to do with the metaphorical and the political. The concept of overpopulation is simply a political metaphor for nationalism and racism. It is an attempt to justify giving to some and denying to others the franchise to reside in any particular area of the globe. The very real issues of inequality of resources, of welfare, of production itself, can only be resolved by confronting the causes of this inequality – namely a world-wide exploitative economic system. It certainly cannot be resolved by further victimizing victims of this system.

The dubious, illogical construct of overpopulation – and one concealing a deeper more racist agenda – can perhaps best be exemplified through some early, little-publicized but remarkable American history. Following its independence the USA was hardly definable in terms of excess of population over resources. Indeed that country is today often described as a land of immigrants. In one respect any justification by the USA to impose its own immigration controls is somewhat bizarre given that the country has itself been built on forced, compulsory migration – namely slavery. However, many of the so-called Founding Fathers were even at the early date of independence strong advocates of immigration control.[35] Thomas Jefferson, the drafter of the Declaration of Independence, argued in his *Notes on the State of Virginia* that Virginia could only ever sustain a population of four million and 'the importation of foreigners' should be banned. George Washington, James Maddison and Alexander Hamilton all opposed the development of the newly created USA through immigration. Support for controls at this time was quite anachronistic and had no material basis. However what it did represent was an early attempt to construct a crude national identity. So Jefferson argued that immigration would only create 'a heterogeneous, incoherent, distracted mass'.

Language such as this is evocative of the aim of both Big Brother and modern controls to create what is in essence a homogeneous, coherent, obedient mass. It is language remarkably similar to some of the more overt racism used to justify modern controls. It bears no relationship to any actual reality. It is both doublethink and Newspeak.

2. INTERACTIVE RACISM
HOW IMMIGRATION CONTROLS OPERATE AS A GAMESHOW

> You cannot answer questions they do not put.
>
> — *Zimbabwean refugee*[1]

SURREALITY TV

On 11 July 2003, the BBC issued a press release advertising a forthcoming production for 23 July:

> *You The Judge*, a live interactive programme hosted by Fiona Bruce and Rageh Omaar which asks viewers to put themselves in the shoes of an immigration official and make difficult choices in four asylum cases on which the Home Office has already decided. The *You the Judge* format…opens up the complexities and heart-searching that goes into making judgements on asylum. Viewers can participate through phone, digital television and text and give their opinions on the merits of each case. They will be able to compare their decisions on the cases with those of the Home Office.

Want to be an immigration officer? Or are you aiming higher and aspiring to be an immigration judge? So become interactive! Tune in to the BBC! Make *actual* decisions on *actual* cases! All cases were summarized on a BBC news release of 23 July.[2] All are true accounts. Try Kadriye's case to start with.

Kadriye

Kadriye was one of 13 asylum-seekers who began a journey to Britain in a container. They were Kurds fleeing south-eastern Turkey. Kadriye says that her husband's political opinions, as well as her Kurdish ethnicity, led them to be persecuted by the Turkish authorities on a regular basis. She says her husband was regularly arrested and tortured, and that they were not allowed by Turkish law to speak Kurdish, let alone have Kurdish names or any education in Kurdish. Eventually, she says, they had no choice but to flee because they feared for their lives. They paid $4000 for what they were told would be a four-hour, 2000- kilometre journey. In Zeebrugge, Belgian smugglers put them on board a P&O Ferrymasters freight container loaded with Italian-made office furniture, supposedly for the last two-hour leg of the journey to England. Instead, after 56 hours, the container arrived in Wexford, Ireland. It was stored on shore for another two days before being transported to the IDA Enterprise Park on the outskirts of Wexford. When police opened the container, eight of the asylum-seekers were dead, including boys aged four, nine and twelve and a ten-year-old girl. They died from suffocation and hypothermia. Kadriye survived but her two children and husband died. Her brother Hussein, who lived in London, brought her to England from Ireland.

Have you come to a decision? Are you part of the 37 per cent of the audience who voted in *You The Judge* and said they would grant Kadriye asylum? Or are you part of the 63 per cent who would have refused Kadriye asylum? Maybe you found it too hard? The Home Office did. In real life they refused the formal status of asylum but nonetheless exercised their discretion and allowed Kadriye to remain 'on humanitarian grounds'; in other words, they simultaneously denied and agreed that Kadriye was in danger – a process known in *Nineteen Eighty-Four* as *doublethink*. Don't worry if you can't make your mind up – you still have three other contestants, all asylum-seekers, to decide on.

Clemence

Clemence says he was being persecuted because he was a member of the MDC (Movement for Democratic Change) in Zimbabwe. He says he and his wife were attacked and beaten by a gang of Zanu PF supporters. Clemence was driven to a darkened cellar room in an unknown location, where he says he was badly beaten with an iron bar on his feet and his head dipped in a bucket. He says he was finally dumped in some bushes and when he got home, he discovered his wife had been in hospital because her injuries were so severe. They only had enough money for one person to flee to England, so Clemence came alone. Later, he says, his wife died from her injuries in Zimbabwe.

Clemence arrived in the UK initially as a visitor. He says he was trying to find the right lawyer and arrange to bring his wife to Britain, which was why he did not apply for asylum until six months later. He says he was also deeply affected by the trauma of his experiences in Zimbabwe. There was no physical evidence of torture, but Amnesty International has claimed beating on the soles of the feet does not cause scarring or physical signs. His lawyers argued that there was a failure to consider the effect of trauma on Clemence's behaviour in assessing credibility.

Forty-six per cent of the audience who voted in *You The Judge* said they would grant Clemence asylum. His first application for asylum was refused because he was not found to be credible. On appeal his case was dismissed. Judicial review was refused, and at the time of the BBC broadcast he was awaiting deportation to Zimbabwe.

The Garza family

Watch and decide on the lives of the Garza family. Dusan, of Roma descent, is married to Agata, a white Slovakian. They have three children. They say that racism in the area near Kosice, Slovakia, where they live, means the family has suffered years of persecution, both physical and verbal, mainly from white skinhead gangs around their village. The final straw came, they say, when thugs attacked Dusan and punched Agata, who was seven months pregnant, in the stomach. The next day, Agata gave birth to Vanesa, two months prematurely. Vanesa subsequently developed cerebral palsy. They say they reported the incidents to the police but the authorities did nothing. They did not move elsewhere in Slovakia because, they say, things are the same for Roma all over the country. So the family waited until Vanesa was old enough to travel and fled to Britain, via France. Vanesa receives treatment on the NHS – the family says she is unlikely to get any medical help whatsoever in Slovakia and her condition may deteriorate substantially.

Twenty-five per cent of the audience who voted in *You The Judge* said they would grant the Garzas asylum. The Home Office refused them asylum.

Abdul

Finally, Abdul's life and freedom is in your hands. Abdul's father was a member of the Party of Democratic People of Afghanistan which opposed the mujahideen and later Taleban governments. Abdul says the Taleban knew that his father was working against them. They twice came to his home and arrested one of his brothers and beat some of the other family members. On another occasion, he says, the Taleban attacked the home with grenades and confiscated all their belongings and land. They moved around Afghanistan, from Kabul to Jalalabad and back, to escape the attacks. In 1998, Taleban police came to their house looking for his father, but arrested him because his father was out. They told him he would be held until his father turned up. During a two-week ordeal, he says he was kept nearly continuously awake, not fed properly and beaten. He was freed on bail to celebrate Eid with his family and decided to flee. He borrowed $9500 from an uncle and paid an agent to take him by car, first to Pakistan, then Iran, where he flew to eastern Europe, got in the back of a lorry, finally entered the UK and claimed asylum at a police station in Hull. He says that the new administration in Afghanistan is just as brutal as the Taleban towards supporters of the old regime – particularly Pashtuns like himself.

Twenty-eight per cent of the audience who voted in *You The Judge* said they would grant Abdul asylum. He was initially refused asylum by the Home Office but after appeal was granted refugee status.

BIG BROTHER

You The Judge is not unique in its trivialization of the experiences of those subject to controls of whom refugees are just one group There was an episode of *Night Stand*, the US spoof talkshow, in which would-be citizens performed variety turns in the hope of winning a green (residency) card. One contestant was a Bangladeshi Robert De Niro impersonator. The immediate analogy with *You The Judge* is the omni-present slogan of Orwell's *Nineteen Eighty-Four*, BIG BROTHER IS WATCHING YOU – Big Brother being the omnipotent leader of the omnipotent party of the omnipotent state of Oceania. Today it is the mass television audience that is watching, spying on, judging, deporting the refugee. *Nineteen Eighty-Four* itself begins with the 'telescreen' moni-toring the movements of the book's main protagonist, Winston Smith – a telescreen that can never be switched off. There is no eject button. However, even Orwell did not conceive of totalitarian rule as family entertainment.

Paradoxically the concept of Big Brother has been resurrected in the last few years whilst being ripped from its literary heritage. It has become known and debased internationally as the title of the original 'reality' TV series of which *You The Judge* is hitherto the most extreme successor. Ascribing 'reality' to such a programme can be seen as either the utter fetishization of life itself and/or a classic example of a mode of thought which in *Nineteen Eighty-Four* is described as doublethink – as thinking two opposites simultaneously (in this case actuality and fantasy) – a mode of thought that will be seen as central to the enforcement of immi-gration controls in that it leads to the loss of all critical, reflective facul-ties.

Ironically, a couple of contestants – one in Australia[3] and one in the UK[4] – have tried to use the TV programme *Big Brother* as an opportunity to counter the modern attack on refugees, thereby ensuring their vilifica-tion and eviction from the series.

The purpose of the present study is to encourage people to press the eject button on immigration controls and, in passing, on programmes like *You The Judge*. The fact that such a programme can be shown at all indicates how immigration controls have become a super-dominant feature of social and political life. The very fact that there exists on any level a relationship between, on the one hand, restrictions on the free movement of people and, on the other hand, reality TV and the fictional, highly imaginative Big Brother reveals the depths of controls within civil society.

IMMIGRATION CONTROLS ANCIENT AND MODERN

There is a dispute as to the longevity of immigration controls. According to one authority, himself an immigration officer: 'Tracing the history of immigration control back to the days of the Norman Conquest, one is conscious that a control of some sort was the rule, its absence the exception'.[5] According to others: 'Worldwide restrictions over all movements across national borders are a product of the twentieth century. In earlier periods…states which imposed restrictions on outsiders generally were the exception not the norm'.[6]

This analytical conflict is more apparent than real. Both arguments are correct in their own way. Prior to the twentieth century, prior to imperialism, there were *ad hoc,* occasional, unsystematic examples of controls that were directed for particular purposes against particular individuals or groups rather than everyone at large. Controls became generalized, and the construct of 'foreigner' (and therefore of 'immigrant', 'migrant' and 'refugee') fully developed, as the definition of the state became clearer and the norms of civil society themselves became generalized.

Much early control was extra-statutory and exercised through the royal prerogative. Those on the receiving end of controls were often those perennial victims of the modern law, Jews and black people. Just as in the modern law, control came as a consequence of popular, violent and reactionary movements on the street. One example was the expulsion, following the Hugh of Lincoln blood ritual murder accusation of 1255, of the entire Jewish community by Edward I (the Jews being accused of ritually slaughtering the boy Hugh and drinking his blood). In 1601, Elizabeth I issued a proclamation banishing 'the great numbers of negars and Blackamoores…who are fostered and relieved [fed] here to the great annoyance of her own liege people'.[7] Feudal legislation was used to control the movement of labour from overseas, in much the same way that the movement of peasants and artisans was controlled within the state. Statutes of Richard III and Henry VIII regulated the number of apprentices coming from abroad and forbade masters to employ more than two journeymen or four servants who were not the king's subjects. These enactments followed Jack Cade's rebellion of 1450 (a people's uprising against the policies of Henry VI) which was imbued with popularist anti-alien sentiment and which was itself followed in 1456 and 1457 by riots in London against Venetians, Genoese and Lombards.[8]

The seventeenth century, the emergence of the power of capital and the consolidation of the state, saw the first tentative steps towards a more comprehensive, though still very weak, system of regulation. There were appointed the Commissioners and Clerks of the Passage whose workings figure in the pages of Pepys' diary. The role of these bureaucrats involved not just the examination of embarking passengers but also the licensing of vessels, control of the postal services and general direction of harbour activities. One report to the Commissioners alleged that immigrants were causing a housing shortage ('no tenement is left to an English artificer to inhabit in divers parts of the cytie and suburbs') and were responsible for rent and food price rises ('soe their numbers causeth the enhancing of the price of vittels and houserents') whilst undercutting manufactured commodity prices ('for working of tape, lace, ribbin and such, wherein one man doth more amonge them than 7 Englishe men can does; so as this cheape sale of theire commodoties beggareth all our Englishe artificers of that trade and enricheth them').[9] These accusations and stereotypes simply predate the modern categorization of the 'undocumented' as being a burden on welfare generally and on the state in particular, whilst being antagonistic to the interests of 'native' labour. The assumption that the ruling elite has ever cared about the interests of labour, native or otherwise, will be seen by many as itself a recurring example of doublethink.

The development of the state such that it was able to build up an apparatus for significant controls can be seen in temporary measures enacted during the war between Britain and revolutionary France. As in much relatively recent legislation, such as the Alien Restriction Amendment Act 1919 following the Russian revolution, a fear of subversion and revolution at home prompted the ruling class into drawing down the shutters on those from overseas. From 1793 onwards, Aliens Acts were passed providing for the registration of aliens, for restrictions on their movements within the country, and for their deportation if necessary. This legislation was somewhat more draconian than even that prevailing today – not least because the return of an expelled alien was punishable by death.[10] The Aliens Acts lapsed with the defeat of Napoleon in 1815 (along with his own deportation to St Helena) and the disappearance of any alleged Jacobin danger. For the next ninety years (years of the explosion of capital) there prevailed a laissez-faire regime as much in the movement of people as of goods. As long ago as 1843, a House of Commons committee argued that immigration was highly beneficial – that is highly beneficial to the British economy.[11]

THE JEWS, THE PHARAOHS AND THE ALIENS ACT 1905

Today's immigration controls are neither *ad hoc* nor temporary. They are universal, permanent and all-pervasive. They began in 1905 with the Aliens Act, a measure aimed at excluding asylum-seekers – the demons being Jewish refugees fleeing persecution in eastern Europe and Tsarist Russia. The ideology of free trade and the free movement of people was so strong that it probably required a racism as powerful as anti-semitism to legitimize controls. Demonization of the Irish had not resulted in immigration legislation, even though from the 1860s the Irish in Britain had been caricatured with typical anti-alien imagery as being 'uncivilized', as 'communicating infectious disease', as aspiring only to 'animal existence', and as coming to the UK only to take advantage of welfare provision (i.e. the punitive Poor Laws!).[12] However, the conspiracy theory of anti-semitism was such that Jews were depicted as not simply taking over the country but the entire world, an ideology powerful enough to overcome the prevalent free trade and free movement ideology.

Arnold White, a fanatical and influential campaigner for controls, was one of many propagandists who expressed these views in bizarre ways – but ways that seemed quite rational to the anti-semite. He was a prolific writer as well as an agitator – and is worth rescuing from history, if only temporarily, for this reason alone.[13] In his 1899 book, *The Modern Jew*, he expressed a type of insanity (resembling clinical paranoia) which has in one form or another characterized apologias for Jew hatred, immigration controls, and controls themselves: 'Jewish power baffled the Pharaohs, foiled Nebuchadnezzar, thwarted Rome, defeated feudalism, circumvented the Romanovs, balked the Kaiser and undermined the Third French Republic.'

The 1905 legislation did not mention Jews as such, any more than the post-1945 immigration control legislation mentioned black people as such. Rather it excluded all 'undesirable aliens'. This generalization was another qualitative break with the past. It reflected a change whereby controls were no longer of limited significance emanating from the royal prerogative to determine movement into and out of the realm. Instead controls entered the modern world, the world of imperialism, global markets and international mobility where the state's primary identity is defined in terms of who can enter and who can remain. Advocates of control are often quite clear about this. In a 1983 parliamentary debate over the immigration marriage rules, Harvey Proctor MP said: 'The main battlefield in defence of national identity has been located in the debates over the marriage rules'.[15] John Stokes MP went further and said:

> Control of immigration into this country is absolutely vital for our national identity and cohesion. It is in my view as important socially as the control of inflation is important economically. Indeed, after defending the nation and keeping the Queen's peace, the government's responsibility for control of immigration is of the next importance. It is of no use being mealy-mouthed on this subject. It is not sufficient to say that control of immigration is in the interests of good race relations. It is necessary in the interests of something even more important than that. The control is necessary for our survival as a nation – so that England, which has survived for 1000 years, with its incomparable history and its contribution to civilisation, can remain recognisably and unmistakenly English.[16]

KINDER, KIRCHE, KÜCHE: THE CONSTRUCT OF STATE IDENTITY THROUGH CONTROLS[17]

There are three constant and interlinked ideological themes within the construct of national and state identity through immigration controls. They are those of race, family and church – themes redolent of the Nazi slogan Kinder, Kirche, Küche (children, church, kitchen). They represent, particularly in their interconnections, an unholy trinity of irrationality.

Central to controls is the ideology of eugenics. This is a confused and pseudo-scientific theory of political biology whereby reality, both nationally and internationally, is perceived as a struggle between races and only the fittest races will triumph. All reputable science has contested the construct of genetically defined 'race'. The best known recent work has been that of the biologist Stephen Jay Gould and his book *Mismeasure of Man*, which challenges both race and IQ tests as the determinant of intelligence. Paradoxically the notion of 'race' is itself racist as it substitutes a meaningless biology for class.[18] Within such a substitution certain groups of people are defined as superior to other groups – this being the defining feature of 'racism'. 'Race' and the existence of separate 'races' is a Victorian (that is, imperialist) invention, with its chief ideologues and popularizers being Francis Galton in the UK, Count Arthur Gobineau in France, and subsequently Houston Chamberlain (who acted as Hitler's adviser on the subject) in Germany. Within this spurious view of the world it has been seen as essential to keep the English (or, depending on the politics, the French or the German or the 'Aryan') race pure – free of dilution and pollution through absorption of the blood of other races. Blood itself becomes no longer a matter of anatomy but of a spurious and reactionary politics. As usual in the struggle for the 1905 legislation, this was best expressed by the obsessive Arnold White in his 1901 book *Empire and Efficiency*: 'What can society do to discharge its duty as trustees for posterity, to preserve the vigour of the race and to raise the practicable ideals of Anglo-Saxons?'[19]

White's dangerous answer to the pointless, meaningless question was immigration controls. This was not just rhetorical. Once the 1905 Act came into force then Jewish refugees (and in particular those with disabilities) were regularly refused admission. Their cases were reported in the *Jewish Chronicle*.[20] It is enlightening to remember names hitherto lost to – or rather suppressed by – history. Examples are Gitel Sholk, aged twenty-two, rejected on grounds of being 'dwarfed and deformed',[21] Jacob Liebman, a butcher aged forty-five, rejected as 'suffering from a dilated heart and senility',[22] and Wolf Relasky, aged forty-seven, rejected on grounds of heart disease.[23] According to the civil servant Edward Troup, who was Permanent Under-Secretary of State in the Home Office from 1908 until 1922, the existence of the Aliens Act had an effect in 'stopping the mass immigration of aliens'.[24]

Of course not every supporter of immigration controls possesses a fully worked-out, comprehensive theory of eugenics, though it is doubtful whether they often or ever challenge the theory. Nonetheless the same quack question as that posed by White (as to how to preserve the 'vigour of the race') with the same quack answer as given by White has bedevilled the debates in and around immigration controls from their inception until today.[25] White was by no means alone in promulgating eugenicist theories in campaigning for the Aliens Act. The journalist Robert Sherard in the *Standard* newspaper described Jews as 'filthy, rickety jetsam of humanity, bearing on their faces the evil stigmata of every physical and moral degradation.'[26] H. Lawson MP argued in parliament that: 'The unrestricted flow will be likely to weaken and violate the whole stream of our national life...and it is not likely to be improved by the introduction of new diseases.'[27]

The post-1945 agitation for control on the movement of black Commonwealth citizens similarly stereotyped the latter as both diseased and therefore genetically dangerous. Between 1955 and 1965 the British Medical Association passed yearly resolutions calling for restrictions, on the grounds that immigration weakened the health of 'the nation'.[28] Another writer in 1966 said: 'The reasons why immigrants are prone to venereal diseases are manifold. Some...come from areas where promiscuity is commonplace...and they continue their accustomed way of life after entering another country.'[29]

Eugenics is still being peddled today. It is what inspired in August 2003 the Conservative Party's consultation paper *Before It's Too Late: A New Agenda for Public Health*. Under the headings of 'The British Timebomb' and 'The Threat From Abroad' – headings imbued with moral panic – this calls for the compulsory testing for HIV of those seeking admission into the UK (including asylum-seekers but excluding British citizens).

FAMILY, CHURCH AND THE STATE

The next element in the unholy trinity defining national identity is the construct of the family – or rather the construct of the white, heterosexual, nuclear family and the destruct of the extended family and all other familial and non-familial relationships. Once again, Arnold White was the most articulate and ludicrous exponent of the relationship between family and nation. In *Empire and Efficiency* he wrote:

> The unit of strong nations is the family. All legislation, habits, ideals, policy or ambitions that increase the welfare and multiply the number of happy families are good for the nation. Things

that stunt, belittle or ridicule domestic life are bad for the nation. This is commonplace but bedrock truth. Turkey is what it is, mainly because the harem replaces family life in the upper or wealthier classes.[30]

Once again the 1905 and subsequent legislation transformed this rhetoric into reality, the reality of 'unhappy families'. These are families not conforming to what passes as the norm in this country and which are divided, deported and destroyed through immigration controls. Following the Aliens Act, the *Jewish Chronicle* wrote: 'A girl has been separated from her fiancé. Fathers and mothers have been torn from son, brothers have been torn from brother and child from parents.'[31]

Within our own epoch, starting with the Commonwealth Immigrants Act 1962, the splitting of families through controls has been a virtual leitmotiv. Perhaps the most extraordinary example is contained in the Immigration Act 1988 which prohibited the entry of second or subsequent wives of polygamous marriages, on the grounds stated by Home Secretary, Douglas Hurd: 'Polygamy is not an acceptable social custom in this country.'[32] What is particularly extraordinary about this is that the part of the Act concerning polygamous marriages was contained in ten sub-clauses and was by far the longest part of the whole legislation (which also slashed rights of deportation appeals and further abolished rights of Commonwealth citizens). However, according to Hurd, only 25 polygamous wives were admitted in 1986. In other words there is one clause for every 2.5 wives, so this must amount to a parliamentary record even in immigration law. Why? Why? Why? The answer is purely ideological – the defence and claimed superiority of the nuclear family.

As early as 1866 the English courts decided that polygamy – seen as a construct of Asiatic or Jewish unions – was to be rejected as not constituting 'marriage as it is understood in Christendom'.[33] This leads us to the third element of the unholy trinity making up the ideological triumvirate of the state and immigration controls, an element relatively sublimated but hugely important. This is Christianity and its Church, and in particular in the UK it is Anglicanism and the Church of England. One reason White, in *The Modern Jew*, gave for exclusion of the Jewish refugees reached the core of anti-semitic theory (or, more accurately, anti-theory), namely that Jews are 'the lineal descendants of the murderers of Christ because of the participation of their ancestors in the greatest crime recorded in history'.[34] Elsewhere, in *Empire and Efficiency*, and this time attacking supposed Roman Catholic influence, he wrote:

> This is a matter which deeply concerns the British Empire and every citizen in it both home and abroad, because the English church is part of the English nation, because the rulers of the Anglican church are the rulers of the Empire.[35]

This hyperbole, this equation between church and state, has been repeated politically in our own time. When Viraj Mendis, a communist under threat of deportation to Sri Lanka, was given sanctuary in a church in Manchester in 1987 the reaction to this was a very pronounced Christian fundamentalist anti-communism. *The Star* and its columnist Ray Mills embarked upon a crusade, literally. On 4 April 1987, Mills categorized Viraj as a 'Trotskyist rabble-rouser...a bearded Bolshie...an atheist and a revolutionary communist and therefore an enemy of both Church and State'. On 21 April 1987, Mills described Viraj as 'the anti-Christ in the house of God'. Mill's Christmas column of 22 December 1987 was headed 'Oh, come all ye Lefties – join an unholy travesty' and again attacked Viraj as 'a revolutionary communist and an atheist'. *The Star* itself carried an editorial on 9 May 1988 condemning everyone who sought sanctuary against deportation, stating: 'How utterly appalling. It is not as if these wretches are Christians; they despise our faith and are fighting holy wars to destroy us.'

CONTROLS EXPERIENCED AS MAD AND MADDENING

It is doubtful whether many or any caught up in the tentacles of immigration controls instinctively and as a first response make any of the above political analysis. Rather more understandable is the response of Sikandar Ali: 'Why? Why? Why?' And this is typical. So an asylum-seeker in detention writes to his doctor: 'I am not feeling well at all. Why am I in prison? Did I commit a crime or hurt somebody? At home in my country I was tortured. I lost a lung and immigration still do not believe me. Why do they mix up the words I said to them?'[36] Detention appears quite random, arbitrary and unpredictable, so many people even give up asking 'Why?'. One detainee simply says 'And if you try to understand you cannot'.[37] Another, questioning how someone can be imprisoned without being charged with any offence, asks: 'When are we going to be sentenced? It's a question without an answer.'[38]

Why? Why? Why? This is also the (apparently) unanswerable question of Winston Smith in *Nineteen Eighty-Four*, whose first act of private rebellion again totalitarianism is to write in his secret diary 'I understand *how*. I do not understand *why*.'[39] The truth is that Winston never even understands *how*, otherwise he would know that Big Brother is already spying on the diary and he would know that individual protest in insufficient He would know that the personal only becomes authentically political when it is collective. As in *Nineteen Eighty-Four*, those destined not to understand *why* can be literally driven mad by immigration controls. This is Winston's fear – fear of being a lunatic because 'Perhaps a lunatic is simply a minority of one.'[40]

Going mad is also the fear of those subject to controls. One of the asylum-seekers already quoted above writes to his doctor: 'I am a man with little time left to live and I am still suffering. If they want the lung I have left I will give it them. ... Immigration think prison is the place to cure me! They have made me crazy. If immigration want to put me in a rubbish bin and throw me in the sea, do it then, I will sign for it.'[41]

The emphasis on signing documents or submitting documents or withdrawing documents is indicative of a system that is itself literally maddening. It is a system where the 'undocumented', those literally without documents or possessing inadequate documents, are reduced to nothingness. This is the fate not just of the immigration *sans-papiers*. It is the destiny of all the 'unwanted' living on the fringes of society. In one piece of 1960s literature, the play *The Caretaker* by Harold Pinter, the search for official papers has become the defining feature of the tramp, the vagrant, the hobo. So Davies, the drifter, who in this divide-and-rule world in which we live is also a racist (condemning the use of the same toilets by black and white people) says that papers proved his existence. In fact they were his existence. They defined who he was. Without them he was unable to move. He was non-existent.[42]

And here is further testimony to the maddening quality of documentation within immigration enforcement, from *The Observer* on 9 August 1987:

> 'D' sought sanctuary in Britain from East Africa where, amongst other tortures, his testicles were crushed. His application for asylum was refused and he tried, with the help of the humanitarian

organization Rights and Justice, to appeal. As time went on, increasing his fears that he would be sent back, he tried to burn himself to death. Then, while receiving psychiatric treatment, he killed himself by jumping from a high window. Rights and Justice closed their file on this case but the Home Office did not. More than a month later it sent a form asking for the dead man's asylum application to be formally withdrawn.

THE LOGIC OF THE ILLOGICAL

Immigration controls are literally a danger to health. They are capable of causing derangement and craziness. It requires huge personal strength for the victim (because those subject to control are such) to perceive that it is not she or he who is crazy but rather the system of controls. In *Nineteen Eighty-Four*, Winston Smith – when eventually interrogated by O'Brien, the party apparatchik and agent provocateur who had initially tricked him into subversion or at least its possibility – is told: 'Your mind appeals to me. It resembles my own mind except that you happen to be insane.'[43] However, it is not Winston Smith, the rebel, who is mad; rather it is the whole system of party rule.

An appropriate entry into the understanding of controls is through the 'anti-psychiatry' movement best known from the works of the psychiatrists R. D. Laing and Thomas Szasz. In his essay *The Moral Physician*, Szasz equated 'immigration authorities and drug-control agencies, prisons and mental hospitals.'[44] In his book, the tellingly entitled *The Manufacture of Madness*, he shows how as recently as 1967 the American judicial system categorized gay men as 'psychopathic' in order to deport them.[45] Laing, in *The Politics of Experience*, saw madness not in the patient but 'in a world gone mad'.[46] It is in *The Politics of Experience* that Laing wrote generally of the existential human condition – 'we are bemused and crazed creatures'[47] – but also specifically that 'Orwell's time is already with us.'[48]

Both the advocates of immigration control and the rulers of Orwell's Oceania justify themselves in slogans and arguments that make sense only within their own distorted logic. Ultimately these slogans and arguments are based on a supreme irrationality which at the same time presents itself as common-sensical. This is the maddening feature of both immigration controls and totalitarianism. In *Nineteen Eighty-Four* it is seen in the brilliantly insane party dogma WAR IS PEACE:

FREEDOM IS SLAVERY: IGNORANCE IS STRENGTH. The party rules through its own inner illogicality. So, when Winston is arrested he asks his interrogator O'Brien whether Big Brother 'exists in the same way as I exist'. He is given the response 'You do not exist'.[49]

In an analogous way, those deemed by the authorities to be in this country without authority ('illegals') are relegated to being outside the law, without status, devoid of existence. They are, literally, the modern outlaw. In the words of *Nineteen Eighty-Four*, they are 'vaporized' – made non-persons and written out of history. Just as the Home Office destroys all memory of the individual by deporting her or him, so in Orwell's novel we read of the woman whose role in the Ministry of Truth was that of erasing from the press the names of people who had been 'vaporized and are therefore considered never to have existed'.[50]

EXAMPLES OF THE ILLOGICAL

Irrationality, the denial of what is real, is a constant feature of controls. It becomes a weapon in immigration control enforcement by breaking down the spirit and the reasoning processes of those subject to it. In this way, human beings become dehumanized. And the weapon of irrationality is not simply and constantly searching new targets, though the old targets never truly disappear; it is also concocting new, spurious and illogical ways to justify these targets. Here are some random examples from the realm of sexuality – examples that will be seen later to be properly described in *Nineteen Eighty-Four* as doublethink.

In the 1980s it was the partners of arranged marriages from, in particular, the Indian subcontinent who wished to come and live in the UK and who were under attack. These partners were confronted by the 'primary-purpose rule' and its requirement on them to show a negative – having to *disprove* that the reason for the marriage was to live in the UK. Imagine yourself in that position (it would perhaps make a good TV games show). The primary-purpose rule was withdrawn after much agitation, but it often re-emerges through the obligation in the immigration rules on couples to prove that they intend to live with each other.

More recently the attack has come against lesbians and gay men seeking asylum on the grounds that they suffer persecution in their country of origin on account of their sexuality.

It is worth pondering on the much broader political question as to why the device of asylum has to be resorted to in order to attempt entry because of sexual orientation. Why should there not be free admission for all, irrespective of the orientation of any? In any event, the courts and the Home Office have here displayed doublethink of classic proportions.

Ioan Vraciu from Rumania was rejected for asylum by the Immigration Appeal Tribunal on the grounds that he couldn't prove he was gay, as he 'does not belong to any homosexual group or club'.[51] In a more recent case, that of Sorin Dumitru, also from Rumania, the tribunal refused asylum on the grounds that sexuality can be kept a secret and there is no need for it to express itself in 'overt and public expression'.[52] The ultimate, crazy, logic of all this is to deny asylum and suggest celibacy! This was the response met by Zia Mehmet Binbasi from the Turkish Republic of Northern Cyprus, when the High Court said that 'the risk of prosecution would be avoided by self-restraint'.[53] All this is reminiscent of – and fits within the logic of – the Junior Anti-Sex League of *Nineteen Eighty-Four* – control of the person through control of their sexuality. Orwell (whose sexual politics were limited to heterosexuality) wrote that the aim of the party was not merely to prevent men and women from forming loyalties that it might not be able to control; rather, 'It's real, undeclared, purpose was to remove all pleasure from the sexual act.'[54]

Another example of this sexual control within immigration controls is so-called 'virginity testing', the warped logic of which decrees that an Asian woman who is not a virgin cannot be entering into a genuine arranged marriage.[55] Agitation has ensured that this has now ceased, yet it is a clear indicator of irrationality posing as political and judicial argument.

In the world of *Nineteen Eighty-Four*, this nonsensical but all-embracing, all-maddening thought pattern is known as 'reality control'.[56] In the world of immigration controls it is everywhere. It is not just confined to sexuality. It is universally maddening. It reached one of its many non-sexual climaxes in the judicial (mis)treatment of Mohammed Zamir.[57] He was declared to be here illegally for failing to declare something he was never asked about and was never given the opportunity to declare, namely that he had married in Pakistan after being given entry clearance to join his parents here. The House of Lords held there existed a 'duty of candour' to reveal all 'material facts', even though no official had said they were material. This effectively transformed the watchword of the immigration service into 'Anything you *don't* say may be taken down and used in evidence against you.' As the asylum-seeker quoted at the start of this chapter so logically declares, you can't answer questions they don't put to you.

The main title of this book — *Deportation Is Freedom!* — is as illogical as any slogan found in *Nineteen Eighty-Four*. However, as already illustrated in the preface, this title is not just a fictional allusion. Rather it is a recurring apologia for immigration controls and a surreal justification for immigration detentions. It portrays the Home Office acting like a Mafia godfather, making offers that detainees cannot refuse. So, Mohammed Ashraf Mughal, a Pakistani citizen, was denied an order of habeas corpus against his wrongful detention on the grounds that he could always agree to be removed to Pakistan and therefore escape the detention.[58] Such are the *doublethink* non-choices given to the undocumented.

UNFAIRNESS: METAPHOR AND REALITY

Confronted by absurdities and destroyed by laws it is no wonder that the instinctive reaction of the victims is to scream out for fairness. This scream is ever present in the testimonies of those confronted by controls.[59] However, the ultimate Orwellian trap of immigration controls is that *there can be no fairness*, because if there were fairness there would be no immigration controls! In whatever way controls may be reconfigured, in whatever way they may be administered, they are inherently unfair, unjust and racist.

It is not surprising that Orwell, in writing *Nineteen Eighty-Four*, at no point contemplated the birth of a 'reformist' movement within Oceania dedicated to retaining the totalitarianism of Big Brother rule but without some of the more blatant authoritarian trappings. Oceania is intrinsically unreformable, intrinsically unfair. It is illuminating to summarize here other points of comparison between the dictatorship of Oceania and the authoritarianism of immigration controls to see how neither is capable of being anything except unfair to those subject to their power.

Central to both is racism. Immigration controls are based on one fundamental racist assumption — that certain people have a franchise on certain territory. So the British assume they have a franchise on Britain, and can control everyone else's movements in and out. This is generalization of the rights of private property on a grand scale. In this context I prefer the aphorism of Pierre Joseph Proudhon, the nineteenth century French anarchist: 'Property is theft'. Of course, in order to justify this national franchise — this national theft — all those who are not of the appropriate nationality or origins are depicted in the most gross, obnoxious and stereotypical ways: they become aliens, they are dehumanised and they become disposable. So it is in Oceania, where there exists 'a continuous frenzy of hatred of foreign enemies'.[60] The latter, when captured, are reduced to the status of 'coloured slaves'.[61] Anti-semitism lurks below or on the surface. Goldstein, the projected enemy of the people, has a conspicuous Jewish appearance as well as name.[62] At the start of *Nineteen Eighty-Four* we see a cinema audience applauding and shouting with laughter at a ship full of refugees bombed somewhere in the Mediterranean – being particularly amused at the sight of a middle-aged woman 'who might have been a Jewess sitting up in the bow with a little boy about three years old in her arms'.[63]

This scene resembles actual events in the Mediterranean in June 2003. Two ships packed with refugees on their way to Italy capsized, resulting in the deaths of an estimated 250 people. The response of the Italian government to this tragedy was to further vilify refugees. Umberto Bossi, chairman of the separatist Northern League Party and a minister in the Berlusconi government, demanded that the Italian navy and coastguard be allowed to open fire on refugee boats. In an interview with the Italian newspaper *Corriere della Sera* in mid-June, he declared: 'I've had enough of these illegal immigrants. After two or three warnings – boom! – let them have it! Forget the palaver.'[64] British racists evoke the same image – a text message to the *Daily Star* from one of its readers suggested: 'Why don't we put all asylum seekers in a boat and bomb it 4 target practice?'[65]

Central to racism is the hyperbolic and brutalizing characterization of *the other*. The alien is reduced to anonymity, to a comic-strip creature. Like the lyrics in the Paul Simon song, the *others* end up a cartoon in a cartoon graveyard,[66] and it is therefore not surprising that some of the worst media examples of racism occur in cartoon form. Unfortunately not unusual was the *Daily Mail* slur on the 58 Chinese refugees found dead in a lorry in Dover amid boxes of tomatoes. The paper ran a cartoon showing a lorry with faces peering out the back surrounded by fruit; the punchline was one refugee saying, 'I hear Mo Mowlam has asked the Queen to move out of Buckingham Palace for us.'[67] Mowlam at the time was a government minister who bravely and publicly had declared herself as suffering from cancer. It is startling to consider who might be amused or laugh at this stuff. In *Nineteen Eighty-Four*, too, racism is projected through the brutalization of image and appearance, through depicting *the other* as a cipher, as a cartoon. On the all-intrusive telescreen there marches the endless columns of the enemy Eurasian army – 'row after row of solid-looking men with expressionless Asiatic faces'.[68]

WAR

In *Nineteen Eighty-Four*, the three superstates of Oceania, Eurasia and Eastasia are perpetually at war.[69] Perpetual war also seems to be the defining feature of the twenty-first century. This is war against state rivals. It is also war against alleged terrorists. Alongside this is constant war against the undocumented. Indeed, all (states, terrorists, the undocumented) are intimately linked, as global military conflict inevitably results in the massive displacement and movement of civilians.

Warfare has always been a central image within immigration controls. As early as 1919, a *Jewish Chronicle* editorial described new immigration legislation as a 'war on aliens'[70] – an understandable description given that, under a subsequent Order, all Jewish aliens were obliged to carry identity cards, to notify the authorities if they were absent from their home for two weeks, to keep out of designated 'protected areas', and to fill in a special register if they stayed overnight at a hotel.[71] Conversely (and re-entering the world of *doublethink*), the alien is allegedly at war against the state, with the vocabulary of 'battle', 'invasion' and 'state security' being constantly used to justify the tightening of controls. Thus in the USA the senior lawyer of the Immigration and Nationality Service has said: 'This is a war. The war is to…open our borders to anybody that wants to come in and to have a world-wide equalization of wealth and property.'[72]

Inevitably, rhetoric turns to reality. A war against those subject to immigration controls ultimately requires militarization of borders. In the UK, the Home Affairs Committee of the House of Commons has recommended a frontier force be established at the ports to police all entrants.[73] However, 'frontiers' are given a wide and elastic definition. As in *Nineteen Eighty-Four*, as in Italy in 2003, the Mediterranean is viewed by British politicians as a prime theatre of war against refugees. A newspaper report has claimed:

> Tony Blair has taken personal control of asylum policy and is considering proposals to mobilise Royal Navy warships to intercept people traffickers in the Mediterranean and carry out bulk deportations in RAF transport planes.[74]

Allegations have been made that a joint British–Spanish initiative ('Operation Ulysses') resulted in twenty-one migrants drowning while trying to cross from the North African coast to the Canary Islands in two separate incidents in June 2003. Their boats capsized after being intercepted by Spanish patrols backed up by RAF Nimrod planes.[75]

THE UNFAIREST ROOM OF ALL

The very idea of 'fair' immigration controls is an Orwellian contradiction of *doublethink* proportions. The transformation of controls into their opposite – that is, from the racist to the non-racist – is an aspiration worthy of the medieval alchemists who believed they could construct gold out of base metals. Controls are by their very nature authoritarian; they never begin from the interests of those subject to them but instead seek to assert power and authority over them.

In his introduction to the latest Labour government white paper on immigration (the tellingly entitled *Controlling Our Borders: Making Migration Work for Britain*), the Prime Minister, Tony Blair, says: 'Those who want to settle permanently in the UK will have to show they bring long-term benefits to our country' – everyone else will be forcibly denied entry or removed. Power in its most concentrated form appears in *Nineteen Eighty-Four* in Room 101. When Winston Smith is caught and imprisoned, his interrogator O'Brien tells him that everyone knows what is in the room without asking or being told, because 'The thing that is in Room 101 is the worst thing in the world.'[76] It is a metaphor for the biggest horror an individual can contemplate being inflicted on her or him.

Once again, television has trivialized and diminished both politics and reality by making a comedy programme called *Room 101*. However, for Winston, living in an Orwellian fictional world that is more real than the television representation, the worst thing in the world is to have a rat attack him by the throat from the inside of his mouth – to have a rat cage wired to his face with the cage door about to open. Today, arguably the worst thing in the world politically and personally is to be powerless and subject to immigration controls, because that is when everything appears to be out of control. There is no need to speculate where the Room 101 of immigration controls is located. It is everywhere. It is every room in which authority and power are exercised.

Room 101 is every room in every British Embassy or High Commission where people from the colonial and neo-colonial heartlands, and from the scattered state remnants of the former Soviet Union and its satellites, are interrogated about their motives for wanting to come to the UK – in much the same way that Winston was interregotated, with his tormentors 'convicting him at every step of lies and self-contradiction.'[77]

Room 101 is, for example, the British High Commission in Dacca, Bangladesh, where entry clearance officers pursue and invent self-contradictions (or 'discrepancies' as they also call them) in order to deny the entry of wives and children into the UK – through the simple expedient of denying that they are in fact 'genuine' wives or children. Discovery of the 'discrepancy' is the entry clearance officer's pot of gold. It is her or his *Eureka!* moment. To quote from one of the entry clearance officers' files:

> Ask the sponsor if he can explain the gap in his child fathering between [first child] and [second child]. It was during this period that he first went to the UK, but he made a visit back to Bangladesh from 28 October 1966 to 22 July 1967, yet no children were born as a result of that visit.[78]

Bangladeshis therefore have the burden of proving not just a double but a triple negative – not only the children who *were* born to them but also the children who were *not* born to them.

Room 101 is every hearing room where immigration appeals are conducted. These appeals – which are essentially exercises in further humiliation – have been well described in the following manner:

> It is at the final stage of the appeal (the adjudication) that the true nature of the immigration process is fully revealed. Like the inquisitions of the witchmania in the 17th century, where the accused would have to prove that they were not in league with the devil, and where the Inquisitor's pronouncements defined once and for all the accused person's morality and their right to live. So in the adjudications or the immigration trials, the sponsor and appellants are accused persons...[79]

However, Room 101 appeals have a unique feature missing from the witch trials: the accused is often a distance of several thousands of miles away. They are trials *in absentia.* Nevertheless, whether or not the accused is present, his or her entire being (or morality) is placed under attack.

Nasreen Achtar came from Pakistan after undertaking a proxy marriage by telephone. She left the relationship after domestic violence. The Home Office claimed that the marriage was invalid and tried to deport her. The adjudicator (immigration judge) said in support of the Home Office:

> She could not possibly have considered herself married as she let her husband beat her up and throw her out while pregnant... having discovered (not surprisingly) that the alliance was a disaster she is resolved to live here on social security...she has brought her troubles upon herself.[80]

Successive governments (including the present one) have systematically curtailed appeal rights, so now, for example, there cannot be an appeal against deportation.[81] It is indicative of the Orwellian world of immigration controls that this curtailment is arguably beneficial to the extent that it prevents further humiliation – except that preserving appeal opportunities does offer a further forum for struggle; Nasreen Akhtar won her case at a further appeal alongside an anti-deportation campaign. What really need to be curtailed, to be dismantled, are immigration controls themselves.

Room 101 is also Dungavel Removal Centre in Scotland, notorious for the detention (after fleeing Turkey) of the four children of the Ay family for over a year before they were deported.[82] Room 101 is also Hairmyres Hospital, where Reza Garikani (detained at Dungavel until taken ill) remained chained to a bed for the duration of the treatment.[83]

Today, and since the late 1990s, perhaps the worst Room 101 in the world is the port town of Dover, a town where no sans-papiers is safe. This is a town without pity (though what the undocumented really need is solidarity, not pity). The local paper, The Dover Express, has assumed a political role against asylum-seekers. In one editorial headed 'We want to wash dross down drain', it stated:

> Illegal immigrants, asylum seekers (when they get asylum are they happy?), bootleggers (who take many guises) and the scum of the earth drug smugglers, have targeted our beloved coastline. We are left with the backdraft of a nation's human sewage and no cash to wash it down the drain.[84]

The hackneyed rhetoric here is redolent of similar provocative (if trite) imagery used a century earlier against Jewish entrants to justify the

Aliens Act: 'This is England. It is not the backyard of Europe. It is not the dustbin of Austria and Russia.'[85]

A public meeting was called in Dover in opposition to immigration. This resulted in a pamphlet, *Dover the Land of Plenty*, which listed 33 reasons why 'we should send them back and close the door'. Reason 13 was 'Pregnant refugee mothers only want brand new equipment for their offspring.'[86]

Protection of Dover against the refugee invaders has now become a national *cause célèbre*. The *Daily Mail* published the address of an asylum-seeking family it described as 'bogus', and their house was subsequently attacked and trashed.[87] The *Daily Telegraph* presented itself as the saviour of Dover in an article 'Strife in the Garden of England'.[88] As one writer has commented:

> The White Cliffs, the Battle of Britain and Churchill's speeches about 'fighting them on the beaches' were all evoked in such a way that Dover again came to be seen as a symbol of national resolve in the face of adversity.[89]

This really is bringing home the war against the perceived alien. Forget the bluebirds of Vera Lynne's famous Second World War song evoking the welcome image of the white cliffs of Dover. Today the lyrics should read 'There'll be *Blackshirts* over the white cliffs of Dover'. However, whatever the lyrics, it is obvious that Room 101 cannot be reformed, cannot be made fair. Like the rule of Big Brother in *Nineteen Eighty-Four*, it has to be abolished in its entirety. The issue is how to accomplish this and avoid the fate of Winston Smith – the fate of defeat and destruction.

3. NEWSPEAK, NEW LABOUR AND OLD RACISM

HOW IMMIGRATION CONTROLS CORRUPT LANGUAGE

I rise to oppose the Migration Amendment (Duration of Detention) Bill 2003…This is another in a long line of Orwellian-titled bills. The government are becoming proficient in the use of the Newspeak language created by George Orwell in his novel *Nineteen Eighty-Four*. They have certainly done their homework. If they are using Newspeak to title this bill, then I will use Newspeak to oppose it. This bill is 'doubleplusungood'. Any average Australian citizen reading the title of this bill and not knowing the nature of the Newspeak government we have, would assume the bill – which is called 'duration of detention' – has something to do with limiting the amount of time someone could spend in detention. This is not the case, of course; Newspeak does not work like that…When the government failed a number of times to get its unfair dismissal legislation through the parliament, it went away, learned all about Newspeak and reintroduced the exact same bill under the title 'fair dismissal bill'…What this bill should be titled, and would be if the government used oldspeak, is 'indefinite duration of detention', because what this bill does is to take away the right of the courts of our nation to release a detainee.

– Australian politician[1]

'BEAUTIFUL THING – THE DESTRUCTION OF WORDS'[2]

The attack on language, and therefore on proper human discourse, is as central to *Nineteen Eighty-Four* as it is to the politics of immigration control. In *Nineteen Eighty-Four*, the instrument of this attack is Newspeak, the bastardized language invented by the party as a vehicle for its own omnipotent rule. One of the workers formulating Newspeak is Syme, who applauds the annihilation of words and describes the new linguistics to Winston, telling him that the whole aim of Newspeak is to 'narrow the range of thought.'[3]

The vocabulary used within immigration control processes is Newspeak as a political method, a method of mind management, a method of thought control. Just as interesting – and frightening – is the fact that the precise examples Orwell gives of Newspeak in *Nineteen Eighty-Four* find a resounding echo within immigration controls. A central example is *unperson* – someone who is deemed by the party to be non-existent, to be purged, to have his or her memory totally eradicated – as in 'Withers, however, was already an *unperson*...he had never existed'.[4] There is an exact equivalent to 'unperson' within immigration control – a person who is *an illegal*. Within all other areas of the law it is the deed that is illegal, but within immigration law it is the person. Immigration law transforms the adjective into the noun and in doing so dehumanizes the individual.

Here are just a few headlines from the *Sun* newspaper: 'Six men on bikes guard us against illegals'; 'Illegals jump NHS queue'; 'Bungle on seven illegals (astonished cops were told to let a bunch of illegal Middle East immigrants go free, because asylum officials were too busy to deal with them)'.[5] The press is here only following the politicians; another paper carries a headline 'Get tough on illegals – Blunkett'.[6]

This constant dehumanizing Newspeak of immigration controls is global. The *Washington Times*, reporting on the deaths of eleven Mexicans who perished trying to enter the USA, described them as 'dead illegals'.[7] The undocumented can thus become double unpersons, by retaining the status of 'illegal' even when actually dead: they thus become posthumous outlaws.

Within immigration controls the lack of status of the 'illegals' is somehow projected as God-given, like the biblical mark of Cain. This is fetishization of law. Illegality is a political construct. It did not descend from heaven (or hell) as some fully formed judicial concept. Yesterday's lawful entrant can become tomorrow's unperson, just like Withers in *Nineteen Eighty-Four* who, whilst still living, was politically eradicated, transformed from being into nothingness. In *Nineteen Eighty-Four* there is a Newspeak word to describe the mechanism of transformation from person to unperson – *vaporization*. People disappeared, always during the night, and their one-time existence was denied and then forgotten. They were 'abolished, annihilated: vaporized'.[8]

Vaporization is what happens either metaphorically (through being classed as an illegal) or actually (through being deported) to those deemed unwanted by the immigration authorities. To be 'an illegal' is to be hidden from reality and then, once deported, to be hidden from history. All this is reminiscent of the eternal warning given by Angela Davis, the American black activist: 'If they come for me in the morning, they will come for you at night.'

It seems quite appropriate in the debate over the repressive Asylum and Immigration (Treatment of Claimants) Act 2004 that David Blunkett, then Home Secretary and Chief Lexicographer, should introduce into the Newspeak dictionary a new non-word to rival 'illegal' but with the same political connotation. This is the demon *clandestines*,[9] a noun transmuted from an adjective that could be straight out of literary science fiction:

> Clandestine: [mock definition] – hidden or secret alien from the planet Clan on a mission to enter Dover disguised as a refugee.

Blunkett stated 'We have separately managed each month to stop 3000 clandestines getting into the country.' This metamorphosis of an adjective into a noun is itself classic Newspeak, the vocabulary of which was ever-decreasing and the grammar of which encouraged complete inter-changeability between different parts of speech such that any word in the language 'could be used as either verb, noun, adjective or adverb'.[10] Blunkett and New Labour are here using the Newspeak of George Orwell to make new law.

THE CRIMES OF THE INNOCENT

Orwell was no biblical prophet. His precise vision of a future world as portrayed imaginatively in *Nineteen Eighty-Four* did not materialize. Nonetheless, much Orwellian and Newspeak vocabulary has entered into popular culture, including music culture. Radiohead have recorded $2 + 2 = 5$ (the insane mathematics O'Brien forces Winston to accept[11]), and the Eurythmics originally recorded the entire soundtrack to the movie *1984* with tracks such as *For the Love of Big Brother* and *Doubleplusgood*.[12] Moreover, many of the bizarre 'crimes' formulated by

Big Brother and expressed in classic Newspeak find a resonance in the modern state, and particularly within immigration controls.

One example is *facecrime*, defined as wearing 'an improper expression on your face'.[13] This has a high-tech echo in the biometric identity-card/passport that the government is intending to introduce and which, according to a Home Office press release, 'can include facial recognition'.[14] However, of all such Newspeak misdemeanors it is *thoughtcrime* that most defies judicial logic (or any logic). How can thoughts be detected, let alone penalized? Nonetheless, Winston was aware when writing his secret diary denouncing Big Brother that whether he went on with the diary, or whether he did not go on with it, made no difference – the Thought Police would eventually get him. This was because he had committed 'the essential crime that contained all others in itself',[15] namely thoughtcrime.

Thoughtcrime is also the essence of immigration law. Throughout the immigration processes the onus is placed on applicants wishing to come or remain in the UK to prove 'intentions'. A prospective visitor has to prove that she or he 'intends to leave the United Kingdom at the end of the period of the visit as stated by him (or her)'. Likewise, a prospective student has to prove intent to leave on completion of studying. Prospective spouses have to prove an intention that the couple will live together (an obligation that would lead to a national uproar if it were a requirement for the documented). Thoughtcrime within immigration restrictions reached its peak (or nadir) with the notorious, though now repealed, 'primary-purpose' rule – the double-negative rule that placed an obligation on prospective spouses to show that the purpose of the marriage was not to circumvent immigration rules.

SEXCRIME

Another Newspeak transgression found within both *Nineteen Eighty-Four* and immigration controls is *sexcrime* (again, a song by the Eurythmics). Orwell writes of Winston that his sex life was defined and confined by two Newspeak words that were counterposed to each other – '*sexcrime* (sexual immorality) and *goodsex* (chastity)'.[16]

In fact what brought about Winston's downfall was not so much the heretical thought as the heretical act – the sex act. This was the essence of his relationship with his lover Julia. They rebelled against Big Brother through sexuality, but it was a a fruitless rebellion as sexuality was outside the party's control and 'therefore had to be destroyed'.[17] And Winston and Julia also had to be destroyed.

The stereotyping of the alien as the totally sexualized subversive is central to justifications for immigration controls. It is a recurring image present at each historic stage in the development of controls. For instance, typical of the agitation before 1905 for the Aliens Act was the assertion made by W. H. Wilkins in his book *The Alien Invasion*: 'Many of the immigrants are young women, Jewesses of considerable personal attraction. Men sharks and female harpies are on the lookout for them as soon as they disembark.'[18]

Similarly, agitation post-1945 (and even pre-1945) against black Commonwealth citizens focused on the identification of those citizens with prostitute and pimp. It is today little appreciated how, right through the war and into the 1950s, Maltese sex barons (known as 'Malts' or 'Epsom Salts') such as the Messina brothers, operating in London's Soho, became the excuse to identify the alien with an allegedly perverse sexuality.[19] From 1956, the British Medical Association passed resolutions virtually every year equating black people with carriers of venereal diseases and calling for immigration control through medical examination.[20] A central motif of the 'race riots' of Autumn 1958 in Notting Hill and Nottingham was that of sexuality. *The Times* tried to explain away the violence against black people as being based on alleged 'misbehaviour, especially sexual',[21] and said of the situation in Nottingham: 'there is also sexual jealousy – the sight of coloured men walking along with white women'.[22] *The Guardian*, at the height of the riots, managed to combine the standard components of liberal journalism – prurience, reaction and racism. It wrote of Notting Hill:

> The most sordid case was that of an English girl who...was quite willing to talk to me about what she called her mixed marriage. I asked her about the stories of English girls being forced into prostitution and she scoffed...A coloured man called for her in a large black Humber...later she was put on her 'pitch' on the pavement in the Bayswater Road.[23]

This ideological stereotyping has had practical implications, such that control of sexuality is a central component of immigration controls. Over two decades ago *The Guardian* carried the headline 'Abnormal sexuality used to ban immigrants'.[24] This was based on Home Office guidelines on exclusion from the UK on medical grounds. The guidelines (to medical inspectors in the UK and medical referees overseas) were themselves Orwellian, in that the so-called medical grounds were not clinically based but were asking doctors to make social and ultimately political judgements concerning 'mental disorder, senility, conduct disorder – e.g. alcoholism, drug addiction, abnormal sexuality...bodily deformity... any person appearing to be bodily dirty...' 'Scandalous sexual behaviour' has been said by an immigration minister to be a reason for refusing citizenship under the good character test.[25]

The ultimate example of immigration control through sexuality control – and vice versa – has already been noted. This was so-called 'virginity testing' for Asian brides seeking entry here. By Orwellian logic, any Muslim woman proven not to be a virgin was deemed to be seeking to circumvent the rules through marriage. We return here to immigration-law Room 101, and the words of one such bride describing her treatment on arrival here: 'He was wearing rubber gloves and took some medicine out of a tube and put it on some cotton wool and inserted it into me. He said there was no reason to get shy...'[26]

This pursuit of the alien through sexuality continues, though virginity testing has supposedly ceased. For instance, the rules relating to entry of a gay partner still remain far more restrictive than for a heterosexual partner. As was noted in the previous chapter, the Conservative Party has issued a document, *Before It's Too Late: A New Agenda for Public Health*, calling for compulsory HIV/AIDS testing for all those subject to immigration controls. This denounced 'sexual or racial politics' that were 'politically correct', and claimed 'the risk to the population comes primarily from those seeking permanent residency in the UK either as an asylum-seeker or through the immigration service.'[27]

All this contains a terrible echo of the medieval attacks, often physical, often murderous, on Jews as being the cause of the bubonic plague that broke out in 1348 and swept the whole of western Europe within eighteen months – in places an estimated two-thirds of the population being ravaged by the plague.[28] One contemporary, Cyriacus Spangenberg, who was a relative sceptic, wrote in the *Mannsfeldischen Chronik*: 'In the year 1349, God visited His punishment upon the unbelieving Jews. Whether they poisoned the wells everywhere, however, I do not know.'[29] Joshua Trachtenberg, writing in 1943, has stated 'to the horrors of the plague itself were added the wholesale massacre of thousands of Jews and the expulsion of thousands more from their homes.'[30] Expulsion in this context meant deportation.

IMMIGRATION-CONTROL NEWSPEAK

The resonance of Orwell's Newspeak – *unpersons, facecrime, thoughtcrime, sexcrime* – within immigration controls is only half the story. The other half is the incessant presence of immigration's own unique bastardized Newspeak vocabulary. Of course, Newspeak exists also outside of immigration law. It exists in misogyny, as in the once-prevalent terminology of 'illegitimate children' – that is, children who are effectively unpersons by virtue of their mother being unmarried.

What is unique about immigration controls is that, far from Newspeak being incidental, it is the linguistic rock on which the processes are built. Here is a dictionary of such vocabulary, in political as opposed to alphabetical order.

As we have seen, coming first is undoubtedly *illegals* – the reduction of humanity literally to outlaws (as in 'tight security has proved to be very successful considering the number of illegals we intercept now compared to the past' – General Manager of the Dartline Shipping Company[31]). The immigration Newspeak vocabulary also contains *illegal immigrant* (as in 'a suspected illegal immigrant has been found dead in a lorry after the vehicle was stopped by police')[32]; and *illegal migrant* (as in 'bill for illegal migrant may force health cuts – services provided by a hard-up health trust may be cut because it must pay a £440,000 bill for the treatment of a failed asylum-seeker'[33]); and *illegal worker* (as in '30 illegal workers arrested in raids…on a flower farm in West Sussex'[34]).

Coming next in the immigration Newspeak dictionary is *bogus*, with its subset *bogus refugee* (as in 'bogus refugees treated better than UK citizens'[35]). Analogous to bogus refugee is *economic refugee* (as in 'how many are genuine and how many are bogus and only here for economic reasons?'[36]). A subset of economic refugee is *economic migrant* (as in 'there was obviously evidence of some economic migrants attempting to use asylum in the EU'[37]). There also exist sub-subsets of immigration Newspeak, and one sub-subset of economic migrant is *illegal economic immigrant* (as in 'Italian government said it was concerned that influx of illegal economic immigrants could be infiltrated by Islamic extremists planning attacks in Europe'[38]). A similar sub-subset of economic migrant is *bogus economic migrant* (as in 'on arrival in the UK, the Roma were quickly labelled as "bogus" economic migrants'[39]).

What is becoming clear is what was stressed in Chapter 1 – namely, the overwhelming meaninglessness of this vocabulary. If all economic migrants are bogus refugees, then who are the bogus economic migrants? Are they genuine refugees? Perhaps the most politically surreal subset of all subsets is *illegal refugee* (as in 'illegal refugees targeted on tubes'[40]). Rights of entry and protection to refugees are supposedly guaranteed by the Geneva Convention, in particular Article 31. However, given that every block (visa requirements imposed by the state, carrier's liability imposed on airline and shipping companies, modern technological surveillance undertaken by numerous agencies) has been placed on 'lawful' entry by asylum-seekers then by a perverse self-fulfilling racist prophesy *all refugees become unlawful.* Rights are transmuted into non-rights. None of it makes sense except as an example of *doublethink* (a concept that is examined further in Chapter 5), whereby every single piece of immigration control vocabulary operates as a synonym for 'unwanted'. Or as Orwell says in *Nineteen Eighty-Four,* Newspeak was designed 'to diminish the range of thought'.[41]

MORE NEWSPEAK, LESS THOUGHT – AND BOGUS GRANNIES

Thoughtlessness within the Newspeak of Big Brother was assisted by diminishing the choice of words 'down to a minimum'.[42] Such is also the case within immigration controls, where these few words and their subsets and sub-subsets are given incessant usage. It is as though they are a never-ending recycled cascade. In fact, what distinguishes immigration Newspeak is often not that the vocabulary is invented, rather that the vocabulary is constantly repeated drivel. No wonder critical thought is impeded.

The designation 'bogus' pre-dates the present hysteria towards refugees and it will undoubtedly post-date this hysteria when new demons are to be found. Right through the 1970s and 1980s, the immigration authorities first constructed and then maintained the idea of the 'bogus child' in order to particularly exclude children from Bangladesh joining parents here, on the grounds that they were not related as claimed, that they were 'not genuine'. According to the British High Commission in Bangladesh: 'Because of the carefully prepared documentation and skilled tuition given to bogus children, the cases can appear at first sight to be genuine.'[43]

'Bogus' within immigration terminology is a blanket expression used to blank-out more than children. There are also 'bogus brides',[44] a concept that is the flip-side of the Orwellian construct 'marriages of convenience' – which are hardly convenient for those couples kept apart through immigration controls.

Perhaps the closest analogy with *Nineteen Eighty-Four* within immigration control literature is the blandly entitled (but fascinating read) *Immigration Control Procedures: Report of a Formal Investigation* produced by the Commission for Racial Equality in 1985. This shows how the informal vocabulary of control as used by immigration officials is replete with concepts such as 'bogus kids', 'bogus boys' and the strangely designated 'courier wives' – that is, mothers who bring 'genuine' children to the UK to join their father but with the intention of themselves returning home, thus forfeiting the right of even the children to remain here as the immigration rules require the presence of both parents.[45] There now also exists the bizarre concept of 'bogus grannies', older women allegedly lying that they are grandmothers in order to be allowed entry to join 'bogus grandchildren'. The following conversation took place on an Australian radio talk-show between the presenter and a lawyer:

> You also refer to something that I wasn't aware was going on, and that is DNA testing by the Immigration Department to weed out bogus grannies…essentially the Immigration Department says they're claiming to come into the country on the basis of family reunion, they're having trouble proving that, so we offer them the possibility of having a genetic test to show that they are in fact related to the family.[46]

What all the above examples show is that globally there exists a profound culture of disbelief as to the motives and intentions of the undocumented. Perhaps one day immigration officials will come up with the ultimate existential bogus family, the ultimate Orwellian nightmare: bogus children, bogus parents and bogus grandparents all living together as one bogus unit.

MIGRANT DAY-TRIPPERS

The culture of disbelief within the immigration process leads to the constant identification of those subject to controls as cheats. *The Sun* newspaper applauded the fact that 'asylum cheats will be tagged under a new crackdown launched yesterday – as figures showed the tide of refugees is rising again'.[47] 'Asylum cheats' are themselves perpetually equated with, and have become synonymous with, 'welfare cheats'. It has been correctly said that: 'Tabloid newspapers have waged a long campaign against so-called foreign "asylum cheats", claiming that many are unfairly milking welfare benefit payments here.'[48]

Cheats has become additional immigration Newspeak for anyone unwanted by the immigration system. Citizens of the ten new European Union states from eastern Europe and the Mediterranean are stigmatized in the same way, evidence of a longstanding racism against, in particular, Slavs and Poles. These EU citizens gained the right of freedom of movement on 1 May 2004. On 18 February 2004, Patricia Hewitt, Secretary of State for Trade and Industry (and, in an Orwellian role reversal, former head of the National Council for Civil Liberties), said to the BBC: 'What we don't welcome is people coming simply with an eye on exploiting our benefit system.'[49]

Immigration Newspeak frequently transcends its *Nineteen Eighty-Four* origins. 'Benefit cheats' themselves become equated with a peculiarly modern form of consumerism. For example, in the debates on the 2002 Nationality, Immigration and Asylum Bill, David Blunkett (as Home Secreatary) denounced those who had gained asylum in an EU member country and then came to the UK as 'benefit shoppers',[50] and he made provision to exclude them from benefits.[51] Parallel to the category of these benefit shoppers are *welfare tourists*,[52] and a sub-category of welfare tourists are *health tourists* – migrants, immigrants and refugees who allegedly come to this country only for NHS treatment.[53] It was propaganda of this nature that led in 1982 to the NHS (Charges to Overseas Visitors) Regulations, which made free hospital treatment dependent on residency status and thus imposed a racist block on the principle that NHS provision should be without charge at the point of service. The essentially political transmutation of patients into 'visitors' in order to limit or deny NHS treatment is Orwellian.

UNIFORMITY AND CONFORMITY

The immigration Newspeak dictionary is perpetually in the process of production and reproduction, depending on who is to be singled out as the latest object of demonization. On the other hand, the vocabulary may remain constant though the victim may change.

In the 1970s, those accused of wanting to abuse the system were partners seeking entry via marriage. Others designated 'abusers' were further family members seeking entry under the so-called (and Orwellian) family reunion rules – better described as family *division* rules. Since the 1990s, the label of 'abuse' has been heaped on asylum-seekers. In October 2003, transit visas were made compulsory for citizens of Pakistan and some other countries en route elsewhere. The Home Office and the British High Commissioner in Pakistan issued a press release describing such air-side transit visas, in which they managed to compare and combine the vocabulary of 'legitimate travellers' and 'genuine refugees' with 'illegal immigration' and 'those seeking to abuse the asylum system'.[54] The message of all this is clear: for many people, simply to seek entry, for whatever purpose, however briefly and temporarily, and without wishing to leave the confines of an airport, is viewed as abusive of the system.

Newspeak is designed to numb the mind. Some immigration Newspeak is now so well used by all sides of the political debate that it can take a feat of intellectual willpower to be able to stand back and understand the real, hidden, agenda behind it – namely the dehumanization of the undocumented. Take the word 'removals'. This until recently was confined to issues of furniture (as in 'furniture removals') and perhaps cargo commodities generally. Now it is used daily to apply to unwanted human beings, as a form of deportation or expulsion. For instance, Labour's 2005 white paper *Controlling Our Borders* has a whole section simply entitled 'Removal', and in fact the word appears 39 times throughout the document. So a vocabulary that was once confined mainly to the transportation of inanimate objects is now best known politically for the forced expulsion of sentient humans.

As Orwell described in *Nineteen Eighty-Four* thoughtcrime would be made literally impossible 'because there will be no words in which to express it'.[55] And as far as immigration controls are concerned, the biggest remaining thoughtcrime is to question the very existence of immigration controls themselves! Within sections of the public imagination controls may need to be 'fairer', to be 'less racist'. But what they cannot be is questioned in principle as being inherently unfair, as being inherently racist. It is taboo even to raise the issue. This is the politically driven orthodoxy that will be examined further throughout this book. It is a politics well understood by Orwell, who wrote 'Orthodoxy is unconsciousness'.[56]

The flip-side of orthodoxy is uniformity and conformity – uniformity with the view of there being no alternative to controls, and conformity to the view of the inevitability of controls. Professor Bhiku Parekh writes:

> For over three hundred years states have claimed and exercised the right to control immigration and emigration...there is no realistic hope of their giving it up. It would therefore be best to begin by accepting the right as an inescapable fact of contemporary life'.[57]

Uniformity and conformity is also the motif of Oceanic society, wherein every citizen could be kept for 'twenty-four hours a day under the eyes of the police'.[58]

In *Nineteen Eighty-Four*, perpetual uniformity and conformity is ensured by perpetual war. The ideal promulgated by the party was a nation of fighters and fanatics all marching forward in synchronized step – 'three hundred million people all with the same face'.[59] Under immigration controls, as will be seen, this ideological monotony is ensured by perpetual media propaganda, lies and distortion.

THE DEMAND FOR LOYALTY

Running parallel to orthodoxy, uniformity and conformity is loyalty to the British state. This is loyalty defined by who can come and who can remain, as enshrined in immigration controls.

The concept of loyalty is rarely discussed within the context of immigration restrictions. However, it has always been organically central to the operation of controls. This is the significance of the 'returning residents' rule, whereby non-citizens with settled status can lose their perhaps hard-won status if they are sufficiently 'disloyal' to leave the UK for more than two years in one stretch. Likewise, the real meaning of the maddening 'primary-purpose' rule and its requirement to disprove a negative was to break the familial link with the Indian subcontinent via arranged marriages and the consequential extended family. In 1970, William Whitelaw, then shadow Tory Home Secretary, attacked Asian arranged marriages on the grounds that 'girls and boys born in this country can seek a fiancé of their own ethnic group from the country from where their parents originally came...a process which could go on forever.'[60] The political aim is to ensure that those living here break all links with their country of origin.

The demand for loyalty is manifestly present within the amalgam of immigration controls and so-called anti-terrorist legislation, which allowed for the indefinite detention without charge or trial of foreign nationals (but not UK citizens) under the Anti-Terrorism Crime and Security Act 2001. As was seen in the preface, the House of Lords subsequently declared such legislation as being in breach of human rights – both by allowing for indefinite detention, and by distinguishing between citizens and non-citizens with only the latter being subject to detention.[61] The government was forced to repeal the objectionable features of the 2001 Act, but in another piece of *doublethink* it did not abandon detention without trial. Instead, under the Prevention of Terrorism Act 2005 it extended it to citizens. In practice this new provision will undoubtedly be confined in its use to those of the undocumented who have managed to acquire what was once considered the holy grail – British nationality.

Another recent example of what amounts to a loyalty oath are the new citizen tests introduced by the Nationality, Immigration and Asylum Act 2002, including the public swearing of an oath of allegiance to the monarchy. Those seeking citizenship are being relegated to a parallel universe that existed prior to the republican revolution of 1642. Yet another contemporary example is the proposed introduction of a national identity card as a way of verifying status and of showing acceptance by the state, a proposal found in the government's 2002 immigration white paper *Secure Borders Safe Haven*. With Orwellian logic, such documents – which are likely to be used to withdraw entitlements from the undocumented – are called 'entitlement cards'.[62] Orwell reveals an appreciation of another significance of such cards, namely their use as internal passports. In *Nineteen Eighty-Four* he writes that for distances of less than a hundred kilometres it was not necessary to get passports endorsed, 'but sometimes there were patrols hanging about railway stations'.[63]

Control of the internal movement of both citizens and non-citizens through passport investigation is central also to the totalitarian society of Jack London's early twentieth-century novel *The Iron Heel*. London writes of 'the introduction of the Russian passport system among the miners, and the denial of their right of removal from one part of the country to another'.[64]

History has now come round in a circle and fact has combined with fiction. Internal passport control, first introduced in Russia by Peter the

Great in the eighteenth century, then again by Stalin in the 1920s, has been reintroduced in 'liberated' Moscow.[65] Back in Europe (and just as in *Nineteen Eighty-Four*), immigration officials are today's patrols hanging about railway stations. Eurostar stations in Belgium and France, as well as the UK, are now policed by British immigration officers. So is the London underground, where immigration officers pose as ticket inspectors – officers whose function is to give the undocumented a one-way ticket back to their country of origin.[66]

THE INVOLUNTARY 'VOLUNTARY' AND THE IOM

As in *Nineteen Eighty-Four*, immigration Newspeak is about the legitimization of control on the freedom of movement, and this legitimization occurs through the madness of stripping language of all meaning. In the battle of ideas around immigration controls there is one dominant political rule of thumb that needs to be learned by the undocumented and their supporters: *If you hear the words 'volunteer' or 'voluntary departure' run a million miles away.* In the 1980s and 1990s, the British government's term for Vietnamese refugees compulsorily and brutally returned to Vietnam from Hong Kong was 'acquiescent volunteers'.[67]

There can never be anything voluntary about the inevitably forced nature of immigration controls. It is emphasized throughout this book that the concept of voluntary departure is *doublethink* in a context where the alternative is often to remain in destitution or detention, or in a limbo simply not knowing one's fate.

The annual statistics on removals produced by the Home Office do not tell half the story; in fact they conceal the story. The Home Office has an ambivalent attitude towards invoking formal removal processes. On the one hand such processes help bolster the statistics. In the debate on the 2004 Act, David Blunkett as Home Secretary boasted of that of which he should be ashamed, namely: 'We have increased the number of removals to 1500 or 1600 a month, which is now over 18,000 on an annualized basis...the total picture is rarely presented in our media.'[68]

On the other hand, removals are often cumbersome and expensive, and can result in adverse publicity. So as an alternative (an offer you can't refuse), the Home Office prefers to 'assist' people to return 'voluntarily' by paying their passage and now giving them poor-law support until they leave – as long as they cooperate in their own leaving. Departure is often facilitated by the International Office of Migration, a body whose

Orwellian role is thus to prevent migration. The IOM describes itself as an intergovernmental body, to which at present there are affiliated 79 member states and 43 states with observer status. Ostensibly the IOM presents itself as an agency designed to facilitate migration; in practice it is a global body designed to help 'repatriate' (i.e. deport) the undocumented of the world.[69]

On its British website the IOM commits itself to 'implementing the Voluntary Assisted Return and Reintegration Programme (VAARP).[70] This is not even an alternative to deportation but is deportation by another name. VAARP has been in existence since February 1999. It is funded by the Immigration and Nationality Directorate specifically to ensure the 'voluntary' departure of asylum-seekers.

The IOM website refers to three voluntary-sector organizations with which it works in partnership on this scheme: YMCA Glasgow, North of England Refugee Service, and Refugee Action. A research paper published by the Immigration and Nationality Directorate (IND) on the scheme declared that 'working relations [between IOM, IND and Refugee Action] were effective and business processes were clear'[71] – which should be seen as an indictment of voluntary-sector collaboration within immigration controls and which is examined further in Chapter 8. The role of Refugee Action and the two other voluntary-sector agencies is, according to the IOM website, to 'offer information…to asylum seekers and refugees who are considering return home'. This is Newspeak. Who are these asylum-seekers who are considering returning home of their own free will? They are mainly refugees refused, or expecting to be refused, or who are too exhausted and poverty-stricken to continue to fight for, the right to remain and who are now forced to contemplate returning to the country of persecution. What is this information being offered? It is not neutral advice, it is the offering of the incentive to quit without first being physically constrained. It is the same Newspeak, the same sanitization of vocabulary, that pervades and defines all immigration control processes.

4. FROM NEWSPEAK TO *AMTSSPRACHE*

HOW RACISM IS SANITIZED BY BUREAUCRATIC JARGON

Officialese [Amtssprache] is my only language.

— *SS-Obersturmbannführer Adolf Eichmann*[1]

On January 20th 1942, 15 men gathered in a villa on the outskirts of Berlin to feast on food and drink and discuss their business at hand. An hour and a half later, the Final Solution had been planned, sealing the fate of millions of European Jews.[2]

NAZI NEWSPEAK

Modern immigration controls are not fascist. Removal centres are not extermination camps – it would be ludicrous and out of all proportion to suggest otherwise. British immigration controls are not yet genocidal. They are still only at the deportation stage. Blaming refugees for housing shortages at home has hitherto justified only removal, not extermination. However, in their profound racism and their brutalization of those deemed unwanted here, controls are arguably a step towards fascism.

It should not be forgotten that, well before the gas ovens were in operation, the dehumanizing of their Jewish and gypsy victims had been legitimized through mass deportations at the hands of the Nazis. These deportations were the responsibility of one Adolf Eichmann, head of the Jewish Affairs section of the *Reichssicherheitshauptamt*, the head office for Reich security. The Nazis and their collaborators had their own Newspeak to explain – to justify – these deportations, and this vocabulary is familiar to our modern ears. So those Jews who, before the war, fled to Poland (or more accurately were forced out of Germany into Poland) were denounced by the Nazis as 'illegal refugees' and were refused readmission to the Reich when the Polish authorities in their turn wanted to deport them back.[3] In supposedly neutral Switzerland it was a crime during the war to 'shelter illegal immigrants' – that is, Jews fleeing Nazism.[4]

The coming to power of the Nazis pre-figured *Nineteen Eighty-Four* by nearly two decades and pre-dated modern immigration laws by even longer. The Nazi leadership was sufficiently conscious (i.e. self-conscious) to formulate a term to describe its own Newspeak – *Amtssprache*, meaning officialese, office-talk, bureaucratic-speak. *Amtssprache* shows in cold blood another aspect of both Newspeak and contemporary immigration-speak. This is the bastardization of language not only to block all critical faculties, but also to sanitize what would otherwise be perceived as unsanitary.

Orwell gave one definition of Newspeak thus: 'No word in the B vocabulary was ideologically neutral. A great many were euphemisms. Such words, for instance, as joycamp (forced-labour camp)...'[5] Likewise, the forced prostitution of women prisoners within concentration camps was organized as 'joy divisions'. And how much further can language sanitize behaviour than to describe the murder of six million people as *the final solution*? In *Nineteen Eighty-Four* this sanitization can be seen in the name of the party's government ministries: the Ministry of Truth (Minitrue) that spreads lies; the Ministry of Peace (Minipax) that organizes war; the Ministry of Love (Miniluv) that preaches hate; and the Ministry of Plenty (Miniplenty) that is responsible for starvation.[6]

Under modern immigration controls, it is a short step down the slippery slope of bureaucratic-speak, down the slippery slope of dehumanization, from being illegal, to being *untouchable* (a word used in *Nineteen Eighty-Four* to describe political outlaws[7], to being *non-human*, to being *sub-human* or, in Nazi-speak, to being *untermenschen* – and therefore disposable without any moral consequences to the disposer.

UP THE WANNSEE

The most grotesque sanitization of human language in history occurred at the so-called Wannsee Conference in 1942, where there was initiated or confirmed (there is an academic dispute as to which) the decision to commit perhaps the greatest crime in human history – the entire destruction of European Jewry. This perversion is the benchmark by which to judge Orwellian Newspeak and contemporary immigration-speak.

In May 1963, Hannah Arendt, herself a refugee from Nazi Germany, published her book *Eichmann in Jerusalem*. Arendt subtitled her book with the telling and frightening phrase *A Report on the Banality of Evil*. This was an account of the 1961 trial in Israel of the Jew-killer Adolf Eichmann, whom the Israeli secret service had tracked down and kidnapped in Buenos Aires a year earlier. Eichmann, who had achieved the middle rank of *SS-Obersturmbannführer*, attended the conference at Wannsee in his role as head of the SS's Jewish Affairs bureau.

What Arendt set out to explain was that Eichmann, a man at the centre of the killing of six million human beings, was not particularly abnormal, was not a devil figure, was not clinically psychotic, was not insane. Instead he was – as he saw himself and argued in his own defence – a functionary, a loyal administrator whose role was not to question orders but to follow them. The orders came down from SS-Obergruppenführer Reinhardt Heydrich (the instigator and lead player at Wannsee), who himself received them from *SS-Reichsführer* Heinrich Himmler, who in his turn was immediately answerable to the *Führer*, Adolf Hitler. The moral content of the orders was irrelevant to Eichmann. His main role at Wannsee seems to have been that of bureaucratic minute-taker, an important role as this required an expertise in the sanitization of the language of mass extermination.

Eichmann did not stand alone in his banality. Indeed, the significance of the banality of evil does not reside in the individual, in the personal. Rather it assumes its significance when it becomes collective and thus highly political. The entire Nazi enterprise was dependent on the unquestioning bureaucratic banality of those operating its machinery, from the clerks who collected and collated the list of victims, to the engineers who designed the death camps, to the civil servants within the transport system who ensured that the trains to the camps ran on time. And another group can also be added to those who colluded without question in this evil – the millions of onlookers, those who saw the trains pass by, and who remained silent. In *Nineteen Eighty-Four* this unreflective bureaucratic banality is best represented by Parsons, Winston's neighbour and fellow-employee at the Ministry of Truth, whom Orwell describes as one of those 'unquestioning, devoted drudges'[8] on whom (even more than the Thought Police) the stability of the party depended.

OBEYING ORDERS

Obedience to orders, deliberate blindness to the (im)moral content of behaviour, is a central motif of Adolf Eichmann's defence, of the functioning of Oceania in *Nineteen Eighty-Four*, and of the operation of immigration controls today. In Orwell's novel, Parsons is arrested for allegedly denouncing Big Brother in his sleep. He tells Winston that it was his little daughter who, after listening in through his bedroom keyhole, reported him to the patrols – but this pleases him as 'it shows I brought her up in the right spirit anyway'.[9]

For Parsons, the will of the party is paramount. His daughter obeying the party is the ultimate in parental achievement, even if this means the death of the parent, of himself. He thus sees no need to question even his own arrest. When Winston asks him if he is guilty he replies: 'Of course I'm guilty!…You don't think the Party would arrest an innocent man, do you?'[10]

Orwell describes this servility on which the Oceanic system depends as 'the human sound-track',[11] the background noise to the entire state. Likewise, the moral basis of reporting immigration offenders to the Home Office is never questioned by the immigration apparatchiks. Nor is the existence questioned by the overwhelming majority of those citizens who live near them (except in terms of the deterioration of the local housing market) of the induction centres, accommodation centres, detention centres and removal centres where the undocumented are segregated from the rest of civil society. Everything pertaining to moral content goes unquestioned. Obedience to orders is all that matters. The head of the Immigration Service Union, an organization of immigration officers that operates as a house union of the Home Office, has been quoted as saying: 'All we do is implement the rules. My members merely carry out what we are told to do.'[12]

What the immigration officers are told to implement is the division of families, the exclusion of refugees, the detention of those charged with no offence, the forced deportation of those guilty of no crime other than being unwanted. What they are told to do is justify the unjustifiable by allowing it to go unquestioned. Countless examples of this can be found in what is itself the blandly titled May 2003 report on *Asylum Removals* by the Home Affairs Committee of the House of Commons.[13] This includes evidence from one of the Home Office's own subcontracted security firms about the case of a child subjected to the deportation process 'who had recently undergone a splenectomy and was under continual medical supervision with tubes and wires coming out of various parts of his body'.[14]

MORE *AMTSSPRACHE*

As was seen in Chapter 3, *removals* is an otherwise innocuous word that has rapidly developed Orwellian undertones. Removals are the end-game of immigration controls. They are the point at which all pretence at niceties are abandoned. They are Joseph Crentsil, who died in November 2001 after throwing himself out of his third-floor window following a break-in by the immigration service. They are Joy Gardner, who died four days after immigration officials and police from the specialist Extra-dition Unit SO1/3 of the Metropolitan police forcibly gagged her with 13 feet of tape and bound her with a leather body-belt, during an attempted deportation in August 1993. At least five other people have died since, as a result of immigration and police raids on homes. Others have committed suicide whilst in detention.[15] They have all become *unpersons – vaporized.*

Removals constitute a world of physical restraints and forcible man-handling. This is a world of violence that is apparently a million miles away from the smooth-talking men and women in grey suits of the par-liamentary bodies that sanction the violence. The same apparent contra-diction between pain and comfort is seen in *Nineteen Eighty-Four* between Room 101 – a room of unrestrained brutality – and the living space of O'Brien, who authorizes the brutality, and where the plushness of the dark-blue carpet 'gave one the impression of treading on velvet'.[16]

This discontinuity between pain and pleasure, with those experienc-ing the pleasure authorizing the pain, reached its nadir at the conference at Wannsee. The movie *Conspiracy* chillingly fictionalizes the banality of the conversations that might have ensued over cigars and claret. Tuesday 20 January 1942, the day of the conference, was a bright, snowy day in Berlin. Wannsee, a gracious and affluent middle-class suburb to the south-west of the city, was a picturebook setting for the discussion of mass murder. There is another literary metaphor that captures the crazy poignancy of this moment in history – a poem found in the diary of Abraham Lewin, written during the destruction of the Warsaw ghetto, in which he wrote that the sun was shining, the acacia was blooming – and the slaughterer was slaughtering.[17]

Today the sun continues to shine while human beings order the construction of tougher and tighter immigration controls; other human beings obey the orders; and other human beings are humiliated, brutalized, detained and deported as a result of the orders – all as a result of the obedience.

RACISTS IN SUITS AND THE LANGUAGE THAT THEY USE

A central feature of the banality of evil is the banality of the language in which the evil is expressed. This is crystal clear in the language of the Wannsee Protocols. These are the minutes, rediscovered in 1947, of the conference at Wannsee – a meeting probably lasting less than half a day in which there was determined the mass liquidation of European Jewry and the methods of its liquidation The protocols are reproduced in Mark Roseman's book *The Wannsee Conference and the Final Solution*.[18] They provide just a summary of the discussion that took place and the genocidal decisions made.

The protocols are a virtual parody of the apparently amoral (but in fact deeply immoral) administrative mentality. The meeting starts with the statement by Heydrich that previous mass deportations 'to cleanse German living space of Jews in a legal manner' had been shown to be insufficient and had 'drawbacks'. There are then sober and calm distinctions made between the quarter-Jew (to be vetted), the half-Jew (to be sterilized) and the full-Jew (to be killed). There are reflections on how to deal with the Jew married to the Gentile, and with the Jew decorated in the first war. Heydrich proposes:

> Jews should be put to work in the East. In large single-sex labour columns. Jews fit to work will work their way eastwards constructing roads. Doubtless the large majority will be eliminated by natural causes. Any final remnant that survives will doubtless consist of the most resistant elements. They will have to be dealt with appropriately.

The representative of the German administration in Poland (*Staatssekretat* Buhler) puts in a plea that the final solution commence in his territory, as 'transportation does not play such a large role there nor would the question of labour supply hamper this action'. However there are competing interests, with others contending that 'the Protectorate of

Bohemia and Moravia will have to be dealt with first due to the housing problem'. And so it goes on.

Banality, the denial of the life force, the rejection of all that offers positive energy, is what characterizes Oceania under Big Brother. So the Ministry of Love (Miniluv) can be entered only through a maze of barbed-wire, a steel door and hidden machine-gun nests.[19] As a literary metaphor this negation of life is well-expressed in Winston's attempt at a smoke in order to calm his nerves before writing his subversive diary. He takes a cigarette from a packet, holds it upright and then watches the tobacco fall on to the floor.[20] Banality is a world where everything is stood on its head and all that is positive falls out and away.

Banality is what defines the already mentioned Home Affairs Committee report on *Asylum Removals*. It is not hyperbolic to describe this document in its (mis)use of language as the Wannsee protocol of British immigration controls. The report has had its own fifteen minutes of fame (or, more accurately, infamy) in the tabloid press. This was as a result of its very first paragraph, which suggested that unless even tougher controls were enacted then there would be Armageddon; that is, 'social unrest' accompanied by the rise of 'extremist parties with extreme solutions'. This led on the day following the report's publication to the *Sun* having the banner headline 'Asylum tearing UK apart', and the *Daily Express* asserting 'Britain facing asylum anarchy'.[21] However, what actually most characterises the report is not this apocalyptic vision as such. Rather it is the way the vision is discussed and sanctioned in the dull, euphemistic, facile, cliché-ridden tones of the bureaucrat.

NEWSPEAK, *AMTSSPRACHE* AND THE HOME AFFAIRS COMMITTEE

In an essay entitled *Politics and the English Language* (published in 1946), Orwell wrote:

> In our time, political speech and writing are largely the defence of the indefensible…Thus political language has to consist largely of euphemism, question-begging and sheer cloudy vagueness.[22]

One of the startling features of the Home Affairs Committee's report is the revealing of the names of those units of the Immigration and Nationality Directorate (IND) of the Home Office which deal with the enforced imprisonment and removal of unwanted humanity. These names are truly Orwellian. For instance there are the Management of Detained Cases Unit,[23] the Removals Co-ordination Unit[24] and the Detainee Escorting and Population Management Unit.[25]

Perhaps even more striking is not so much the language of the Home Office but that of its subcontractors in the realm of force or threats of force. A substantial degree of immigration control is enforced by private security firms, many of which are part of multinational companies, and all of which are essentially mercenaries in a war against the undocumented. Several of these gave oral and written evidence before the Home Affairs Committee. These were Wackenhut UK Ltd (which manages Tinsley House Removal Centre at Gatwick and the detention centre at Manchester Airport), Premier Detention Services Ltd (which runs Dungavel House Removal Centre in Scotland), UK Detention Services (which is responsible for Harmondsworth Removal Centre), Loss Prevention International Ltd (which 'escorts' deportees overseas), and Group 4 Falck Global Solutions (which runs Campsfield House Immigration Centre, Oakington Reception Centre and Yarl's Wood Detention Centre). Evidence was given that the latter is listed on the Copenhagen Stock Exchange,[26] which is as though a part of the Nazi SS had been floated as a publicly owned company in the period of mass deportations prior to the death camps. Now for the price of a share everyone can be a stakeholder in immigration control. It will be seen in Chapter 8 that this is now the reality, and to a greater or lesser extent we are all immigration officers now.

The oral and written evidence of these security institutions show a common and fundamentally amoral/immoral attitude towards their role as agents of immigration repression. And this attitude is continually expressed in bureaucrat-speak, in *Amptssprache*. The representative from Wackenhut UK Ltd implicitly adopts the 'obeying orders' (i.e. obeying Home Office orders) justification. He describes his firm as 'a demand-led organization who respond to the challenges and tenders put out by the Immigration Service', and that 'the efficiency of targets' is not its responsibility but that of the Home Office.[27] Just as the Wannsee Protocols were obsessed by the most efficient way of disposing of European Jewry, so the UK Detention Service is concerned to show that it has 'increased the throughput' from detention to deportation.[28] The Director of Operations of Premier Detentions Services Ltd speaks in similar sanitizing vein when he boasts that a new facility at Logford House would contain 'design features…specifically geared to improving the processing proce-dures for removal'.[29]

The Wannsee Protocols (in the penultimate paragraph of the minutes) declared that 'the final solution should be carried out…without alarming the populace'. This touching regard (unnecessary as it so happens) to the possible sensitivities of the local population at seeing the machinery of evil again finds a resonance in the Home Affairs Commit-tee's report. The Chief Executive of Loss Prevention International Ltd asserts that it would be 'more humane to remove more people on chartered aircraft because it can be done out of the public eye'.[30] Indeed: look away, or walk away, and thus hear no evil and see no evil appears to be the dominant advice given to their employees by all the security mer-cenaries, so the chain of denial can go lower and lower. The representa-tive from Loss Prevention International Ltd claimed that employees have no idea how those they have 'escorted' to certain countries are treated by the authorities there, and gave testimony that:

> Down in Lagos, for instance, the agreement that we have there is that we actually hand the returnee over to the ground staff of either British Airways or Virgin Atlantic, the two airlines flying in there. Standing right next to them are the Nigerian immigration officers who watch that process, then we walk away from it.[31]

Ultimately it is the banality of language that predominates. Thus, Group 4 describes the control and punishment of its prisoners in this way:

> We are able to incentivise detainees in terms of good behaviour and conforming with the regime that is actually on offer at the centre but there is an appropriate system of sanctions…good behaviour is a sign of good citizenship, disruptive behaviour is the contrary.[32]

BANALITY, INSANITY AND CLICHÉ

If, as Hannah Arendt asserts, Eichmann was not psychotic but normal in his obedience to orders, then other questions remain. This is because Eichmann gave orders as well as following them. He was part of a pecking-order, albeit near the very apex of the ladder. It was, as argued above, the whole pecking-order that was collectively banal in its methodical, bureaucratic approach to mass extermination. This collective banality can itself be viewed as systemic insanity – the whole system was insane. It ultimately had no other *raison d'être*, contained no other moral values, than its own existence. It was characterized by the absence of logic and of rationality. The systems prevailing in the real Nazi Germany and in the fictional Oceania were both banal and insane, both bad and mad. The same applies to immigration controls today.

Arendt in her book describes how Eichmann at one point in his trial apologized to the judge for not being able to explain some obscure point. His apology consisted of the statement 'Officialese [*Amtssprache*] is my only language'. Arendt comments: 'But the point here is that official-ese became his language because he was genuinely incapable of uttering a single sentence that was not a cliché.'[33] And today it is the power of cliché, of officialese, of *Amtssprache*, that helps maintain the horrors of immigration controls by deadening the critical faculties not just of the perpetrators but also of the onlookers (who then look away). Through the corruption of language, both perpetrators and onlookers abrogate the very asset that renders them human – the power of critical (i.e. moral) thought. Orwell says of Newspeak in *Nineteen Eighty-Four* that the intention was to make speech 'as nearly as possible independent of con-sciousness'.[34] Likewise, Arendt quotes Eichmann as saying with regard to the mass genocide discussed at Wannsee, and in which he was deeply implicated: [Who am I] to have my own thoughts in this matter?'.[35]

Immigration Newspeak pervades immigration control enforcement – even where the language is not designed for a wider public consump-tion. A letter from the (Orwellian-titled) Immigration Service (IS) Enforcement Policy Unit to the (Orwellian-titled) Asylum Processes Stakeholder Group refers to the scenario where the IS has 'collected a child from a school in order to reunite him/her with other family members prior to removal from the United Kingdom'.[36] This is true Newspeak – the achievement of family unity in order to effect expulsion. *Deportation is freedom!* The letter goes even further. It concludes by stating:

> Families do, of course, have the option of departing the United Kingdom voluntarily once their application has been refused and all their appeal rights exhausted. This option would negate the risk of family members being separated at the point where the IS are required to enforce their removal.

Voluntary departure is immigration Newspeak for voluntary deporta-tion, but without the IS having to go through the hassle of procedures.

Such removal, by preserving family unity throughout, is being projected as a superior form of liberty to forced removal. It can best be described under the Orwellian slogan of *deportation is doubleplusgood freedom!* [37]

5. FROM *AMTSSPRACHE* TO DOUBLETHINK

HOW BUREAUCRATIC JARGON ENFORCES REALITY CONTROL

On the cell door it was written 'deportee'. I questioned it. 'It doesn't matter,' they said. 'I'm not a deportee,' I said. 'Detainee, deportee – it's the same,' they said.

— Immigration prisoner[1]

I am made to feel as if I smell and there is zero tolerance for the non-existent smell of an asylum-seeker.

— Kamwaura Nygothi, Kenyan asylum-seeker in the UK[2]

THE NEGATION OF THOUGHT

Leon Trotsky, the Russian revolutionary, frequently referred in his writings to the need for 'a battle of ideas'.[3] Elsewhere he wrote 'Only the truth is revolutionary'.[4] Oceania, and its domination by Big Brother and the party, represent the direct opposite of this philosophy. Oceania embraces the rejection of ideas and the denial of truth – the negation of philosophy. This anti-philosophy is expressed through *doublethink*: 'Doublethink means the power of holding two contradictory beliefs in one's mind simultaneously, and accepting both of them'.[5]

Doublethink is a mode of thought that is essentially thoughtless and which is based on the mindset linguistics of Newspeak, a mindset which resists 'the temptation to take thought'.[6] Big Brother exercises power through the transformation of perception, through making mind-games appear real, through subverting the psyche, through creating a world of anti-logic and anti-rationality, through legitimizing madness as a way of being and of seeing. This is doublethink.

Chapter 1 of *Nineteen Eighty-Four* is a literary *tour de force* in illustrating how doublethink operates as a multilayered force in corrupting all modes of thinking. The very first sentence of the very first paragraph sets the time, with the twelve-hour clock striking thirteen. There then follows a cascade of irrationality posing as normal and rational: the Thought Police (whose role is to prevent not just heretical but all thought); hate week (organized by Parsons, who is later hated and tortured in the Ministry of Love); the Ministry of Love itself (with its 'hidden machine-gun nests')[7]; Winston living in Victory Mansions, drinking Victory gin and smoking Victory cigarettes (though Oceania never achieves any conclusive victories and its population is politically defeated); unrelenting racism (where anger is directed outwards against the 'enemies of the state, against foreigners'[8]). Then there are the lunatic doublethink slogans, the most significant being IGNORANCE IS STRENGTH. The significance of this is that the real Oceanic truth, the truth as enforced but never expressed by Big Brother, lies in its reverse – knowledge is death (mind death in the case of Winston and his lover Julia) to those who ever manage to get even close to the understanding of reality.

FREEDOM IS SLAVERY!

Doublethink was not an invention of Orwell, he simply but brilliantly conceptualized it. Doublethink is the ever-present political reality of oppressive societies. It is political control through schizophrenia. It is the ultimate in political alienation. It is dialectics gone out of control. In Marxist dialectics, thesis and antithesis are resolved in synthesis. In doublethink there is no such synthesis. Instead, mutually contradictory ideas simply represent parallel thought processes going in opposite directions in the same brain. And it doesn't even require a totalitarianism to enforce control in this way. Orwell's literary achievement was to transform an implicit form of social control found in what pass as democracies into an explicit one found in dictatorships. In an essay on the demise of literature under despotism he wrote: 'To be corrupted by totalitarianism one does not have to live in a totalitarian country. The mere prevalence of certain ideas can spread a kind of poison.'[9]

This poison is today being spread in Britain's own backyard. So war can be declared on Iraq for having weapons of mass destruction, when everyone (including the war-makers) knows that such weapons do not exist. They are *unweapons*. WMD has itself attained the virtual status of a Newspeak acronym – meaning something that has a political but not a material reality. Alternatively 'peace' can be proclaimed by the war-makers at a time when the media is redolent of news from Iraq of bombings, killings and outright murders – from all sides. This announcement of peace (as though such an announcement of calm can itself alter the reality of conflict) is then used as a justification to threaten to deport asylum-seekers back to a *pacified* Iraq.[10] On the other hand, the declaration and continued support of war – supposedly a war against international terrorism – is an excuse for the strengthening of the state back at home with the enforcement of the Terrorism Act 2000 and (in an Orwellian switch in title) the Anti-Terrorism Act 2001, now replaced in part by the Prevention of Terrorism Act 2005. At the same time the Minister for Immigration and Nationality has been renamed, if only temporarily, the Minister for Immigration, Nationality and Counter-Terrorism (and who in Newspeak may well be referred to as a *Mininacto*).[11] In this way, war becomes 'peace' and peace becomes 'war'. Or, as the slogan proclaims in *Nineteen Eighty-Four*: WAR IS PEACE.

It gets worse and it gets crazier. A USA spokesperson in Iraq has claimed that the Iraqi people continue to wage war on American troops as 'these people [the Iraqis] hate freedom'.[12] This must be the first war in history where one side is fighting against its own liberty. Again there was a slogan, the third and final slogan, for this in *Nineteen Eighty-Four*: FREEDOM IS SLAVERY. This is the point at which doublethink reaches 'reality control'.[13]

THE DOUBLETHINK OF IMMIGRATION CONTROLS

In reading, watching and listening to the media and the politicians on the subject of immigration controls one's immediate reaction is astonishment as to how anyone can be deceived by all this rubbish. At least this would be an immediate reaction except that all of us have to some extent or another been politically corrupted and mentally exhausted by the perpetual onslaught of dangerous junk masquerading as an apologia for control.

The only explanation for this corruption and exhaustion is the power of racism, as expressed through the mind-disturbing properties of doublethink. And it has all been legitimized so quickly. The first legal controls were introduced only a century ago (the Aliens Act 1905).

Agitation for such controls began seriously only in the 1880s with the arrival of Jewish refugees and their denunciation as economic migrants. Prior to that it would have been the advocates of control who were viewed as unhinged and a minority. The popular acceptance of controls has occurred with such speed both because of the unrelenting campaigns for their imposition and because these campaigns have brought together the most reactionary aspects of imperialist ideology – racism, nationalism, sexism, homophobia – all of which involve doublethink.

As a practising lawyer, the most common example I have heard of such doublethink is the cry of the asylum-seeker asking how fear of death after deportation can be proven without his actually agreeing to be sent back and killed. There are numerous refugee testimonies to the effect of 'If I'm sent back, I'll die anyway'[14] or 'What use am I to anyone dead?'[15] It is not unknown for death to follow deportation – such as happened to John Reyes-Prado, a Columbian who was refused asylum and was subsequently shot dead by right-wing paramilitaries.[16] All this is a reminder of the 1960s satirical hit song *I Feel Like I'm Fixing To Die Rag*, about the Vietnam war, and its rallying cry to be the first one on the block to have your boy brought home in a box.[17] Or, as Orwell wrote in *Nineteen Eighty-Four* about those arrested by the Thought Police: 'They were corpses waiting to be sent back to the grave.'[18] This is also an echo of the aphorism of the German revolutionary, Eugen Levine: 'We are communists living on borrowed time.'[19] Levine was correct as far as he was concerned: he was executed by right-wing militia in 1919 after the unsuccessful German revolution.

In the last twenty years, doublethink has attained the status of 'good practice' by Home Office advocates and apparatchiks in immigration cases. This really is the point at which badness meets madness. It can be seen in case after case. In the 1980s, Anwar Ditta and her husband Shuja waged a campaign to bring in their children from Pakistan – a campaign that eventually achieved success and international publicity. Initially the Home Office asserted that the children were not related as claimed – that they were, in immigration Newspeak, 'bogus'. Then quite spectacularly the Home Office asserted that Anwar herself was bogus and that there were 'two Anwar Sultana Dittas, – one who married Shuja Ud Din in Pakistan and the other whom Shuja Ud Din married in the UK in 1975.[20] Having to prove one's own identity *and* to disprove a hypothetical identity of someone else in Pakistan is the essence of lunacy. In fact it is *doublelunacy*.

THE GREAT IMMIGRATION CONTROL SWINDLE

In another typical case from the same period, Ijaz Ul Arfeen was refused entry to the UK from Pakistan to marry Arfarna Amin, on the grounds that this would be a *marriage of convenience*, another doublethink concept. (The destruction of relationships through immigration controls is, as we have seen, highly inconvenient to those in the relationship.) It is instructive to look at the questions asked by the Entry Clearance Office (ECO) to Ijaz, which seem designed not just to confuse but ultimately to disorientate and unhinge:

> [Q] Would you marry your fiancée if she had lived in Pakistan? [A] Yes I may have gone to her house or she may have come to mine. We would have discussed it. [Q] What would have happened if she had lived in Karachi, whereas you live in Lahore, and she had wanted you to join her in Karachi? [A] I would have gone to Karachi as my firm has an office there. [Q] What would have happened if she had wanted you to join her in Mirpur? [A] I would have gone to join her if she had wanted and found a job. [Q] What would have happened if she had wanted you to join her in Pindi? [A] I would have gone as my company has an office there as well. [Q] Who would have joined whom if your fiancée had lived in the USA or Canada? [A] If necessary I would have joined her and found a job. [Q] Would you be prepared to follow your fiancée anywhere? [A] Yes, provided work was available. [Q] How do you propose to support your fiancée in the UK? [A] I would do any sort of work.[21]

Even an invited television audience would, presumably, have found in Ijaz's favour. However, the ECO concluded that he was marrying only in order to find work in the UK.

The 1986 pamphlet *But My Cows Aren't Going to England* shows the extraordinary lengths to which ECOs in Bangladesh went in denying visas to wives and children of men settled here. One file was discovered with a note by an ECO warning other officers not to handle this particular case, as 'I want to do this re-interview myself. Hands off'. Another note on the file from a senior officer seeking to refuse entry said 'Well done, looks as if you've hit the jackpot again.'[22] In the vocabulary of *Nineteen Eighty-Four* this was, as far as the ECO was concerned, not so much doublethink as *doubleplusgoodthink* – whereas for the mother and children it was definitely *ungood*.[23]

Doublethink was reinforced as the norm within immigration processes with the discovery in the late 1980s of DNA as a way of 'proving' parentage. This was translated into the practice of the giving of blood to get into England – the Dr Mengele version of immigration restrictions.[24] Doublethink was central to the employment of DNA in controls because it led not just to the admission of some children but also paradoxically to the further global division of families. This development was explicitly political, with the Home Office embracing new and cruel strategies to refuse entry. Here are just three examples. Numerous children (particularly those from Bangladesh) had been trying for years to show their parentage. However, those who had reached the age of eighteen were still refused admission even after positive DNA tests had proved they had always been 'related as claimed' to a parent or parents in the UK. Now they were excluded on the grounds that they were 'over-age'. Second, the Immigration Act 1988 declared that admission was to be refused where the father in the UK had 'recourse to public funds', irrespective of the fact that the father may have been in work at the time of the initial application. Third, British children of whatever age should in law be allowed entry – except that the 1988 Act denied entry to people without passports, and embassies in the Indian subcontinent routinely refused passports. These are all examples of the great DNA swindle.[25]

And 'swindle' – meaning the dashing of any positive expectations – is the operative word within immigration controls. The truth is that, whatever their objective political analysis of controls, most people still retain some subjective expectation of justice or fairness – a belief that is itself an instance of doublethink. So the swindle continues, is intensified, to this day. Refugee applications provide numerous examples. A common one is the refusal to grant asylum to women who are raped as part of a military conflict. Fernande Tchibinda from Congo Brazzaville was raped at the instigation of the military. The appeals adjudicator, in refusing her asylum, dismissed the rape as being simply 'the actions of soldiers who were out of control in a civil war situation'.[26] Maybe this is correct in the perverse sense that soldiers are by definition out of control in any conflict, though in fact rape is routinely and consciously used as a military weapon. However, once again the real issue – and the one that leads to immigration-control doublethink – is why anyone should have to justify their reasons to come or remain here. Why should proof of persecution or proof of parentage or proof of anything be required?

EXTENDING THE LITERARY METAPHOR

Swindle, mind-games, double-cross and doublethink pervade all aspects of what remains of the immigration appeals system. It is a system where the onus of proof is on the appellant, where effectively there is being conducted a trial without formal charges, where (in applications from abroad) cases are heard in the absence of the appellant. The authors of *But My Cows Aren't Going to England* compare such trials to the inquisitions of the seventeenth century, where 'the accused would have to prove that they were not in league with the devil, and where the Inquisitor's pronouncement defined once and for all the accused person's "morality"'.[27]

The present study aims to show how *Nineteen Eighty-Four* can be used as a metaphor to describe and understand immigration controls. However, neither Orwell nor his novel have a monopoly on metaphor as a way of appreciating the frightening, claustrophobic world of doublethink. The writings of Franz Kafka provide many symbols for the literally Kafka-like nature of controls in action. And of all Kafka's writings, it is *The Trial* that is most evocative of the apparently incomprehensible world in which the undocumented find themselves – a world where immigration controls are themselves quite out of control and are certainly out of the control of those subject to them.[28]

The Trial, published in 1925, tells the story of Joseph K, who is charged with an offence of which he is not only innocent but which *is never explained to him*. One analogy with immigration controls is the accusation of entering into a marriage of convenience, an inexplicable accusation in as much as it places the burden of proof on the accused to somehow show that a marriage is 'genuine' – whatever that means. *The Trial's* opening sentence suggests the paranoia so reminiscent of that governing immigration controls: 'Someone must have been telling lies about Joseph K, for without having done anything wrong he was arrested one fine morning.'[29] When asked why he was being arrested he is told 'We are not authorized to tell you that.'[30] When eventually he obtains a legal adviser, the adviser asks him what it is all about. Joseph answers 'That's just the snag...I don't know that myself.'[31] Joseph, in trying to understand the legal tentacles crushing him, provides a very good description that could equally be applied to immigration controls:

> an organization which not only employs corrupt warders, stupid Inspectors, and Examining Magistrates of whom the best that can be said is that they recognize their own limitations, but also has at

its disposal a judicial hierarchy of high, indeed the highest, rank, with an indispensible and numerous retinue of servants, clerks, police and other assistants... And the significance of this great organisation gentlemen? It consists of this, that innocent persons are accused of guilt, and senseless proceedings are put in motion against them.[32]

Euripides, the Greek dramatist, put it more succinctly: 'Those whom the gods wish to destroy they first make mad.' And madness comes from doublethink. It has been well documented how refugees seeking freedom in this country can suffer severe psychological disorder when they are put in detention as asylum-seekers, and thus become doubly *unfree* – unfree in their own country and unfree here.[33] The *cris de coeur* from asylum-seekers at the start of this chapter further illustrate this maddening process, with the immigration system regarding it as irrelevant whether a detainee is at any particular time subject to deportation, and with all refugees being stereotyped as smelling. Perhaps it is the sheer arbitrary nature of detention that is the most mentally disturbing – the not knowing *if* or *why* or *where* or *how* or *when* or *for how long* detention may occur. One detainee interviewed by a psychiatrist is quoted as saying:

> And if you try to understand you cannot. Even the immigration officers say they cannot understand. If you come with your brother they give your brother release and they hold you. You are the same. Yes, he is lucky. You come from the same house, the same country, the same mother and father and you talk the same language, take the same airplane and you come here and have the same story, they release one and to the other one they say no.[34]

Immigration detainees are charged with no crime, let alone convicted of any offence. Likewise, in *Nineteen Eighty-Four* there can be arrests for transgressions that are not even prohibited: 'In Oceania there is no law'.[35] This is the political madness that can drive its victims to personal madness, or (what may amount to the same state of mind) to abject compliance with the system. The latter was the fate of Winston and Julia arrested and tortured in the Ministry of Love for love-making – pure doublethink.

6. FROM DOUBLETHINK TO THE PROGRAMME THAT DARE NOT SPEAK ITS NAME

HOW IDEOLOGICAL OPPOSITION TO IMMIGRATION CONTROLS IS ITSELF CONTROLLED AND SILENCED

There is no doubt that the asylum system is being abused...The government will not allow our controls to be abused with impunity. ...the risk of immigration abuse is significant.

– Fairer, Faster, Firmer, *Home Office document, 1998*[1]

Migrants do not compete for jobs with existing workers... Migration brings huge benefits...One of the issues which troubles the public most in relation to immigration and nationality is a belief that entry into this country and residence is subject to abuse...This White Paper intends to refocus the agenda onto the wider issues of migration: on the global reality of increasing international mobility

– Secure Borders, Safe Haven, *Home Office document 2002*[2]

DOUBLETHINK AS THE CORRUPTION OF IDEOLOGY

Doublethink does not reside passively in the daily operation of immigration controls, in court judgments and in bureaucratic decisions. It is allowed to reside in these daily spheres precisely because every single justification for the very existence of controls is itself defined by doublespeak: there never is and never can be any reason for controls based on rationality. The usual ideological justifications presented are essentially anti-ideological. They are against reason. This is quite clear in the most racist – the most explicit – impulse behind controls, namely the preservation of British heritage or British nationalism or British blood. All these eugenic concepts are problematic beyond the point of rationality. They assume the most fundamental irrationality of all, the concept of 'race' – a pseudo-science that substitutes a false and meaningless biology for human relationships.

There is what might be described as a second-tier, and more socially acceptable, argument for controls, one that masks the real racist agenda. This is the so-called Malthusian justification, namely that the country is overcrowded and incapable, either economically or spatially (it is always unclear which), to incorporate a further increase in population. Malthus, the first professor of political economy in British university history, devoted his career to attacking both the urban and rural poor for causing overpopulation. His *Essay on the Principles of Population* was a literary winner amongst the bourgeoisie and went through six editions from 1798 to 1826.

Malthus positively advocated the eviction of the Irish peasantry from the countryside on the grounds that 'the land in Ireland is infinitely more populated than in England; and to give full effect to the natural resources of the country, a great part of the population should be swept from the soil'.[3] His wishes were met in part not just by death and emigration caused by the famine of the 1840s but by an English and Irish landlord class that deliberately transformed the island from a wheat-producing nation, protected from foreign competition by the corn laws, into a huge pasture for wool-producing sheep . There was nothing natural about this Irish 'overpopulation'; it was engineered.

Malthus opposed all forms of social improvement in England, Ireland or anywhere on the grounds that 'We are bound in justice and in honour to disclaim the right of the poor to support'.[4] Karl Marx was later to describe him as 'a shameless sycophant of the ruling classes'.[5] Malthus' ideas acted as an inspiration for both the Poor Law of 1834 (better described as the anti-poor law because of its assault on the poor) and for the first and all subsequent immigration control pieces of legislation. Indeed, as was argued in Chapter 1, the most obvious flaw in the Malthusian position is that if this country were overcrowded in 1905 (when the Aliens Act was introduced) then it surely would, at least in a metaphorical sense, have sunk by now with the repeated 'floods' of immigration. This emphasis on space, or the lack of it, is redolent of the Nazi concept of *Lebensraum* used to justify the invasion of the USSR in order to provide land for the pure German *volk* – hardly an advert for rationality.

Population theory conceals a third-tier racist agenda, one that is paradoxical and based on extreme doublethink emanating if not from Malthus personally then from Malthusian ideas that are antipathetic to welfare. This agenda is justified by a spurious argument based on welfare itself – that is, *the other*, the *alien*, the *foreigner*, taking, stealing or usurping *our* jobs, *our* housing, *our* benefits. As early as 1888, one newspaper campaigning for controls against Jewish refugees ran an editorial proclaiming 'Surely our own people have the first claim upon us.'[6] Such an argument is posited on a world view which is essentially racist, presupposing a superiority of 'us' over 'them'. It leaves unexplained (because it is inexplicable) why the British (whoever they are) should be able to assert a franchise over Britain and its material wealth. This argument as a justification for controls is used mainly by politicians who (and a media which) do not normally express interest in the welfare of ordinary working people, British or otherwise.

REACTION IS REFORM!

It is not surprising that the whole system of immigration controls, first legitimized by doublethink, should invoke doublethink as a way of making itself consistently more repressive. Numerous examples can be seen in the parliamentary debates over the Asylum and Immigration (Treatment of Claimants, etc.) Act 2004.

This Act is frightening in its consequences. For instance it abolishes the right to appeal an immigration decision from an Adjudicator (an immigration judge) to the Immigration Appeals Tribunal – which it achieves by the simple expedient of abolishing the tribunal.[7] It makes it an offence, punishable by imprisonment, for any non-British or non-EEA national arriving at a UK port not to have a passport.[8] This reinforces the criminalization of refugees by again contravening the central principle of the Geneva Convention – that asylum-seekers should not be punished for their method of entry.[9]

Under the Act, immigration officers are essentially afforded the status of police officers by being given the powers of entry, search, seizure and arrest without warrant for a series of alleged offences – from bigamy to theft – supposedly uncovered when exercising a function under immigration legislation.[10] Powers of fingerprinting are also increased.[11] For the first time there is allowed the electronic tagging of all those subject to immigration controls where residence restrictions are imposed, where reporting restrictions could be imposed, and in some cases where immigration bail is granted.[12] This satellite technology further criminalizes all *sans-papiers*. There is enlarged the power to remove a claimant to a 'safe third country' through which she or he has passed and of which she or he is not a national, without substantive consideration of an asylum or, in certain cases, human rights claim.[13] Another writer has already recognized that the construct of 'safe third countries' in effect reverses the flows of established transnational migratory paths and turns them into transnational corridors of expulsions.[14]

After a time it becomes genuinely difficult not to believe that the legislation did not come straight from the pen of George Orwell. A new criminal offence is created (which can carry a sentence of two years' imprisonment) – an offence of failing to co-operate in one's own removal from the UK![15] In Britain today the choice for those subject to immigration controls is now either imprisonment or expulsion – *Deportation is freedom!*

Doublethink rests in a central justification given for the legislation. The Act is projected as a 'reform'. Beverley Hughes, the then Minister for Immigration, said in parliament that the new law 'is the next essential stage in our programme of reforms to the asylum and immigration system'.[16] A Home Office press release of 27 November 2003 is headed *Final Phase of Asylum Reform…*[17] Ignoring (if that were possible) the near-convergence of 'final phase' with 'final solution', this is a complete bastardization of the word, vocabulary and concept of 'reform'. The construct of reform connotes progress, enlightenment, positive development, human improvement and social advance. Immigration controls, on the other hand, are about negativity, reaction, obscuranticism, pain, misery, disress, enslavement – the control of people. The conflation of the two is grotesque.

It is legitimate to ask how deportation can be freedom. But yet how can it be anything else when the alternative is imprisonment? And how can reaction mean reform? But again, how can it mean anything else when racism is dragging society backwards in time to a new dark age? The identification of reaction with reform is a supreme example of doublethink in its requirement to 'use logic against logic'.[18]

MORE DOUBLETHINK APOLOGIA

The Asylum and Immigration (Treatment of Claimants, etc.) Act 2004 is the creation of a highly confident government that believes a century of parliamentary and media Newspeak and doublethink, plus a top layer of New Labour spin, has generated enough support for immigration controls that the undocumented can be simply trodden on. Another dreadful image from *Nineteen Eighty-Four* springs to mind: *'If you want a picture of the future, imagine a boot stamping on a human face – for ever.'*[19]

This confidence is shown by the ease with which further double-think apologias are used to justify putting the boot in, apologias that in any event have all been heard before. They are repeated like a mantra, as though the repetition of madness can somehow be justified as sanity. A classic example is that articulated by the Labour Home Secretary in justifying the 2004 Act – namely, the legislation is 'in the interests of good race and community relations'.[20] This is a regurgitation of what, for example, was said by a Tory Home Secretary, Douglas Hurd, in introducing the Immigration Act 1988, namely 'Immigration control is essential if we are going to have good community relations'.[21] All this is essentially blaming the victims of racism for racism. It is equivalent to arguing that mass redundancies are in the interests of good industrial relations.

Most outrageous of all – what in *Nineteen Eighty-Four* might well achieve the superlative *doubleplus-doublethink* – is the assertion that the greater the demonization of the refugee and the tougher the immigration controls, then the less chance there is of fascism and the British National Party growing in strength, this being the same fascism and British National Party that consistently demonise the undocumented and campaign for the toughening of controls. It is now difficult to distinguish the puppet from the puppeteer, the Labour Party from the BNP, and who is pulling whose strings. In a question and answer session at the 2003 Labour Party Conference, the then Minister for Immigration, Beverley Hughes, stated: 'The BNP feed on people's fears and use that for their own racist political objectives. It's imperative that we sort out the asylum system and have a fair, robust process the public can have confidence in.'[22]

Hughes called this 'a progressive approach to migration'. This is simultaneously doublethink and political cowardice, where fascism is opposed to racism, where racism is defined as progressive, where repression is equated with fairness. It's the same doublethink and cowardice that led Neville Chamberlain down the road to appeasement in his dealings with Hitler and the Nazis in the 1930s.

THE DOUBLETHINK OF SOCIAL RACISM AND ECONOMIC RACISM

There is a passage in *Nineteen Eighty-Four* which describes Winston's work of fabrication in the Ministry of Truth whereby the process of continuous alteration was 'applied to...every kind of literature'.[23]

No British government has yet resorted to rewriting literature or book burning. Even New Labour has not had a literal (as opposed to metaphorical) recourse to what existed 'in thousands or tens of thousands'[24] throughout the Ministry of Truth – namely, *memory holes*. These holes had a specific technological function in the construction of deceit and the destruction of truth. Whenever it was perceived that any document was due for destruction it was an automatic action to 'lift the flap of the nearest memory hole and drop it in'.[25] Once in it was confined to the flames and to oblivion.

However, New Labour has achieved the closest approximation to the memory hole, that being a complete shift not in the perception of the migrant but in the need of the British economy for migration. This shift has not been articulated as such; rather, the past has been simply obliterated through being unacknowledged. So we arrive at doublethink, which is clearly seen by comparing the two quotations at the start of this chapter. In 1998, just after Labour came back to power, the white paper *Fairer, Faster and Firmer* crucified the migrant as the villain by attacking those 'facilitating economic migration by people who are not entitled to enter the UK'.[26] By 2002, with the publication of *Secure Borders, Safe Havens*, the villain had been metamorphozed into a hero, the devil had become a god: 'migration can bring considerable benefits to the UK'.[27] Of course this is not a recipe for an open-door immigration policy. Instead it is for a policy of selected entry, the chosen being those perceived as of economic value. This again is the migrant as an unperson, but now also as a commodity. Semret Feshaye, an Eritrean asylum-seeker, expressed it this way:

> We came here to seek asylum, but we are being reduced to non-people...The Home Secretary has announced he is changing the rules about who can claim asylum... Does the Home Office prefer us to disappear into the underbelly of British

society? Not seen, not heard and working for shadowy bosses in the jobs many British people don't want to do for a fraction of the minimum wage. We are a useful source of cheap, unregulated labour that can boost the economy.[28]

There is nothing new about this. The contradictions between the two white papers are just superficial. They are both about *capitalist-think*. Immigration controls have never been simply about excluding and expelling migrants and their labour, though this has often been the dominant factor. Rather, as their name suggests, they are literally about controlling this labour in accordance with the needs of capital. In New Labour Newspeak, such control is euphemistically known as 'managed migration'. Beverley Hughes clarified the Newspeak when she said 'this government's policy is to welcome migrants where this helps our economy'.[29] The real contradiction here, the actual doublethink, has been between social racism and economic racism – the social racists want neither labour nor the presence of the alien, the economic racists want the labour and tolerate the presence.[30]

Put another way, this is a conflict between those who want to limit immigration to the perceived needs of capital and those who are for zero entry. Sometimes it is the economic racists who prevail, as under New Labour and its 'managed migration'. At other times it is the social racists who triumph. A classic example of the latter was the Commonwealth Immigrations Act 1962 (the first post-war controls on black people). This was passed as a direct consequence of neo-fascist activity, the Notting Hill riots of 1958, but at a time when there was a shortage of labour in London transport, the hospital services and catering. So, just before the passing of the Act, the *Times* argued against the imposition of restrictions on the grounds that 'Britain's essential services could not carry on without immigrant labour'.[31] For the undocumented this has resulted in a situation of neither open door nor closed door, rather a revolving door.

FAIR, FAKE, FACILE

The conceptualization and construction of 'fairness', 'justice', 'tolerance' and 'equality' by the Home Office in the justification and administration of immigration controls is an exercise in irrationality and mind control. There is an English phrase (which has its own racist roots) that equates to

Orwell's doublethink and which appropriately describes this nonsensical conceptualization – namely, *double Dutch*.

For instance, outside Lindholme removal centre the Immigration and Nationality Directorate, in the manner of Big Brother, has its own doublethink slogan: BUILDING A SAFE, JUST AND TOLERANT SOCIETY. This slogan appears also in much Home Office immigration literature. Lindholme is run by the prison service. It holds up to 112 men aged 21 and over. A prison inspectors' report in April 2003 revealed that staff routinely imposed random strip-searches after visits. Detainees are also strip-searched on admission to the centre as a matter of routine, without any reason given. Staff at this former prison treat detainees as offenders, though they have not been convicted of any crime. There is a prison atmosphere with detainees being made to wear prison clothes. Their own money is withheld from them and channelled into prison-like 'incentive schemes'. The report describes poor food, heating and healthcare, and intimidation and hostility. Detainees there do not feel safe.[32]

With similar madness, the immigration rules define themselves as fair and non-discriminatory, declaring:

> Immigration Officers, Entry Clearance Officers and all staff of the Home Office Immigration and Nationality Department will carry out their duties without regard to the race, colour or religion of persons seeking to enter or remain in the United Kingdom'.[33]

These are the rules that allow for the division of families, for deportations, for denial of entry, for detentions, and for exclusion of refugees.

The government chose to call its first white paper *Fairer, Faster and Firmer*, as though firmer and fairer could ever be equated in this racist context. This was a context where the white paper led in 1999 to the notorious Immigration and Asylum Act, the removal of the undocumented from the welfare system and the confining of asylum-seekers to a new poor law.

NO FAIRNESS WITHIN RACISM

It should come as no surprise that the Home Office indulges in doublethink. However, this indulgence reaches the status of *doublethink-doubleplus* when exercised by those who are in some way partially critical of controls, those who consider that controls can be maintained whilst rendering them 'fair' or 'non-racist'. The assertion that there can be fair, non-racist controls once again involves the use of logic against logic. This is not simply because controls themselves are inherently racist – with the construct of border restrictions and of borders themselves being based on the vilest nationalism. Neither is it simply because controls are the product of imperialism – with limitations on the movement of labour being imposed just at the point when technology had provided labour with cheap international travel through rail and steam. It is not even because, as will be seen later, controls result from fascist and proto-fascist agitation – though it would be remarkable if legislation based on such origins could be sanitized and made non-racist and equitable. Rather, controls, however redefined, however reformulated, are inherently unfair precisely because they are an attack on the free movement of those excluded from the reformulation.

NO JUSTICE WITHIN RACISM

This inherent injustice is quite manifest from a critique of a book published in 1994 and which became the bible for New Labour's immigration rhetoric. The book was *Strangers and Citizens* (subtitled *A Positive Approach to Migrants and Refugees*), edited by Sarah Spencer and published by the Institute for Public Policy Research.[34] Spencer calls for 'non-discriminatory, fair' controls[35] and attempts to construct such controls. However this (re)construction inevitably leads to exclusion, so only 'genuine' visitors[36] will be admitted, and only 'legitimate' refugees[37] and only marriage partners where there is no evidence of 'abuse' of controls.[38] Spencer herself admits that 'Whatever policy is adopted, some will be excluded'.[39] She is correct – and those excluded will be the colonized and neo-colonized workers of the third world washed up like flotsam in the imperialist heartlands. The reason for this inherent unfairness resides in Spencer's own explicit support of the inherent nationalism of controls, namely: 'In immigration policy, government has the right to put the interests of its existing residents, including members of ethnic minorities, before those of individuals who want to settle here.'[40]

This differs in no way from the explicitly exclusionist rhetoric that we have seen was used against Jewish entrants in 1888: 'Surely our own people have the first claim upon us.' Spencer's inclusion of 'ethnic minorities' in the definition of existing residents, far from being a stand against racism, actually seeks to draw into support for controls those of the undocumented whose stay here is being tolerated at least for the time being. Within all this self-imposed thought control there is nowhere considered an international viewpoint, one that does not privilege British residents, a viewpoint that is against controls *in principle*.

Throughout Spencer's book there is a futile search for a rational system of controls. Likewise, another critic of restrictions has recently called for a 'sane and fair' asylum policy.[41] All this misses the point. Immigration control can never be about rationality or sanity. It can only ever be about oppression and exploitation, which are inevitably both irrational and insane.

THE MEDIA AS THOUGHT CONTROL

In *Nineteen Eighty-Four*, Orwell recognized that the technology of print made it 'easier to manipulate public opinion'.[42] But the real manipulator of opinion in Oceania, the purveyor of Newspeak and doublethink and the destroyer of critical faculties, was the daily, ritualistic Two Minute Hate and the yearly carnival Hate Week. These were spectacles of reaction directed towards the fictional or stereotypical alien such as Emmanuel Goldstein, the designated enemy of the people, with his 'lean Jewish face'[43] or the figure of a Eurasian soldier 'with expressionless Mongolian face'.[44] Hate has material consequences, and one consequence in the novel was that 'an old couple who were suspected of being of foreign extraction had their house set on fire and perished of suffocation'.[45]

In Britain today it is the press that legitimizes and spreads the doublethink anti-ideology of immigration controls. The press assumes the role of the daily Two Minute Hate and surpasses the role of the Hate Week in its hyperbolic and condemnatory language against those subject to controls. For some sections of the media, every day is Hate Day and every week is Hate Week. The attack on the alien goes across time. One paper in particular has consistently and historically, for over a century, supported controls against the undocumented, irrespective of the identity of the latter. So join the *Daily Mail* guessing game! See if you can guess the year of the three following *Daily Mail* quotes:

> It was 8-10pm on Christmas Day when the first mob struck. There were around 150 of them, howling and yelling as they made their way to the French mouth of the Channel Tunnel.

The way stateless Jews from Germany are pouring in from every port of the country is becoming an outrage.

There landed yesterday at Southampton from the transport *Chesire* over 600 so-called refugees, their passages having been paid out of the Lord Mayor's Fund. There was scarce a hundred of them that had, by right, deserved such help, and these were the Englishmen of the party. The rest were Jews…They fought and jostled for the foremost places on the gangways…When the Relief Committee passed by they hid their gold and fawned and whined and in broken English asked for money for their train fare.

These quotes go back through time and appear timeless: 27 December 2001, 20 August 1938 and 3 February 1900.

Today we have the same or analogous quotes appearing virtually every day. For instance, the *Daily Express* has reproduced 20 of its front-page articles attacking asylum-seekers under the caption 'We told you so.'[47]

The issue is not simply one of constant repetition of Newspeak and doublethink. It is also that the doublethink becomes more and more divorced from rationality and from sanity. A headline in the *Sun* proclaims: 'Asylum-seekers steal the Queen's birds for barbecues'. The front-page story appeared under the title 'SWAN BAKE' and a picture of a swan. The article claimed: 'Callous asylum-seekers are barbecuing the Queen's swans, the *Sun* can reveal. East European poachers lure the protected royal birds into baited traps, an official Met Police report says.'[48]

Some of the so-called reporting, and in particular the methods used, is reminiscent in style of Nazi propaganda in the notorious *Der Stürmer*. We have already seen how today's refugees and migrants are sometimes caricatured through cartoon, and this is essentially no different from the way Jews were caricatured. In July 1936, *Der Stürmer* showed a cartoon entitled 'Unfruitful' of a voluptuous Jewish woman with the caption 'lost to the German race'. The *Sun* has portrayed the comic-strip of 'Mr Asylum Seeker' who 'dreamt of a country where he could get a free house, go to hospital for free and where his children would get a free education'. Mr Asylum Seeker 'goes through Belgium but most of his friends are stopped and sent home…so on he travels to Britain where he knows he can slip through a net with very big holes in it'.[49] Which cartoon is the more vile?

It is a common doublethink fantasy of the press (and politicians) that racism is not the product of racists but is a consequence of the presence of those subject to racist hatred. In the 1930s, the *Daily Express*, in a leader asking rhetorically 'Shall All Come In?', stated:

> We need to ask, for there is powerful agitation here to admit all Jewish refugees without question or discrimination. It would be unwise to overload the basket like that. It would stir up elements here that fatten on anti-Semitic propaganda.[50]

The (anti-)logic of this is that the way to defeat racism is to get rid of the victims of racism. Doublethink (*doublethinkdoubleplus*) again becomes a self-fulfilling prophesy. A central institution in stirring up racism, in fattening up the racists, is the press itself. Perhaps it is not surprising that the fascist British National Party on its website has posted a recent front-page *Daily Express* article linking asylum-seekers with terrorism, stating 'British press is helping to spread BNP message'.[51] And again, this message of hate has material consequences. This is the same message with the same brutal consequences as in *Nineteen Eighty-Four* – for example, arson attacks on a refugee hostel in Ireland[52] and the racist murder of Firsat Dag, a Kurdish asylum-seeker, in Glasgow.[53]

EXTENDING THE METAPHOR: WITCHES AND MORAL PANIC

The press acts as a vehicle for a witch-hunt, comparable not only to the daily hate of *Nineteen Eighty-Four* but also to the anti-communist McCarthyite witch-hunt of 1950s USA, and to the actual witch-hunts of medieval times. This is why Arthur Miller's play *The Crucible* (written at the height of the McCarthyite period) provides another apt metaphor for immigration controls.

The play describes the seventeenth century witch-hunt in Salem, Massachusetts. Just as today an almost impossible burden is imposed on those subject to controls to show their presence here is 'legal', so the judge in Salem demands of the accused: how she knows that she is not a witch.[54] Just as today asylum-seekers and all others subject to control are made to appear as demons or devils, so in *The Crucible* Miller writes that the whole country was talking witchcraft.[55] Another author, Lillian Hellman, correctly described McCarthyite America as existing in *Scoundrel Times*.[56] We live in similar times today, courtesy of the power of the press, politicians, patriotism and passports.

The press is, perhaps more than any other institution, responsible for enforcing near conformity and uniformity on the political question of immigration controls. It is the consistency of the outpourings of Newspeak and doublethink nonsense that dumbs and numbs all critical faculties, leading to a sheep-like acceptance of immigration controls as being somehow natural.

This successful attack on the intellect is made very clear today in the fact that many writers and commentators who are manifestly opposed to controls cannot bring themselves actually to state this; or if they do state it then the statement is surrounded with so many caveats as to become meaningless. They have taken a vow of silence. Professor Michael Dummett in his book *On Immigration and Refugees* proposes that 'national frontiers should everywhere be open'. He then immediately deprives this of all content by reverting to neo-Malthusian arguments about overcrowding, saying:

> In two rare cases a state does have the right to exclude intending immigrants: that in which people are in genuine danger of being submerged, and that in which the number wishing to come would bring about serious over-population.[57]

Professor Vaughan Robinson concludes another book by launching a rousing attack on 'the moral panic that currently exists about "our" ability to maintain the purity of our national and local space'.[58] It is quite remarkable that the existence of immigration restrictions, which are the prime mechanism for the control of national space, is then left unquestioned. Indeed, Robinson – in what can only be described as a doublethink act – calls for 'a more efficient removals system for those who are abusing the system'.[59] It is as though an unreserved, un-nuanced, unequivocal call for no immigration controls would be to cross some politically uncrossable Rubicon. The self-imposed mind control of *Nineteen Eighty-Four* has become virtually synonymous with immigration controls.

Another writer says that 'the radical alternative, and the one that many of us feel in our hearts is the right one, is the idea of "no borders": people should be free to go wherever they please'.[60] However, the mind controls the heart and the same writer simply does not argue the case for no controls but apparently accepts the need for 'forcible returns' and to regard open borders as not being a 'realistic alternative' to closed borders.

Belief in controls and all their justifications has become what Orwell described as 'lunatic credulity'.[61] Just like gay romance in the 1894 poem 'Two Loves' by Alfred Douglas (ironically himself a racist and anti-semite), the abolition of controls – all controls – has become via doublethink the programme that 'dare not speak its name'.

7. PROLES AND POOR LAWS:
HOW THE UNDOCUMENTED ARE OUTSIDE THE WELFARE SYSTEM

The government has taken away from me: a chance to work / a place to live / food to eat, and to feed my family / health services, to support me when I am ill / my passport, so I can't go anywhere else / the chance of finding a solicitor / because they say I have no case for asylum and if they give me nothing I will go back to my country. I can't go home. It is not safe. I am trapped here, with nothing...forever.

— Asylum-seeker's poetic account of his situation[1]

How can I run away when I have a baby and no money? Where could I go?

— Detained asylum-seeker[2]

PARALLEL UNIVERSES

Apartheid still exists, and it exists in Great Britain. There is a complete separation on the level of welfare between those with an acceptable immigrant status and those without such status. Asylum-seekers, the latest demonized class of entrants, are reduced to the level of the unacceptable, to the *harijan* (untouchables) of the imperialist heartlands, to social and welfare pariahs. However they are not alone. All migrants and immigrants devoid of the correct documentation are reduced to destitution and are forced to exist outside of the support of the welfare state. They have become the 'proles' of Orwell's *Nineteen Eighty-Four* — just about tolerated because of the work they do (juristically often defined as illegal labour) but otherwise ostracized.

As is written in the novel, 'The proles are not human beings'[3] and, as the party slogan puts it in typical doublethink: PROLES AND ANIMALS ARE FREE.[4] Substitute the *undocumented* of fact for the *proles*

of fiction. In *Nineteen Eighty-Four* the proles have no access to the life of
the ruling, dominant, party, either the privileged Inner Party to which
O'Brien belongs or the unprivileged Outer Party of Winston. Likewise,
the modern undocumented have no access to mainstream welfare
provision. In this sense they have become an underclass. In many other
senses they have been abstracted from the class system altogether and
exist in a segregated form. Like the proles, they live apart from the rest of
society, surviving in their own dimension on the other side of the under-
neath.

This segregation has taken two interlocking forms. First came the
exclusion from welfare of those subject to immigration controls. This
exclusion has been a process over several decades. However, it became
cumulative and generalized with the three pieces of legislation in the
1990s to which reference has been made: the Conservative government's Asylum and Immigration Appeals Act 1993 and Asylum and
Immigration Act 1996, followed by Labour's Immigration and Asylum
Act 1999. The latter removed access to means-tested, family and disability benefits.[5] It confirmed that social housing – including both mainstream council housing and homelessness provision – would be unavail-
able to those subject to immigration controls. Finally it made much
community care provision[6] dependent on immigration status, thus drawing
social workers into the orbit of control enforcement.[7] Combined with the
need to prove the 'adequate support and maintenance without recourse
to public funds' requirements of the immigration rules (which are
defined in terms of welfare benefits[8] and housing provision), this placed
the undocumented in a scissors grip worthy of the creator of Big
Brother: no entitlement to benefits because of immigration status, yet
even a potential attempt to claim such benefits resulting in deportation
because of immigration status.

The flip-side of this segregation is the creation of a new poor law
reminiscent of that prevailing in the nineteenth century (and lasting well
into the twentieth century[9]) for the 'undeserving poor' – namely, a
national, punitive scheme based on isolating the undeserving/undocu-
mented from the rest of the community and keeping them in a position
of impoverishment, degradation and powerlessness. This modern
scheme – with a very old pedigree – was introduced by New Labour in
its 1999 legislation and was tightened by the Nationality, Immigration
and Asylum Act 2002. It is based on enforced removal (euphemistically
known in Newspeak as 'dispersal') of 'destitute' asylum-seekers to any

part of the UK at a maintenance level (more Newspeak) deliberately below the poverty level at 70 per cent of income support.

Dispersal is 'voluntary', which is both Newspeak and doublethink in that refusal to be dispersed will be met by homelessness and the withdrawal of the so-called maintenance. Eligibility (i.e. being in the state of both homelessness and hopelessness) for the poor law removes a dependant child and members of the child's family from the protection of a significant part of the Children Act 1989 – namely Section 20, which requires a local authority to 'safeguard and promote' the welfare of children 'in need'.

The scheme applies only to asylum-seekers. All other migrants and immigrants are excluded even from the poor-law safety net. They become the most undeserving of the undeserving. In the world of the damned the asylum-seeker is privileged!

NASTY NASS

The poor-law scheme is administered by the Home Office. The bureaucratic arm created for this purpose is the National Asylum Support Service (NASS). This is further doublethink as NASS provides neither a service nor support to asylum-seekers; its main function is to demoralize asylum-seekers and, ultimately, force them out of the country through poverty. This interconnection between welfare and removal, between internal and external immigration control, is seen in a NASS pamphlet *The New Asylum Support Scheme*, issued in March 2000. Here it is made quite clear that NASS is not neutral when it comes to the expulsion of failed asylum-seekers, and particularly the expulsion of failed asylum-seeking families with children. The pamphlet states: 'It is, therefore, important that we develop our removals capacity to ensure that we can effectively remove such families from the country.'

There is no contradiction in fact between welfare and removal. This is because NASS is dealing with the *withholding* of welfare. As such it has a crucial role in the whole enforcement process, by starving out the undocumented. In fact, just as the Home Office is at the centre of immigration controls enforcement, so NASS – a body nominally (i.e. by name) designated to support asylum-seekers – is increasingly becoming the central, most important agency in this operation. More doublethink.

A new mechanism of NASS administration was introduced by Labour in its 2002 Nationality, Immigration and Asylum Act.[10] This is the so-called 'accommodation centre' that will lead in future to the near-total physical (as well as legal) segregation of those asylum-seekers who are intended to be involuntarily housed in such centres (many will still be dispersed to ordinary housing). These centres have still to be built (and it was announced in June 2005 that none will be built for at least another five years), yet the very commitment to build them is a threatening signal to refugees. Living in the centres will be involuntary in that the alternative will again be homelessness. In essence they will perform the function of open prisons. They will run alongside the closed prisons of removal centres (previously and correctly known as detention centres) reserved for the damned of the damned – that is, asylum-seekers and non-asylum-seekers whose next stop is deportation and another country. Accommodation centres will also create an educational apartheid in that children placed there will have no access to state education.

In September 2002, a report on these new institutions, the appropriately titled *Asylum City*, was produced by the Asylum Coalition of which the Transport and General Workers Union is a member. In his introduction, the General Secretary of the union described accommodation centres as 'a parallel universe, one created to ensure that asylum-seekers remain separated from our society'. Orwell could not have put it better.

PURSUING THE SEGREGATION

Deprivation of housing, welfare benefits and community care support does not represent the totality of the segregation.[11] It represents only segregation from the state. However, there is another form of segregation of the undocumented, this time, ironically, from those progressive forces who otherwise should be their supporters. As in *Nineteen Eighty-Four*, even protest itself often appears to be stage-managed in order to conceal more than it reveals.

In *Nineteen Eighty-Four*, Winston never knew whether there existed the revolutionary 'Brotherhood' against Big Brother. In the course of his interrogation after being imprisoned he is told that as long as he lived it would remain an unsolved riddle in his mind.[12] Today there is often ignorance of the existence of the undocumented amongst those fighting for positive change in other areas of society. This ignorance, which is actually self-induced, simply confirms the segregation. For instance, there has been recent mass campaigning against the withdrawal of student grants and the imposition of student fees. However, this agitation does not protest against – rather it simply ignores – the facts of internal immigration control against students without the appropriate immigration status. The Education Act 1944 (generally seen as a landmark in establishing a democratic access to education) excluded from grants students not 'ordinarily resident' in the UK, and differential fees for overseas students were introduced in 1967 through administrative guidance.

Likewise there is constant agitation to preserve what is seen as a guiding principle of the National Health Service, namely that treatment should be free at the point of need. This ignores another reality: since the National Health Services Amendment Act 1949 there has been provision for the making of regulations to exclude from free hospital treatment those 'not ordinarily resident'. Such regulations were in fact made in 1982[13] and were strengthened in 2004[14] when failed asylum- seekers were redefined as 'not ordinarily resident', and there is now propaganda to extend these restrictions to general practitioners.[15]

The whole concept of 'not ordinarily resident' is a designation appropriate both for the proles and the vaporized non-persons of *Nineteen Eighty-Four*. It refers politically, and the jurisprudence flows from this, to the alien, the other, the outsider, the unwanted, the pariah. And both main political parties, Labour and Conservative, have fantastical plans for future geographical segregation of the unwanted. David Blunkett, as Labour Home Secretary, proposed that all asylum-seekers be imprisoned in 'processing centres' outside of the European Union.[16] Oliver Letwin, Tory shadow Home Secretary, trumped this by suggesting such processing take place on some 'remote island'.[17] This echoes another piece of forgotten history – the plan by Edward Heath, the then Tory Prime Minister, over thirty years ago to dump 57,000 Ugandan Asians (many with British passports) threatened with expulsion by Idi Amin. He is reported to have said: 'Find some islands to put them on and the further away the better.'[18] Bermuda, the Falklands, the Solomon Islands were all approached – and all in their turn refused help.

Forcibly transporting asylum-seekers to islands or zones has even more ugly resonances. In the period 1938–40, the Nazis planned to ship the *Untermensch* to Madagascar. In today's political reality it is the undocumented, those unwanted by the immigration authorities, who fulfil the role of the *Untermensch* – and who have to be segregated either through welfare deprivation or geographically, or both, from civil society. And of course the most vivid forms of segregation are deportation or refusal of entry.

One relevant case, that of Mukesh Patel, contained what might be described as the ultimate Freudian slip and thereby achieved double-think status. Mukesh, whose entire family lived in the UK, suffered a severe spinal defect. He was refused entry on the grounds that 'One of the considerations with a disabled person is that they should be able to stand on their own feet.'[19]

PURSUING THE METAPHOR

In *Nineteen Eighty-Four*, the economic deprivation and social segregation of the proles is described in the following way: 'The Party taught that the proles were natural inferiors'[20] who must be kept in a state of powerlessness and treated like animals. Hidden allusions and analogies to the proles (and to the modern immigration proles, the *sans-papiers*) can be found throughout historical and creative literature. For instance, Gareth Stedman Jones in a seminal work of history, *Outcast London*, describes the segregation of another underclass and the consequent moral panic created by this segregation:

> In the second half of the nineteenth century, Victorian civilization felt itself increasingly threatened by 'Outcast London'. Stripped of the mythology which surrounded this phrase, 'Outcast London' symbolized the problem of the existence and persistence of certain endemic forms of poverty, associated under the generic term, casual labour. London represented the problem of casual labour in its most acute form, and the fears engendered by the presence of a casual labouring class were naturally at their greatest in a city which was both the centre and the symbol of national and imperial power. Such fears permeated conservative, liberal and socialist thought alike.[21]

Stedman shows how, particularly in London's East End, 'casual labour' frequently became synonymous with 'sweated labour', and this itself became synonymous with 'immigrant labour'. In the case of tailoring, for instance, 'Irish workers were conspicuous in the East End slop trade from the 1850s onwards'.[22] Likewise, the East End became the sweatshop home of Jewish labour in the tailoring, cabinet-making and footwear industries, this combination of class and national origins furthering the process of geographical segregation and the making of ghettos and ghetto culture.

FROM DICKENS TO DETENTION

Within the realms of creative literature the nineteenth century also provides the most vivid creation and recreation of a social and welfare apartheid, which foreshadows our contemporary immigration poor laws generally, and the modern removal and accommodation centres in particular. This is the workhouse of Charles Dickens' *Oliver Twist*, the workhouse being the central component of the poor law and the only alternative to starvation for the unemployed. The story is best known for the hungry Oliver's 'rebellion' in daring to ask for more food:

> For more!' said Mr Limpkins. 'Compose yourself Bumble and answer me distinctly. Do I understand that he asked for more, after he had eaten the supper allotted by the dietry?' 'He did sir' replied Bumble. 'That boy will be hung,' said the gentleman in the white waistcoat; 'I know that boy will be hung'.[23]

The comparison to the immigration accommodation centre is prescient. No-one pretends that removal centres entail anything other than forced detention. However, in classic doublethink, accommodation centres (like other dispersed accommodation) are depicted as 'voluntary' even though the alternative will be destitution and a life on the streets. This doublethink is ironically described by Dickens through the deliberations of the board administering the workhouse: 'So they established the rule, that all poor people should have the alternative (for they would compel nobody, not they) of being starved by a gradual process in the house, or by a quick one out of it.'[24] The board then justifies the punitive regime of the workhouse by standing reality on its head:

> They found out at once what ordinary folks would never have discovered – the poor people liked it! It was a regular place of public entertainment for the poorer classes, – a tavern where there was nothing to pay – a public breakfast, dinner, tea, and supper, all the year round.[25]

In an almost surreal equation with this extract from *Oliver Twist*, and utterly devoid of irony, is some of the evidence given in the House of Commons Home Affairs Committee's report on *Asylum Removals* by the private companies responsible for running detention/removal centres.[26]

Children incarcerated at Dungavel are described by Premier Detention Centres as enjoying 'a very positive experience'.[27] UK Detention Services at Harmondsworth describe themselves as 'envious' of the quality of the food provided to the detainees,[28] and the representative from Wackenhut UK Ltd (responsible for Tinsley House removal centre at Gatwick and the detention centre at Manchester Airport) agreed that 'a comfortable tummy solves a lot of problems'.[29]

Who needs Dickens when we have Wackenhut? And who needs Wackenhut when we have *Nineteen Eighty-Four* and the Ministry of Plenty? This was the ministry that issued a promise that there would be no reduction in the chocolate ration during 1984, though in reality the chocolate ration was to be reduced from thirty grammes to twenty.[30] In Oceania the unreal statistics continually came from the telescreen declaring that 'As compared with last year there is more food.'[31]

This literary madness is now in competition with material reality. So Harmondsworth, of which we are told we should be 'envious', has at the time of writing witnessed a suicide by hanging followed by an uprising of the detainees who took control of the institution and tried to burn it down before being overwhelmed by Tornado squads – made up of prison officers trained in quelling riots.[32] Who would be envious of conditions provoking such individual desperation as suicide and such violent collective action in pursuit of freedom? These are conditions more befitting the lunatic asylum of popular imagination than accommodation for those wishing political asylum. The crazy and the undocumented, both deserving of support and solidarity in their own right, are rapidly becoming identified as one entity.

What is clear is that the British state needs the UK Detention Service and all the other private prison operators to act as a deterrent to the undocumented – not simply to keep the undocumented apart from civil society, but to legitimize this segregation through a process of brutalization, of which hunger and/or inappropriate diet is but one manifestation. The testimonies of detainees on the issue of nutrition are highly revealing. In September 2002, the Maternity Alliance with others produced a pamphlet *A Crying Shame* (about pregnant asylum-seekers and their babies in detention).[33] The second quotation at the start of this chapter is taken from this devastating document, which provides what can only be described as the ultimate indictment of immigration controls.

Here are what some of the other detained mothers say:

> I started to be sick, I can't eat. You know the food they gave us in detention, every time I smelled it I started to vomit. All I could take was milk and water. I used to cry and tell [the midwives] 'I can't eat, and I'm very concerned; when I can't eat what will happen to the baby?'

> Breakfast there is only 8–9 o'clock, lunch is 12 to 1, and dinner is 6 to 7. So by later, by late night when I was feeling hungry, there is nothing – overnight there is nothing. It is not easy.

> We don't eat good here. Sometimes I eat just once a day because it's not nice food. I can't breastfeed.

All those, the undocumented of every description, segregated in this and other ways, have been described elsewhere as *margizens* – non-citizens 'truly living on the margins of prosperous Western societies'.[34] It is perhaps more accurate to say that these *margizens*, these contemporary proles, have now been forced well beyond the margins into a nether world of a totally different reality: into a parallel universe.

IMMIGRATION CONTROL, WELFARE CONTROL, POVERTY CONTROL

There is an apparent paradox at the heart of immigration controls. The question to be asked is why the first two major movements for immigration controls, and the internal welfare controls that ran alongside them, coincided with the first two stages in the development of the welfare state. Intuitively it would have been thought that the supposed universal, humanitarian values of welfare would have led to a more, not less, generous attitude towards open borders. One lesson to be learned is not to trust intuition, only political analysis.

The Aliens Act 1905 (against Jews) and the Commonwealth Immigrants Act 1962 (against black people) were enacted or enforced in periods of welfare expansion. The Aliens Act came into force in 1906, the time of the great, reforming Liberal government which introduced those milestones in welfare of state pensions (the Old Age Pensions Act in 1908) along with sickness and unemployment benefit (the National Insurance Act in 1911). Controls against black people, starting with the Commonwealth Immigrants Act, were enacted precisely at the time of the flowering of the welfare state; indeed they were first enacted by the government of Harold Macmillan, whose avaricious slogan was 'We've never had it so good'. Inevitably and deliberately, those excluded from the country were excluded from the country's welfare. Even those who managed to gain entry were confronted by internal controls – by entitlements being linked to immigration or nationality or residency status and therefore not being entitlements at all. The hidden history of the Liberal government's welfare benefit reforms is that they were restricted in this way,[35] and the whole history of the post-war welfare state has been one of linking entitlement to status.[36] Why has this been the case?

There are several answers and many lessons to be learned. First, welfare is neither humanitarian nor universal. History shows it to be built on the basest nationalism and racism. For instance, it is a trite but true observation that what was created post-war was a *national* health service, not an *international* health service.[37] Second, this provides the resolution of the seeming paradox whereby welfare reform coincides with immigration control. Both are built on xenophobia and national chauvinism. Third, the present dismantling of the welfare state is occurring differentially with those subject to immigration controls being amongst the first to be excluded. This is the significance of the present wave of external and internal controls starting in the 1990s. Fourth, welfare, like immigration restrictions, is itself used as a form of control – or more accurately, destitution and poverty (that is the denial of welfare) are so used.

Control through poverty is at the heart of the class basis of immigration controls. A recent Court of Appeal case (the case of 'T') illustrates this, as well as illustrating an Orwellian understanding of the concept of 'human rights' such that it effectively becomes equated with 'human wrongs'.[38] Section 55 of the Nationality, Immigration and Asylum Act 2002 excludes from even the NASS-administered poor-law regime those refugees who do not make an asylum claim 'as soon as reasonably practical'. This has been interpreted by NASS as requiring a claim to be made *on arrival*, which many refugees are understandably reluctant to do before obtaining advice. Section 55 also contains an exemption to its own exclusion provisions where there would otherwise be a breach of the Human Rights Convention (such as Article 3 – prohibition against inhuman or degrading treatment).

In the Court of Appeal case in question, a Malaysian refugee was refused NASS 'support' by virtue of Section 55. As a consequence he sought shelter by living rough at Heathrow airport. His plight was described by one lower-court judge as follows:

> [The] Article 3 claim is based on his circumstances when 'living' at Heathrow. He found it difficult to rest or sleep because of the noise and the light and because he would be moved on by the police. Any ablutions were confined to public lavatories and he was unable to wash his hair or his clothes or to bathe or shower. He developed a problem with his left eye and also a cough. He carried his belongings around with him in holdalls and became increasingly worried. [His solicitors] referred to difficulties there and to T's health being affected. They referred to his becoming increasingly demoralized and humiliated. They also referred to his fear of sleeping on the streets lest he might be attacked and have his papers stolen.

In spite of all this, the court held that T had not suffered degrading treatment. He was therefore left with no support whatsoever. At one point the court described T as being mentally ill and as believing that his acts and thoughts were constantly watched. This is a direct reminder of *Nineteen Eighty-Four*, of the Thought Police. First the system *accuses* you of being mad, then it tries to make you believe you *are* mad, and then it actually does *drive you mad*. Winston, during his interrogation by O'Brien, reflects that there was no idea that he had ever had, or could have, that O'Brien had not known, scrutinized and discarded, in which case how could it be true that O'Brien was mad? 'It must be he, Winston, who was mad.'[39]

Whatever T's mental state, the truth is that his acts and thoughts, like those of all the undocumented, were and are subject to investigation at any time by the modern Big Brother – that is the Home Office and its multitude of powerful agents, immigration officers, the police, NASS, the courts, who collectively are the O'Brien of immigration controls.

MORE HISTORY, MORE POOR LAWS

Poverty has always been a method for controlling the poor. For instance, sixteenth-century Justices of the Peace had the power to order the unemployed (and in theory anyone else) to work in the fields at harvest time and to command that those caught begging 'be tied to carts and dragged through the town, whipped until they were bloody, have the "gristle" part of their ears cut off, be branded on their face or breast and, for the most unreformable, be hanged.'[40]

However, the most vivid comparison between the modern undocumented and the historic undeserving remains with the Poor Law Amendment Act of 1834 (which is why the NASS-administered scheme can correctly be designated a poor law, controlling the refugee, the migrant and the immigrants). As has been seen, the latter two catagories are controlled by the scheme precisely because they are outside the 'safety net' of the scheme, and so remain ghettoized in their own destitution. In this respect they find themselves in an analogous position to those nineteenth-century unemployed, now forgotten, now unknown, whose dignity led to an active refusal to enter the workhouse. There is a reminder here of Bob Dylan's lyric that 'when you got nothing, you got nothing to lose...'[41]; and another reminder of Janis Joplin (whose original group was tellingly called *Big Brother and the Holding Company*) who sang that 'freedom is just another word for nothing left to lose.'[42]

Just as asylum-seekers receive 'maintenance' at below income support level, so the unemployed under the nineteenth-century poor law were to be maintained below the level of income of the worst paid – known as the principle of 'less eligibility'. Similarly, just as the level of nutrition in removal centres is below the average (and presumably will likewise be the case in the new accommodation centres in order to continue to act as a deterrent to refugees), so the less-eligibility principle ensured, that in the workhouse, 'only the cheapest fare be served in the house: an ample fare might be served only if it did not render the condition of the burdensome poor more desirable than that of the self-maintaining poor'.[43] Another Commissioner spelt out the centrality of poverty control when he said: 'I wish to see the Poor House looked on with dread by the labouring classes...For without this where is the stimulus to industry?'[44]

In the same way, the NASS system, with its accommodation centres, its dispersed housing, its maintenance below poverty level, is also conceived as a stimulus – a stimulus to the undocumented to keep out of, or be driven by poverty from, the country. This is the ultimate segregation. It is directly comparable to the workhouse whose intolerable conditions were designed to drive inmates back on to the job market. The regime of the old poor law was that of a cashless economy, as workhouse inmates received no wages for their (usually pointless) labour. Likewise, when the NASS scheme was first introduced asylum-seekers were not 'supported' with money but instead were given vouchers and thus locked into a pre-capitalist cashless system.[45] Within the workhouse, unpaid work of the most demeaning and unproductive nature was compulsory. Under the modern poor law, paid work is prohibited for the asylum-seeker. Both compulsion and prohibition are complementary and constitute a common system of control – control through impoverishment.

Now, with the Asylum and Immigration (Treatment of Claimants, etc.) Act 2004, this control has come historically full circle. The Act (through Section 10) has imposed forced labour (i.e. slavery) on a category of failed asylum-seekers, those rejects who cannot yet be physically deported because they are too ill to travel, or don't have the appropriate documents, or (another example of doublethink in respect of a failed asylum-seeker) are considered 'unsafe' to return to the country of origin. Under the 1999 immigration and asylum legislation and subsequent NASS guidance there is residual provision to offer this group the most primitive ('hard case') support and accommodation.[46] This has now been reduced to an actual relationship of slavery by making receipt of such minimal help dependent on the compulsory undertaking of so-called 'community services'. This is exactly the same judicial punishment that courts can inflict on convicted criminals, except that asylum-seekers have been found guilty of nothing other than seeking asylum. As an alternative to deportation this enforced labour exactly mirrors Big Brother's crazy slogan: FREEDOM IS SLAVERY!

MORE ANALOGIES

The Victorian poor law, however harsh, however draconian, drew no distinctions based on nationality. The dreaded workhouse was 'available' to all nationalities. This principle had been established in a court case prior to 1834, prior to the overtly punitive nature of nineteenth-century welfare, when it had been decreed in respect of 'foreigners' that 'the law of humanity, which is anterior to all positive laws, obliges us to afford them relief, to save them from starving'.[47] This is patently more progressive than the present NASS regime.

However, immediately upon the arrival of Jewish refugees in the 1880s relative progress turned to absolute reaction. As early as 1888 the House of Commons established a Select Committee on Emigration and Immigration (Foreigners). This wrote to every parish and township asking about the numbers of non-citizens dependent on the poor law.[48] Ideologically this was the precursor of the modern relationship between immigration status and welfare.

The historical and political comparisons continue. A defining feature of the workhouse system was the deprivation of civil rights – the right to freedom where to live, the right to be with family (men and women were kept apart), and the right not to exist under a punitive, regimented regime. Today, the NASS scheme is based on forced dispersal, which often means separation from close family and an intolerable regimentation. For instance, periods of absence of more than a week from dispersed property have to be reported to NASS and can be undertaken only with the permission of NASS.[49] It will be seen in the next chapter that 'supported' asylum-seekers have to constantly provide NASS with an unprecedented amount of private and personal information. In its role as a social and economic segregationist, NASS has in effect taken on an analogous function to the hated Poor Law Commissioners of the 1834 legislation and the Thought Police of *Nineteen Eighty-Four*.

The analogy goes even deeper, and once more enters right into the heart of local government. Under the nineteenth-century poor law, parish relief (i.e. the workhouse) could itself be denied to those who could not show they were 'settled' in the area. Those so denied could be removed (deported) back to the parish where they had settlement.[50] This led to struggles between parishes over denial of obligations. Likewise today, local authorities are engaged in similar disputes, again based juridically on concepts of settlement. In one case it was held that an asylum-seeker who was housed in a dispersal area did not acquire a local connection there.[51] This meant that a successful asylum-seeker who was eligible to apply for rehousing as a homeless person and who moved to another local authority was eligible for rehousing by the new authority of his/her choice. That council could not lawfully compel him or her to return to the dispersal area. Harrow and Kensington wanted to remove/deport a homeless refugee back to Glasgow and the court refused. Within the reactionary context of the whole scheme of internal controls this was a progressive decision. Precisely because it was progressive, the government reversed it at the first possible opportunity, in the 2004 legislation. This now compels those granted asylum and who otherwise would be homeless to continue to live in the dispersed areas – a recipe for permanent segregation and ghetto creation.[52]

A prominent civil servant and political economist writing critically of the conditions in the Manchester cotton industries just before the 1834 poor laws argued that treating labour (i.e. people) as a mere commodity without feelings or consciousness was 'a folly…allied to madness'.[53] The very construct of the alien and the attempted apartheid of the undocumented, particularly as contained within the forced dispersal regime, is a similar madness.

THE FINAL SEGREGATION

The political and anti-human, anti-humanitarian madness continues to the point where deportation – the final segregation – is seen (often correctly) to be a release from the oppression of internal control. Under the Nationality, Immigration and Asylum Act 2002, NASS poor-law support and a whole new raft of community care legislation can be withheld from failed asylum-seeking individuals or families or persons 'unlawfully' in the UK who have failed 'to cooperate with removal directions'.[54]

This is the ultimate Orwellian demand: help in your own removal or the Home Office will starve you out anyway. *Deportation is Freedom!* This provision was tightened in the Asylum and Immigration (Treatment of Claimants, etc.) Act 2004.[55] It was seen in the previous chapter that this criminalizes those who do not assist in their own removal. The 2004 legislation has now decreed that NASS and community care assistance terminates once the Secretary of State has certified that a person has failed 'without reasonable excuse to take reasonable steps to leave the UK voluntarily' – that is, even before removal directions (the legal requirement on which deportation is validated). Once more it can be seen that the construct of 'voluntary departure' is fraudulent. It is more like a response to blackmail, to an offer that can't be refused.

ECHOES OF A GENOCIDAL PAST

The issue of children's rights becomes important here. For a local authority to maintain its obligations to the welfare of children in such non-returning families, they may have to be placed into the care of that local authority under the Children Act 1989. With the logic of *Nineteen Eighty-Four*, Beverley Hughes, the then Minister responsible for immigration, speaking in the Standing Committee on the 2004 Act, said that children can avoid being put into care by joining their parents in leaving the country: 'Returning home is an available remedy for every family to whom the measure might apply'.[56]

Hughes provided a spurious humanitarian twist to the doublethink Home Office preference for this so-called 'voluntary departure', saying:

> Members have heard me speak about enforced returns, but have
> they been out with an arrest team and seen what this means?
> With families, it is always done with mixed teams of men and
> women who are specially trained, and it is done very well, but if
> one imagines someone turning up at people's front door at 4 or 5
> in the morning and getting them and their children out of bed
> and taking them to a place of detention, ready to go on a plane...
> this is an experience that one would want to avoid, however well
> and professionally it is done by immigration officers, however
> kindly people are spoken to.[57]

Hughes' concerns seem more about the sensibilities of immigration
officers than the plight of asylum-seekers. Although expulsion is manifestly not the same as extermination, Hughes' words have a resonance of
a genocidal past. This is a past when Heinrich Himmler, the Nazi leader,
addressed the SS officers whose role it was to implement extermination.
He was answering the argument (itself doublethink in an ideology of
Jew-hatred) that there were some 'good Jews' who should be permitted
to live:

> Not one of those who talk like that has watched it happening, not
> one of them has been through it. Most of you will know what it
> means when a hundred corpses are lying side by side, or five
> hundred or a thousand are lying there. To have stuck it out and –
> apart from a few exceptions due to human weakness – to have
> remained decent, that is what has made us tough.[58]

Genocide and removal are not the same. But the bureaucratic mindset
behind both is often indistinguishable. It is the mindset of 'the banality
of evil'.

8. WE ARE ALL IMMIGRATION OFFICERS NOW
HOW BIG BROTHER IS EVERYWHERE

You just look at the shoes. Third World punters posing as experienced international travellers have a blind spot when it comes to footwear and usually get it hideously wrong

— Tony Saint, Sunday Observer[1]

CORRUPT CONTROLS AND MURDEROUS METAPHORS

There are many simple metaphors that can be devised to describe the day-to-day, hour-to-hour operation of immigration controls and the British state. I have described them elsewhere as a 'vortex into which is sucked and then spun out all those the nation defines as "unlawful" – those modern outlaws whose labour is unneeded (or no longer needed) and whose presence is unwanted'.[2]

Controls are nominally the responsibility of the Home Office alone. In reality they have now developed to such a point that the entire state machinery along with its civic and social components – welfare workers, local authority employees, the so-called voluntary sector, business enterprises, individual citizens – have to a greater or lesser extent become part of the administration of controls. Immigration restrictions are no longer enforced just by what Friedrich Engels, the collaborator of Karl Marx, described as the 'bodies of armed men',[3] though many of these overtly repressive bodies directly managed by the Home Office (police officers, immigration officers, prison and detention officers, private security firms) are crucial to their physical enforcement.

Imagine a wheel with the Home Office at the centre but with a myriad of spokes emanating out with messages constantly passing back up and down and between the spokes. Or think of a series of concentric circles designed to protect the imperialist heartland, with the Home Office being chief designer and architect. Each of these circles is arranged in the round like the stagecoaches of the early American colonizers and they exist politically for very much the same reasons – to protect the expropriators from the dispossessed.

The modern logistics of protection are strung out globally. The outermost circle consists of the visa sections at British Embassies, High Commissions and Consulates, whose role is to deny visas to the unchosen. Moving inwards, the next circle is by definition mobile and peripatetic. It consists of the carrying companies of the world – airlines, shipping firms, rail companies, road hauliers – which began operating in 1987 as agents of immigration control by virtue of carriers liability legislation.[4] This financially penalizes carriers for transporting passengers without the appropriate documentation and so is part of the privatization of controls. Moving inwards again, the next circle is occupied by those direct guardians of the motherland's shores, the immigration officers, greeting new arrivals with detention and departure. The next circle of defence is within the country itself and consists of the comprehensive apparatus of the daily machinery of controls – the 'bodies of armed men'. And so it goes on. There is a circle of employers (every employer in the land) who since 1996 have been coerced into the role of control enforcers under threat of being fined for hiring undocumented labour.[5] There is a circle of marriage registrars: since 1999 these have been given the responsibility not just of conducting marriages but of 'shopping' participants to the Home Office for immigration purposes.[6] Further, under the Asylum and Immigration (Treatment of Claimants, etc.) Act 2004 there has been created a special class of marriage registrars authorized to conduct marriages involving the undocumented.[7] There is a circle of internal welfare controllers – the 'soft cops' – who are reduced to refusing welfare and reporting those refused to the Home Office. Then there is the orchestrator of internal controls, the National Asylum Support Service.

A further circle (more like a hoop of fire) is occupied by the so-called Community Legal Services whose ostensible role is to provide legal aid for the undocumented and their legal representatives but whose actual function is to deny financial help. Since April 2004, legal-aid lawyers are allowed only five hours to prepare for asylum cases and three hours to prepare for other immigration cases.[8] So much for the rule of law. One is reminded of Bob Dylan singing (in *It's All Right Ma*) that money doesn't talk, it swears.

It gets worse. In a pilot scheme introduced in the North-West of England, the middleman (Community Legal Services) has been dispensed with and the Home Office itself allocates legal representatives to asylum-seekers.[9] Talk about being an arbiter in your own case!

At the very centre of these circles within circles is always the Home Office, the star of the immigration control galaxy and providing the ideological and juridical impetus to the universe around it. Perhaps ultimately the most vivid metaphor for immigration controls is to imagine a many-fanged monster of the deep. If one fang doesn't poison the undocumented then another will probably do the job. If none of the poison works then some deadly limb will throttle the victim. There is no point in cutting off any particular fang or limb, the whole monster has to go.

BIG BROTHER AS LEGAL FETISHIST

The Home Office sometimes appears almost as a substitute for the state itself, pulling the strings of all other statutory and extra-statutory agencies. The Home Office as puppeteer is indeed another apt image. In the Orwellian-sounding *Home Office Group Corporate Plan 2004–5* we learn of the strategy to 'increase removals...working with other governments and other government departments' and to 'build relations with local government and the voluntary sector...to better coordinate action on removals'.[10] In *Nineteen Eighty-Four*, the allegorical equivalent to the Home Secretary is Big Brother, at the epicentre of all repression. Big Brother controls the party. Big Brother controls the state. Big Brother *is* effectively the party and the state. One is reminded of the polemic by Trotsky against Lenin before the former became a Bolshevik:

> In the internal politics of the party these [Lenin's] methods lead the party organization to 'substitute' itself for the party, the Central Committee to substitute itself for the party organization, and finally a 'dictator' substitutes himself for the Central Committee.[11]

On the first page of *Nineteen Eighty-Four* we are introduced to the slogan BIG BROTHER IS WATCHING YOU, which could quite easily be applied to the British state. Maybe a modern slogan could be HOME OFFICE RULES – UK. Winston, in his secret diary, keeps repeating his own slogan: DOWN WITH BIG BROTHER.[12] But on the last page, in the last lines of *Nineteen Eighty-Four* we read that Winston 'loved Big

Brother'.[13] His individualistic rebellion, his relationship with Julia, has been crushed. The contemporary undocumented remain uncrushed, but not for want of effort by the Home Office.

Hate is the mechanism by which Big Brother controls the system, not simply by attacking the objects of hatred but by dehumanizing those who hate. At the climax of the Two Minute Hate the participants break into a sheep-like chant 'B-B...B-B...B-B' in worship of Big Brother 'as an act of self-hypnosis'.[14]

Racism today fulfils a similar role of dehumanization. The contemporary equivalent of the repetitive obeisance to the authority of Big Brother can be found in those enforcers of external and internal immigration controls who implement restrictions on the grounds they are 'obeying orders' and refuse to countenance either themselves or anyone else disobeying them because they are 'the law'. The same applies to the supporters and onlookers of controls who invoke obedience to the law as a moral imperative. This amoral obedience and worship of the law ('legal fetishism') is what sustains immigration controls and has been examined in Chapter 4. Big Brother, like law itself, assumes the persona of the immortal. During his interrogation Winston asks whether Big Brother will ever die, and O'Brien replies 'Of course not. How could he die?'[15] Similarly, immigration controls are usually presented as somehow eternal – without beginning or end, a part of nature itself.[16]

BIG BROTHER AS OMNIPRESENT

Big Brother, like the Home Office, is everywhere, is omnipresent. Like the Home Office and Home Secretary, he operates through state and non-state agencies, through the various ministries of Truth, Love, Plenty and Peace, through the Inner party and the Outer Party. Winston, like the vast majority of members, is confined to the Outer Party and denied the privileges of the elite leadership.[17] Then there is the Junior Anti-Sex League, a startling precursor of modern immigration control via sex control. There are the Spies, the youth organization where children screen and arrest parents – and which now also forms the subject matter of a U2 song (*The Wanderer*) which describes how men can't walk or freely talk, and sons turn their fathers in. There are the deliberately manipulated Two Minutes Hate and Hate Week. There are the Thought Police (in particular): 'only the Thought Police mattered'.[18]

A combined force of Spies and Thought Police is reproduced in the Nationality, Immigration and Asylum Act 2002. Public bodies such as the police, the Inland Revenue and port medical inspectors are given an obligation to supply information on the undocumented to the Home Secretary.[19] However, Big Brother ultimately relies on 'private' individuals spying on each other, thus ensuring that 'privacy' in Oceania is doublespeak. Parsons' seven-year-old daughter denounces someone after 'she spotted he was wearing a funny kind of shoes...So the chances were he was a foreigner'.[20] At that point the Oceanic state and the individual have become indivisible.

The 2002 Act also requires private employers and financial institutions to disclose information on those subject to immigration controls.[21] Contemporary immigration controls are now frequently dependent on the individual *whistleblower*, acting on her or his own initiative and without any legal obligation. Such a whistleblower is a maverick and may be operating within the immigration service itself. An example is the low-grade civil servant whose claim that undocumented people from eastern Europe were being allowed entry led to the resignation of the Minister for Immigration, Beverley Hughes – a victory that none of the campaigns against controls had been able to achieve.[22]

There is now both an opportunity for, and a pressure on, ordinary citizens to 'shop' those without 'correct' immigration status. This is also the storyline of Arthur Miller's 1955 play *A View From the Bridge*, in which Eddie Carbone informs on his fellow Italian immigrants.[23] The *Sun* newspaper invites its readers to inform on refugees who have (legitimately) claimed backdated benefits,[24] a call that led the government to restrict such payments in its 2004 legislation.[25]

Spying is official government policy, as shown in the 2002 white paper *Secure Borders, Safe Havens*. Buried within this document under a section called 'removals' is a proposal designed to transform Britannia into Oceania. The Home Office declares its intention to 'set up a confidential Immigration Hotline to enable members of the public to report immigration abuse'.[26]

Now the expansion of the control ring has reached a point whereby everyone can become their own immigration officer. Everyone can become Parsons' daughter, a Go Home Office stool-pigeon!

COLLUDING AND REFUSING – IN THEIR OWN WORDS

Central to the immigration Big Brother, and a recurring theme in its growth and reproduction, is *collusion* and *co-option* – that is, the drawing into its orbit and employing as its agents a continually deepening layer of personnel. A vivid example of this is described by James Fergusson in his recent factual study *Kandahar Cockney: A Tale of Two Worlds*. Fergusson describes an immigration appeal against the deportation of an Afghani refugee where both the adjudicator (the judge) and the Home Office presenting officer (the lawyer) are non-British in origin. The judge is Bengali, the lawyer a refugee from Kosovo – both of whose countries have been devastated by imperialism and whose citizens are regularly deported from the UK. Speaking in a manner as much existential as political – whilst purporting to be legal – the state lawyer says:

> But if the Home Office were to grant refugee status to every victim of the civil wars going on in the world it would be like opening the floodgates. Even I can see that. Even as a victim of civil war myself.[27]

The iconic and best known, though perhaps no longer the most significant, representation of immigration controls is the immigration officer – the custodian of the gate into the UK and the pursuer of those deemed to be on the wrong side of the gate. It is not inappropriate that the only non-fictional book written by an immigration officer about the work and the service is called *The Key in the Lock*, by T. W. E. Roche.[28] This confirms what has been long suspected about the ethics and politics of not just individual officers but of the service itself. Perhaps the most striking feature of the book is its revelation of the self-image of the immigration service. Like the army and the police, it sees itself as a collegiate body, as some sort of swashbuckling, Boy's Own entity, answerable to no-one except itself. So Roche thanks 'that great company of people who have been my colleagues in the Immigration Branch…to which I have been so proud to belong'.[29] Later on he writes of the origins of the service (in 1906):

> A considerable pride attached to being members of this 'founders' club. They were breaking new ground, setting up traditions, building an *esprit de corps*, and creating what would nowadays be described as a 'public image'.[30]

Roche supports the 'obeying orders' thesis in defence of the 'unpleasant' nature of much of his job, quoting with approval the statement that 'The Immigration Officer does not make the law, but it is his duty to apply it.'[31] In fact, immigration officers constantly try to make and strengthen the law. Roche himself reports how a petition of support was sent to Enoch Powell MP when the latter was campaigning in the late 1960s to exclude East African Asians and was at the height of his notoriety – with the *Evening Standard* carrying as its headline 'Airport's watchdogs back Enoch'.[32] The then Labour government responded to this racist agitation by passing the restrictive Commonwealth Immigrants Act 1968.

FROM ROCHE TO ORWELL TO MARCUSE – AND BACK AGAIN

Roche has a very clear, if very crude though typical, political justification for controls:

> The roots of alien control, in fact, go deep down into the soil of history to the purely animal defence of home against the invader…in the last resort in the taking up of weapons to repel the enemy.[33]

The acknowledgement that controls can be described as 'animalistic' (wild, untamed) is ironic, but even this isn't true because most animals thrive on the migratory process.

What is true is that, given that human migration is itself perpetual, then the specious equation of migrant with invader is a recipe for perpetual war on the former. Within this scenario there can never be a choice between war and peace, only between war and never-ending war. This is a direct reminder of *Nineteen Eighty-Four*, of the ceaseless and meaningless military campaigns between Oceania, Eastasia and Eurasia – 'war had been literally continuous'.[34] It is also a reminder of how all wars are ultimately justified in Newspeak, as in government propaganda in the 1950s about a 'clean bomb' and 'harmless fallout'. In the rhetoric of the Vietnam war in the 1960s and 1970s, the destruction of villages was labelled a 'pacification programme', village refugees were 'ambient non-combat personnel', and simultaneous carpet-bombing of Cambodia was 'air support'. Similar Newspeak is the more recent naming by the USA of one of its most frightening ballistic weapons as the Peacekeeper Missile. In his seminal book of the 1960s, *One-Dimensional Man*,[35]

Herbert Marcuse specifically refers to the 'Orwellian language'[36] of the then cold war, quoting contemporary political captions such as 'Labor is seeking missile harmony' and consumerist adverts such as one selling a 'Luxury fallout shelter'. Marcuse writes (in language which otherwise could be describing Newspeak) that:

> The spread and the effectiveness of this language testify to the triumph of society over the contradictions which it contains, they are reproduced without exploding the social system…The syntax of abridgement proclaims the reconciliation of opposites… The unification of opposites which characterizes the commercial and political style is one of the many ways in which discourse and communication make themselves immune against protest and refusal.[37]

Roche, in writing about immigration, manages to combine the language of war with that of the crudest stereotypes. The West Indian 'invasion' was just a 'surprise' but that from the Indian subcontinent was a 'veritable shock' consisting of the 'bewildered, gregarious, defensive', just like 'those Russian Jews'.[38] The right-wing politics of the service and those it recruits is shown by their extracurricular scabbing role in the 1926 General Strike, with 'some of the high-spirited young "bloods" of the Immigration Service entering into the spirit of the thing, unloading coal wagons, helping discharge cargoes and even driving cranes'.[39]

> The Orwellian nature of Roche's eulogy of immigration officers can be seen in a purported quote he gives from some traveller: 'I've been refused entry by many countries in my time, but never so pleasantly as by the British.[40]

FURTHER TESTIMONY FROM WITHIN

As something of a counterpoint to Roche, there has recently been written a newspaper article, 'They shall not pass'[41] and a novel, *Refusal Shoes,*[42] by a former immigration officer, Tony Saint, who is not so much disillusioned with the service but appears to have had no illusions from the start.

Saint's newspaper article paints the following picture of the internal life of the service. It is not perceived by its members as a desk job, rather it's a 'siege', 'the Alamo', 'a way of life'. He describes how a hardcore of headhunters 'held a private competition to see which of them could rack

up the most refusals in a year. There was a chart on the notice board
which allowed you to follow the action. There was a pint in it for the
winner.'

At points there is a strange identity between Saint's article and
Nineteen Eighty-Four. In Orwell's novel, alleged 'foreigners' are distin-
guishable, even to seven-year-olds, by their shoes – wearing the 'wrong'
sort of shoes leads to vaporization, to becoming an unperson. And it is
the same at the immigration desks of Heathrow Airport. To quote further
from Saint's article:

> Immigration officers are expected to come up with substantive
> reasons for refusing passengers entry but more often than not the
> decision rests on the subject being seen to be sporting a pair of
> suede winklepickers or plastic crocodile brogues. As systems go,
> it's by no means the least reliable and, once you understand the
> premise, Spotting Refusal Shoes is a game that anyone can play at
> the airport to while away the time.

Refusal Shoes, the title of Saint's novel, is a literary exposé of immigration
controls. We learn of things we would prefer otherwise not to know,
such as that unannounced visits by immigration officers (the modern
Sex League) to ascertain the genuineness of relationships are known
as 'mattress sniffing'.[43] Imprisonment of the undocumented 'has become
a totemistic practice among immigration personnel, priapic proof of
dedication to the cause. To them, the thought of one empty immigration
detention space is an abhorrent vacuum'.[44] The detention cell has
become the fantasy of the immigration officer and the Room 101 of the
undocumented.

THE PUBLIC AND COMMERCIAL SERVICE UNION

Immigration officers are a minority within the Home Office's immigration restrictions apparatus. The majority consists of civil servants
working unseen within the Immigration and Nationality Directorate.
These bureaucrats and apparatchiks are ultimately responsible for
making decisions on asylum applications, on extensions of stay and on
removals. The chief civil servant responsible for all this apparatus is the
Permanent Under-Secretary of State at the Home Office, a highly
political post. Sir Edward Troup, Under-Secretary from 1908 until
1922, wrote in his book *The Home Office* that if it had not been for

controls 'the whole social condition of the country would have been altered substantially for the worse'.[45]

However, the power of workers within the immigration apparatus does not derive just from the might of the Home Office. These workers are organized in another way which supports and strengthens controls. Paradoxically (and regrettably) this way is through trade union membership. There are two unions relevant here, one relatively benign, the other utterly malign.

The first and by far the largest is the Public and Commercial Service Union (PCSU). This major civil service union has its own Immigration Staff Branch which is divided into regional constituencies and which, according to its website, 'represents all grades in the Immigration Service, up to and including Assistant Director '.[46] It is problematic and arguable as to whether the labour movement should be welcoming into its ranks those whose role is to enforce a regime that is so explicitly racist and repressive as to warrant comparison with *Nineteen Eighty-Four*.

Working for the immigration service is not an 'ordinary' occupation. It is an occupation that those on the receiving end would like to see destroyed and closed down. There could in fact emerge (and may well have emerged) a situation where one PCSU member in the Immigration Staff Branch is obliged to deport another PCSU member. This is obviously not a viable situation. The only conceivable progressive reason for unionization is to challenge and undermine controls from within; and, given the number of people involved in internal welfare controls whose involvement forms only part of their job and who are members of other unions, this would seem the most appropriate way forward. However, it is not a way forward yet recognized by any union, so it will have to be fought for politically.

The PCSU Immigration Staff Branch does not view its main, or any purpose, as representing a challenge to controls. Its main concerns are the everyday conditions of its members. In expressing these concerns, the PCSU inevitably legitimizes the politically illegitimate. In its written evidence to the House of Commons Home Affairs Committee report *Asylum Removals*, it expresses 'discontent with the system for removing failed asylum-seekers', but it does this not from the perspective of the refugee but rather 'on the basis of improving the working conditions of members of the union'.[47] It offers no principled objection to controls or their implementation; rather it criticizes the IND's 'business plan' and 'the setting of unrealistic targets'. The latter term refers to the forced and potentially violent removal of human beings. This is the banality of language, the sanitization of the unsanitizable, thriving within the labour movement.

The PCSU normalizes immigration controls by regarding workers within the immigration service as 'ordinary' employees undertaking ordinary employment. This is made clear in the November 2003 edition of the union's *Journal*. The General Secretary, whilst condemning 'prejudice' against asylum-seekers, compliments union members in the immigration service as undertaking a 'professional job' to which the PCSU 'has given and will continue to give 100% support'. Various workers within the service discuss their job. One, an enforcement officer, refers to it as 'worthwhile' and himself as 'compassionate'. The *Journal* gives a typical example of his work:

> It's 6.15am and on a nondescript South London street the fleet of unmarked vans could belong to any number of early risers, builders perhaps or council workers. The Immigration Services arrest team don't announce their arrival, relying instead on undercover intelligence and the element of surprise.

This elevates (or reduces) the vocabulary of *worthwhile* and *compassionate* to Newspeak.

THE IMMIGRATION SERVICE UNION

At least the PCSU is a member of the Trade Union Congress with its own open website. The Immigration Service Union (ISU) is or has neither. It is effectively the house union of the IND, working for much of the time in secret and encouraging its members to operate as political shock-troops for the Home Office.[48] The ISU broke away from the predecessor of the PCSU in 1981 after the latter had called for the repeal of the Immigration Act 1971. In 1985, the ISU met senior civil servants to argue that restrictions be placed on the rights of members of parliament to intervene on behalf of passengers refused entry.[49] Following this meeting, in April 1986 the Home Office introduced guidelines limiting MPs' rights to intervene (for instance by reducing the time in which removal would be deferred).

During this period the ISU embarked on a campaign for pre-entry visas to be imposed on arrivals from Nigeria, Ghana and the Indian subcontinent. It cooperated with the *Sun* newspaper, which carried a half-page headline 'The LIARS' sub-headed 'Whoppers Asians told at

Heathrow'.[50] The *Daily Express* reported that the ISU was preparing politically to have entry clearance introduced and that 'union chiefs are set to ballot their members about moves that would bring Heathrow to a shuddering halt'.[51] The ballot was set for 2 September 1986. On 1 September the Home Office agreed to the imposition of visa control. *The Independent* then described the ISU as virtually running Heathrow Airport and that it and not the Home Office had given written instructions to its members on whom to allow into the UK and whom to keep out.[52]

ARE YOU, OR HAVE YOU EVER BEEN, AN UNDOCUMENTED ALIEN?

Inquisitions – that is, the obtaining through terror by state and quasi-state authorities, such as the church, of information and 'confessions' – has been a feature of much of history. The Spanish Catholic court of Torquemada is probably the most notorious example. One of its more modern manifestations occurred in the 1940s/1950s in the USA. This was the House Un-American Activities Committee (HUAC) which was referred to in Chapter 6.

HUAC was dominated by that most Svengali of characters, Senator Joseph McCarthy, and subjected its victims to the constant, repetitive mantra: 'Are you, or have you ever been, a member of the Communist Party?'. The committee was a combination of the Thought Police and the Spies, which is somewhat ironic given that those hauled before it were in effect being accused of spying for the Soviet Union. HUAC, along with the USA immigration authorities, operated a form of immigration control in reverse, by confiscating the passports of citizens it judged (without trial) to be subversive and thereby confining them within the country's borders. This was the fate of the actor, singer, scholar, athlete and communist Paul Robeson.[53]

In the UK, today's closest analogy to HUAC is the National Asylum Support Service (NASS). Through its involuntary dispersal scheme of 'destitute' asylum-seekers, NASS has the authority to demand the most personal of information. Under the Asylum Support Regulations 2000, dispersed refugees are obliged to provide to NASS, in writing, details of any of the following changes in circumstances:[54] whether she or he is joined in the UK by a dependant / receives or gains access to any money / becomes employed (which is now in any event legally prohibited) / becomes unemployed / changes name / gets married / starts living with a person as if married / gets divorced / separates from a spouse or from a person equivalent to a spouse / becomes pregnant / has a child / starts to share accommodation / moves to a different address / goes into hospital / leaves school / goes to prison or is otherwise held in custody / leaves the UK / ...dies.

This is literally womb-to-tomb surveillance.

THE LOCAL STATE

Today's immigration restrictions could not function without the active support of local government. There is a long history of *ad hoc* collusion between the local authorities and immigration controls.[55] For instance, in 1915 the London County Council linked entitlement to school scholarships to immigration status,[56] and in 1920 it prohibited aliens from council employment.[57] However, in 1993 the then Conservative government launched an initiative ensuring that the local state, along with other parts of the state machinery, would in future have a comprehensive, integrated role in their capacity as immigration Big Brother. This was the so-called Efficiency Scrutiny, the purpose of which was to 'examine the efficiency of existing arrangements for co-operation between the Home Office's Immigration and Nationality Division and other central and local government bodies'.[58] Subsequently, the IND issued its October 1996 guidelines through a Home Office circular entitled *Exchange of Information with the Immigration and Nationality Directorate of the Home Office*, the stated purposes of which were to identify 'claimants who may be ineligible for benefits or services by virtue of their immigration status' and to 'encourage local authorities to pass information to the IND about suspected immigration offenders'.[59]

This pact with the devil was consolidated via the Asylum and Immigration Act 1996 and its mirror image in name and intent, the Immigration and Asylum Act 1999. The 1996 legislation removed welfare state benefit and housing rights from the undocumented,[60] thus obliging local authorities to provide support under the National Assistance Act 1948 and Children Act 1989. This support was provided unwillingly and only as a result of litigation against local authorities. In one of the first cases, the local authority argued that an asylum-seeker without food or shelter had no need of care or attention, a truly Orwellian notion of welfare provision.[61]

Instead of agitating politically for the restoration of rights irrespective of immigration status, local authorities took a position of welcoming whatever relieved them of their obligations to refugees and other *sans-papiers*. So they greeted with approval the imposition by the 1999 legislation of a national poor law and forced dispersal scheme. This legislation, as we saw in Chapter 7, also made much local authority care-in-the-community provision dependent on immigration status, prompting further investigation of such status by the local state acting as our contemporary Spies.

The Association of London Government, in its written submission to the House of Commons Special Standing Committee on the Immigration and Asylum Bill, stated: 'the primary purpose of social services is... not the support and maintenance of destitute asylum-seekers'.[62] The use of the phrase 'primary purpose' reads like a slip of the tongue, like Newspeak, given this was the formulation notoriously once used in the immigration rules to exclude partners of arranged marriages. Similar endorsements to the poor law were given by the Local Government Association and Kent County Council.[63] This was not a political situation where local authorities were coerced or even seduced into colluding with reaction. Rather they were equal partners in promoting it as a way of avoiding their own statutory obligations under the National Assistance and Children Acts. If they had resisted, if they had pulled the plug, if they had fought to break the links between services and status, if they had refused to volunteer property for the dispersal scheme, then maybe the scheme would not have got off the ground.

It is still not too late for this to be considered and acted on. Unless and until local government does break the link in this way, then it remains morally and politically responsible for the Big Brother internal immigration control regime that exists at local level and is described below.

ASYLUM TEAMS

The process of removal needs to be open and in order for it to be effective. There needs to be close liaison between local authority asylum teams, private accommodation providers and immigration officials.[64]

This startling statement – which in effect is an open incitement to local government asylum teams to participate in the deportation process – was part of the written evidence by Sheffield City Council to the House of Commons Home Affairs Committee on asylum removals. It demolishes a modern Orwellian myth, namely that Asylum Teams fulfil their own self-image and are allies of asylum-seekers. They are no more allies than is NASS. Rather they act as puppets of NASS within the local state. The manager of the Asylum Team in Bury, Lancashire, has congratulated NASS on its 'good work'.[65] Indeed, that particular team has recently circulated a draft document, 'Bury welcomes asylum seekers and refugees', the declared aim of which is 'to develop trust and confidence in the immigration and support systems'.[66] These are the same systems that deport, deprive, humiliate, degrade and evict the undocumented. Some basis for trust! Some welcome!

The construct of the local authority Asylum Team in most major metropolitan centres is emblematic of the doublethink of controls themselves. One study has shown that workers within the teams normally have a subjective commitment to supporting asylum-seekers.[67] Work descriptions may encourage this. The remit of these teams, as in Manchester, may include offering support through the statutory duty still remaining on councils to conduct assessments of need in line with legislative responsibilities and to commission and review services (including accommodation).[68] The job description of a worker in the Bolton team requires him/her 'to treat everyone with dignity and respect'.[69] However, the proper realization of such a commitment is not objectively possible. A social work member of one such team has said 'the reality of our work is not what it is taught to be'.[70] For instance, there may be an assessment of the needs of an undocumented person, but there is no obligation to then meet those assessed needs. The same worker went on to say: 'social workers are increasingly drawn into the dirty work of social policy'.

This collusion is inevitable not least because Asylum Teams are financed through the Home Office (under Section 110 of the Immigration and Asylum Act 1999), but also because they are designed to administer the forced dispersal scheme, and because they therefore fully co-operate with NASS, and because there is a monetary incentive here in that council property employed to house asylum-seekers is often otherwise unlettable or voided (Newspeak for 'not fit to live in'). A background paper produced by Bolton says it 'makes financial sense' to be involved in the dispersal scheme. What ultimately damns Asylum Teams is that they are responsible for ejecting failed asylum-seekers from council properties into which they have been dispersed. Helping in evictions, and thus creating homelessness, is part of the Bolton job description. Court proceedings are unnecessary as dispersed asylum-seekers have no security of tenure and are not protected by the Eviction Act 1977 from being thrown onto the streets.[71] According to a government minister, if an asylum-seeker refuses to vacate a property 'the police may be called'.[72] It is at this point that the supposedly benevolent Asylum Team becomes synonymous with the 'bodies of armed men'.

Recently, Camcorder Guerillas, a group of alternative video producers, made a film (*Welcome!*) of the eviction of asylum-seekers in Glasgow.[73] At the launch of the video a Glasgow councillor stated that if the council refused to carry out Labour's policy of enforced destitution they would be acting illegally.[74] This is legal fetishism – putting obedience to the law above the interests of the undocumented. It is the 'obeying orders' defence, but this time given by those (Labour politicians) complicit in making the orders! Nowhere in the limited literature produced by Asylum Teams do forced dispersal and its consequences (forced eviction) appear as problematic. Concepts such as 'dignity' and 'respect' in this context lose rational meaning and are reduced to Newspeak, obliterating critical thought and rendering 'unorthodox opinion...well nigh impossible'.[75]

LOCAL AUTHORITIES AND IMMIGRATION SLAVERY

It is sometimes difficult to get precise information about the operational work of Asylum Teams. They function like a state secret. The deputy leader of one local authority, Bury, has justified this by saying: 'There is naturally some reticence at disclosing detailed information because many of those who would seek this information are clearly malevolently intentioned, e.g. BNP.'[76] Though well-meaning, this contrasts with a statement from a government minister: 'If a member of the BNP sought information from NASS their enquiry would be handled in the same way as others.'[77]

Local authority workers constantly refer to immigration control as a sensitive issue. This is the real reason for the reluctance to disclose information. Immigration controls have achieved an almost unique status

within political discourse, so that functionaries have become too fright-
ened and embarrassed to discuss their own functions. It is doubtful
whether this is through fear of fascist groups like the BNP. Rather it is
embarrassment at the nature of the work itself (which the BNP could
well support).

What the British National Party could support with glee are the
explicit deportation functions now given to local authorities. It was seen
in Chapter 7 that the Nationality, Immigration and Asylum Act 2002
lists the categories of persons no longer eligible for community-care legislation. It also allows for regulations to be enacted 'enabling' some of
these persons (those granted refugee status abroad and EEA nationals) to
leave the United Kingdom. *Deportation is freedom!*

Under the regulations it is local authorities who are given the
responsibility to implement these deportations 'at the lowest practicable
costs'.[78] In one case a judge opined that these provisions disturb the con-
stitutional balance, because 'Immigration policy is the concern of the
Secretary of State. Welfare provision is in the main the concern of the
local authorities.'[79] In fact the two have become identical. They have
become identical through the local state joining, in the vocabulary of
Nineteen Eighty-Four, the Spies. The 2002 Act imposes an obligation on
local authorities to supply to the Home Office the whereabouts of immigration 'offenders'; and what could be more demoralizing than the realization that, as a worker who opted for local authority employment as
relatively socially useful labour, one has become a member of the Spies?

It gets worse. Welfare is being replaced by slavery (euphemistically
called 'community service') and local authority workers are destined,
unless they resist, to become slave-masters and slave-mistresses. It was
seen in Chapter 7 how the 2004 legislation transforms a category of
failed asylum-seekers (those unable to return home) into a pool of forced
labour as a price of their being given a roof over their heads. Local
authorities are specifically designated as an agency that can contract for
the use of this slavery.[80] This is directly analogous to the hiring out to
local parishes, for instance for road repairs, of workhouse labour under
the nineteenth-century Poor Law. In the committee stage of the 2004
Act, Lord Rooker said in the House of Lords that community service
might involve refugees 'contributing to the upkeep or maintenance of
their own accommodation'.[81] This is a formula for the free repair of
otherwise unlettable property, which can then be rented out at a profit
once the slave is deported. In immigration Newspeak, Rooker called this

forced labour 'social cohesion'. It is more like social disintegration and feels like a direct echo of the 'coloured slaves' of Oceania to which allusion was made in Chapter 2.

THE VOLUNTARY SECTOR: NORMALIZING THE ABNORMAL

> The Investigations Team will deal with fraudulent cases (which include illegal working and car ownership), harassment and anti-social behaviour. At present, until this team is fully up and running, any information regarding possible investigations interest can be directed through the RMT (Regional Management Team).[82]

This was a message posted on a local electronic smartgroup set up by Refugee Action in Manchester. It was sent by a worker at the North West region of the National Asylum Support Service. Its aim was to persuade members of the smartgroup (mainly voluntary sector and refugee organizations) to act as informers – to assist in investigations on 'illegal working' and, bizarrely, on illegal car ownership, (presumably on the assumption that the destitute should not have the privilege of possessing personal transport). A subsequent NASS email said the agency sought to 'provide a helpful, friendly service'.[83] It was seen in Chapter 4 that a central feature of Newspeak vocabulary in Nineteen Eighty-Four was that it was not 'ideologically neutral' because a great many words were euphemisms.[84] The metamorphosis of forced dispersal, for which NASS is responsible, into an activity that is 'helpful' and 'friendly' and which provides a 'service' is classic Newspeak and doublethink, corrupting not just its users but everyone subjected to it.

None of NASS Newspeak was perceived as contradictory or dubious by Refugee Action.[85] The point of this anecdote is that it is an illustration of the normalization of the abnormal. The forced dispersal scheme, the removal of welfare provision based on immigration status, NASS itself – all these have at one time or another been fought against and opposed. Now they are seen as legitimate. It is not known whether any voluntary sector group has so sold its soul to the devil as to participate in NASS investigations and become a snitch. However, the indefensible has been defended by at least one local authority Asylum Team. The team manager at Bury has written that 'we work with NASS investigations on an individual basis'.[86] The language is plain. It is no longer Newspeak, it is betrayal of the undocumented.

VOLUNTARY-SECTOR STAKEHOLDER CULTURE

Under the guise of democracy and accountability, the Home Office has sucked large sections of the voluntary sector into both establishing and implementing immigration control policy. It has achieved this through creating its own front organizations, so-called 'stakeholder groups'. It is difficult to know what is more remarkable, the number of these groups set up by the Home Office (or its minions) or the number of voluntary-sector organizations willing to participate, or the utter lack of reflective discussion within and by the voluntary sector of this collusive practice.

The Immigration Law Practitioners Association, the organization of immigration legal advisers, regularly sends out minutes of these Home Office front organizations. At the last count they included the Immigration and Nationality Directorate User Panel, Local Stakeholder Asylum Casework Group (North), Asylum Processes Stakeholder Group, Immigration Appellate Authority Stakeholder Group, National Refugee Integration Forum, Entry Clearance User Panel, Illegal Working Steering Group, National Asylum Support Forum, Work Permits (UK) User Panel Meeting, Asylum Support Adjudicator User Meeting, Detention Users Group, Advisory Panel on Country Information, Business Users Panel, and Inter-Agency Co-ordination Team. Some of there titles are, of course, Newspeak. So, the Detention Users Group is not composed of detainees but of Home Office prison 'estate' officials, and of concerned and otherwise excellent voluntary-sector groups such as AVID (Association of Visitors to Immigration Detainees) and BID (Bail for Immigration Detainees). There is a wide range of voluntary-sector agencies working in these stakeholder groups. They include law centres, Citizens Advice Bureaux, trade union representatives, student organizations, the Refugee Legal Centre, the Refugee Council and the Immigration Law Practitioners Association.

Participation in Home Office front groups is neither politically viable nor justifiable. Any theoretical gains achieved – perhaps learning information, maybe ameliorating some excesses – is offset by the further legitimization of immigration controls caused by such involvement. The voluntary sector is reduced to being a very junior partner in developing strategies for immigration controls. It has become, to borrow the title of another Bob Dylan song, *only a pawn in the game*.

SEATED WITH SATAN[87]

> It is the responsibility of the accommodation provider to evict asylum- seekers who refuse to leave. Voluntary-sector agencies are advised to ensure that procedures for evictions are included in the contracts they have with accommodation providers.[88]

> Where a refusal letter is issued the voluntary sector will be expected to evict the individual the following working day.[89]

It is not only local authorities who evict asylum-seekers. So do those parts of the voluntary sector who provide 'emergency accommodation' under the poor-law scheme − that is, temporary accommodation pending a decision by NASS as to whether the asylum-seeker is 'eligible' for poor-law forced dispersal.[90] A major reason for lack of eligibility − and therefore ejection on to the streets − is the notorious Section 55 of the Nationality, Immigration and Asylum Act 2002, which creates a poor law within the poor law by denying NASS 'support' to those who apply for refugee status out of time (i.e. not on arrival).[91] Whilst publicly opposing Section 55, major voluntary-sector agencies are secretly evicting asylum-seekers under it − classic, awful doublethink.

There are six major voluntary-sector agencies (collectively referred to as the Inter Agency Partnership, or IAP) which are financed through NASS. They are paid not only to provide emergency accommodation but also to offer advice on the NASS scheme to asylum-seekers. There is a lot of money involved here. For instance, in the financial year 2002/3 the Refugee Council was given £11,000,000 out of an overall grant of more than £24,000,000 to all six agencies.[92] A further £95,000,000 was reimbursed to the agencies for previous work undertaken. Serious issues are raised by any involvement in the poor-law administration. Involvement at such a high financial level in itself sanctions as normal, as unextraordinary, as acceptable, the whole scheme. The major issue raised is how such collusion can possibly be justified, and how in particular it can be justified by a social sector that historically has acted as an advocate of the oppressed.

Various apologias have been given. They all amount to self-delusion, to doublethink. Similar doublethink can be used to explain away collusive participation in stakeholder groups fronting for the Home Office. Some such justifications were given by the Director of Asylum Advice at Refugee Action in a letter to the National Coalition of Anti-Deportation

Campaigns (NCADC) after the latter had criticized Refugee Action for being complicit in the forced dispersal of a pregnant woman from Liverpool.[93] Whatever the truth of this particular allegation, the response to it by Refugee Action did try to confront the general accusation of voluntary-sector collusion, saying that 'If Refugee Action and the other agencies withdrew, the government would very likely put this service out to private tender.' The suggestion here is that the tender (for advice and temporary accommodation) would go to security firms such as Group 4. However this is not necessarily a worse alternative. Group 4 involvement would at least be a step towards clarification. It would highlight and thus clarify the repressive nature of the scheme. What is objectionable is not the organizations running the poor law but the poor law itself.

Another justification put forward is that, by working within the system, it is possible to influence it. The Refugee Action letter says:

> It is not very often that a refugee is able to speak to government; we can help with this both directly and indirectly. As an example, one of our caseworkers, who is himself a refugee, was able to speak directly to the minister, Barbara Roche.

The concept of operating within the system to change it is in fact the latest manifestation of the argument that controls can be sanitized and made fair. This is an illusion which refuses to recognize the political realities. Forced dispersal, evictions, homelessness and deportations are still the norm in spite of chats with ministers. All collusion does is further legitimize an already incredibly powerful system.

A third attempt at justification comes in another letter from the Chief Executive of Refugee Action, namely that 'we must abide by the law'.[94] Once more, abiding by the law in this context means being part of a process that humiliates and impoverishes asylum-seekers. Have we now reached a point where voluntary-sector groups are going to contract-in for the administration and use of the new slave labour scheme? Lord Rooker has said:

> We envisage that the community activity scheme could be delivered by a range of partners in the public or private sector... We would be happy to see the voluntary and community... sectors involved in this way...Consultation should take place with...the National Council for Voluntary Organisations.[95]

In fact the YMCA in Liverpool attempted to take advantage of this slave labour scheme but was forced to withdraw after protests from local community organisations.[96] Refugee Action has, to its credit, said it will refuse to participate in this particular scheme.[97] However, not to engage in slavery is the least that should be expected. The voluntary sector needs to mount a far greater challenge than this if it is to disentangle itself from the sticky web of collusion.

CHALLENGING THE LAW

Some would say it would be better to challenge and break the law. Instead of advising on dispersal, mount pressure to stop NASS from dispersing! Instead of evicting from emergency accommodation, refuse to subcontract such accommodation and then resist all evictions attempted by private (or local authority) landlords! Instead of advising on the NASS scheme, advise on how to campaign for the restoration of full benefits not linked to immigration status! Instead of colluding, disrupt! Instead of becoming a slave-master, unite with the slaves!

This presents another way forward. It is a way that would be supported by all opponents of Big Brother in *Nineteen Eighty-Four*, not just Winston and Julia but also Goldstein and (if it really exists) The Brotherhood – with the latter indulging, or accused of indulging, in 'sabotage, heresies, deviations'.[98] It is a way already adopted by those of the undocumented who organize anti-deportation campaigns, who go on hunger strike, who break out of detention centres which imprison them. It is a way of resistance that, as will be seen in Chapter 10, has been followed ever since there have been controls.

No-one who comes in contact professionally with immigration controls can come away with totally clean hands. This is because controls are politically filthy. Even as an adversarial lawyer, I often felt that simply appearing in court on behalf of the undocumented was somehow giving credence to the system. There may in fact come a time when mass non-cooperation by immigration lawyers could help severely undermine the system – and perhaps that time has already arrived. Ian Madonald QC recently created a fundamental precedent in this respect by refusing to be part of the panel of lawyers who represented detained alleged terrorists before the Special Immigration Appeals Commission. This was on the basis that he fundamentally opposed the legislation (the now-repealed Anti-Terrorism, Crime and Security Act 2001) allowing for such detention without trial of non-British nationals[99]. His difficult but brave refusal to act as a lawyer was subsequently followed by the similar resignation of Rick Scannell QC. These constitute precedents for withdrawal by lawyers from wider aspects of immigration control representation. Such decisions, by leaving the undocumented unrepresented, raise some deep moral and political issues. However, as was said by Mario Savio, the American student activist of the 1960s:

> There is a time when the operation of the machine becomes so odious, makes you so sick at heart, that you can't take part…and you've got to put your body upon the gears…and you've got to make it stop.[100]

Or, as was even more famously said by the British philosopher Edmund Burke, born in Ireland two hundred years previously: 'All that is necessary for the triumph of evil is that good men do nothing'.[101]

9. THROUGH THE MEMORY HOLE

HOW HISTORY IS REWRITTEN AND THE DEPORTEES FORGOTTEN

> Become historians yourselves! Don't depend on the hands of strangers! Record it, take it down and collect![1]

I REMEMBER, THEREFORE I AM

There is no personality without memory – without true memory. In *Nineteen Eighty-Four*, Big Brother rules through the fabrication of memory and therefore through the destruction of the personality. Reality is dominated by the party's hideous, absurd, surreal slogan: 'Who controls the past controls the future: who controls the present controls the past'.[2] So the party, depending on its present alliances, determines whether its previous wartime enemy was Eurasia or Eastasia.[3] It determines whether or not revolutionaries (or, in its doublethink mindset, counter-revolutionaries) such as Jones, Aaronson and Rutherford were in one place, whilst convicting them of sabotage in another place.[4] It determines whether the past exists. It allows O'Brien , during his interrogation of Winston, to put a paper down the memory hole at the same time as telling Winston 'I do not remember it.'[5]

The annihilation of memory is portrayed as the ultimate violence, the final abuse of the human spirit because, if the party could destroy the past by claiming certain events never happened nor certain people ever existed, then that 'surely, was more terrifying than mere torture and death'.[6]

Ironically, Winston himself works in the Records Department at the Ministry of Truth, inventing lies and despatching all written evidence of the truth down the memory hole chutes. In particular, Winston despatches statistics into oblivion, and 'statistics were just as much fantasy in their original version as in their rectified version'.[7] In just the same way, government ministers today juggle the immigration figures to appease the racists, belching out a constant parade of statistics showing decreases in the number of asylum applications or the asylum applications granted. The point has been reached where the Prime Minister is now so doubtful of his own figures that he has launched a public inquiry, which must be the equivalent of *doubleplusdoublethink* or triplethink.[8] It is only after making love to Julia and reading Goldstein's secret book (itself perhaps a forgery by O'Brien) that Winston realizes 'sanity is not statistical'.[9]

Winston's initial act of personal rebellion, the writing of a diary, was an exercise in retention of memory, retention for the future: 'For whom, it suddenly occurred to him, was he writing this diary? For the future, for the unborn.'[10] He was mesmerized by what he considered, correctly, would be the destruction of the diary, and therefore of memory, because he always knew that the diary 'would be reduced to ashes and himself to vapour'.[11]

The parallel with Ray Bradbury's novel *Fahrenheit 451* is here striking. In this, Guy Montag is a firefighter whose job is to burn books, which are the source of knowledge and therefore, it is claimed, the source of conflict. Fahrenheit 451 is the temperature at which paper ignites – and so the temperature at which memory disappears.[12]

THE BIG LIE ABOUT FREE ENTRY OF REFUGEES[13]

A most remarkable feature of the history of immigration restrictions is how from the very beginning they have been distorted, fabricated or plain obliterated, often quite deliberately. This is history told from the point of view of the victors – who control the present. And the victors have been those so driven by racism as to successfully implement that most racist of constructs, immigration controls. They have made such constructs appear *normal*. In this age of supposed multiculturism, and an age still reeling with the last remnants of the guilt of the holocaust, any acknowledgement of true history would lead to great embarrassment by many of its participants or their predecessors. So it has been suppressed. The only people who could show pride in their involvement would be the fascists, and as will be seen they have not remained silent.

Imagine a Zen mantra transposed into a reactionary chant; then you will be able to imagine the repetitive lie spun by repeated governments as to this country having a history of free entry for refugees. The mantra is *Nineteen Eighty-Four* Newspeak designed 'not only to provide a medium of expression for the world-view…but to make all other modes of thought impossible'.[14] It is also classic doublethink because the assertion of an historic free entry for asylum-seekers is employed only whenever the government is planning to restrict entry even further. In fact, even the start of such a chant is warning of more restrictions to follow. Here are examples of the deceit within a two-year period (1985–87) concerning mainly, but not exclusively, Tamils trying to escape Sri Lanka:

> The United Kingdom has an honourable record in giving refuge over the years to hundreds of thousands of people who have suffered persecution in their own countries. (Jeremy Hanley MP, in a debate imposing visa controls on Sri Lankans)[15]

> We have an enviable record on the treatment of genuine asylum-seekers. (David Waddington MP, Minister for Immigration, subsequent to 64 Sri Lankan Tamils stripping naked at Heathrow airport and thus preventing their own removal)[16]

> The United Kingdom has always adopted a generous and liberal policy towards those seeking asylum. (John Wheeler MP, in voting for the Immigration (Carriers Liability) Act making it even harder for Sri Lankans and other refugees to come here)[17]

Though all the above speakers were Tories, Labour apologists for controls have taken up the same mind-numbing chant. For instance:

> The UK government has a longstanding tradition of giving shelter to those fleeing persecution. (Home Office white paper, *Fairer, Faster and Firmer*, introduced prior to the Immigration and Asylum Act 1999, which established the notorious NASS)[18]

> We have a proud tradition of welcoming people. (Beverley Hughes MP, Minister for Immigration, in the debate on the Asylum and Immigration (Treatment of Claimants etc.) Act 2004, the main purpose of which was to exclude people)[19]

REMEMBER THEM!

The lie behind the chant is a monstrous one. Far from this country having an open door for refugees, the very first comprehensive piece of immigration control, the Aliens Act 1905, was aimed at Jews fleeing religious and political persecution in eastern Europe and Tsarist Russia. The Act had no other rationale.

If proof were needed of this it can be seen in cases decided after 1905 – cases reported weekly in the *Jewish Chronicle* with names that should now be retrieved from the memory hole, remembered and honoured. Remember Aaron Hecht Milfore from Sokorow, rejected even though 'one of his children, he said, had been killed in a pogrom. His family then 'fled in a state of panic and frenzy and in the confusion he had become separated from them'.[20] Remember also Feivish Feldman from Vilna and an ex-soldier, rejected even though he had been 'arrested for refusing to fire on Jews'.[21] Remember also Pichas Serachim from Surazh, rejected even though he had 'become entangled with the revolutionary movement…upon one occasion he was chosen by lot to shoot a supposed police spy. Serachim missed the mark, ran and escaped'.[22]

The 1905 Act legitimized all that followed, not least the pre-war exclusion of Jews fleeing from Nazi Germany, annexed Austria and conquered Czechoslovakia. It is no exaggeration to say that the fate of Jewry in these countries was effectively sealed when the UK imposed visa controls on German/Austrian nationals in May 1938 and then later on Czech nationals. Of course some Jews, a small minority – mainly children brought here in the *kindertransport* – did gain entry. But we should remember those denied entry. The full story of exclusion is documented by Louise London in her book *Whitehall and the Jews 1933–1948*.[23] Remember the two Jews gripped by police in the photograph on the cover of Louise London's book: refugees from Czechoslovakia being marched away from Croydon airport on 31 March 1939. They were detained at a police station and put on a plane to Warsaw. The pilot refused to fly after they had threatened to kill themselves, but they were deported the following day. Remember them.

Remember them in order to retain critical faculties in the face of the constant mantra of claimed freedom of entry for refugees – a mantra which those wanting to acquire British citizenship will be forced to chant as part of the citizenship tests introduced by the 2004 legislation. This is made clear in a document, entitled *The New and the Old*, which is the work of the Orwellian-named Life in the United Kingdom Advisory Group.[24] This is another body appointed by the Home Office to collude in the operation of immigration controls, this one consisting of the 'great and the good' from education and the race industry. The document, in its own internal doublethink, speaks the language of liberal pluralism but advocates the crudest uniformity. It is imbued with a one-sided and false view of history, stating: 'historically this country has had a good and tolerant record...[to] those coming to a free country to better themselves and refugees fleeing oppression'. This extends the big lie to a supposed welcome to 'economic refugees' – conveniently omitting the fact that, from the Commonwealth Immigrants Act 1962 onwards, black individuals, families and communities have been systematically destroyed by immigration controls.

The understanding of British history that is to be taught to would-be citizens is an uncritical and deceitful interpretation, one where 'to be British seems to us to mean that we respect the laws, the elected parliamentary and democratic structures, traditional values of mutual tolerance, respect for equal rights'. So much for any critical view of history where to be British is to promote racism, colonialism, bloody oppression, closed borders and suppression of truth. All this is to go down the memory hole, to be replaced by Orwellian indoctrination that is to be a *sine qua non* for the acquisition of citizenship.

TRAGEDY AND FARCE: TRADE UNIONS AND FASCISTS[25]

It was Karl Marx, in *The Eighteenth Brumaire of Louis Bonaparte*, who wrote that history repeats itself once as tragedy, twice as farce. The repetition of the campaign for immigration controls against black people in the second half of the twentieth century, which echoed that against Jews in the first half, is just tragedy. The constant repetition into the twenty-first century of the deceitful mantra of a welcome to refugees has achieved the status of farce. Moreover it is tragedy and farce whose real facts are largely hidden from history, though much of the history is still within the participants' lifetimes. This memory hole matters politically because, as Marx also wrote in the same essay, 'the tradition of all the dead generations weighs like a nightmare on the brain of the living'.[26]

The role of (some) trade unions has been central to the enactment of controls.[27] This makes embarrassing reading to those trade unionists who in recent years, and under pressure from an increasingly loud *sans papiers* voice, have begun to make some limited criticism of controls.[28] Major Jewish immigration to this country began after 1882, the year the May Laws were enacted by Tsar Alexander Third confining and deporting

Jews to the land area within Russia known as the Pale of Settlement. As early as 1892, controls against Jewish refugees was the official policy of the Trade Union Congress as expressed in a resolution at its conference. W. H. Wilkins, the fanatical campaigner for controls, in his book *The Alien Invasion* published in 1892, named 43 labour organizations (not including the TUC) advocating restrictions.[29] The issue of immigration controls was included in a list of questions to be asked of all parliamentary candidates and which was compiled by a special conference of the TUC held in Manchester in 1896.[30]

All this was very much replicated following the arrival of black Commonwealth citizens to the UK from the late 1940s. The TUC General Council report to the 1955 Congress stated that a TUC delegation had visited the Minister of Labour and told him that 'the government must have a policy which could ensure that the rate of immigration could be controlled'.[31] The 1956 General Council report stated: 'This year the National Union of Railwaymen have pressed for some form of immigration control'. In 1957 the Transport and General Workers Union voted for controls.[32] The 1958 Congress was a significant one if the TUC were ever to take up a position of opposition to controls. This is because Congress met just after the 'race riots' (that being popular Newspeak for racist pogroms) in Notting Hill and Nottingham. In classic doublethink, the TUC General Secretary (Tewson) condemned the 'riots' whilst the General Council report blithely said 'This year apprehensions have been expressed about the numbers of immigrants from Pakistan' – and called not just for controls but also raised the racist, stereotypical spectre of the diseased alien by declaring 'a medical examination should be included within these immigration controls'. It was this conference that legitimized a mode of thought that is now almost universal – it is the victims, not the perpetrators, of racist attacks who should be penalized, by controls and exclusions. Four years later came the first Commonwealth Immigrants Act.

The 1958 pogroms were pivotal in ensuring the 1962 legislation. This was because they were not just 'spontaneous' outbreaks of racism. Rather they were orchestrated by explicitly fascist organizations with the demand for immigration controls. For instance, Oswald Mosley's Union Movement circulated a leaflet around West London stating: 'Protect your jobs. Stop coloured immigration. Houses for white people – not coloured immigrants'.[33]

There is more hidden (that is, suppressed) history to recover. Not
only was the 1962 legislation a result of organized fascism. So was the
Aliens Act 1905. A major influence behind this was the aptly-named
British Brothers League which flourished between 1901 and 1905 in
that traditional stomping ground of British fascism, London's East End.
The Brothers had the capacity to mount huge and violent rallies. A
typical event, attracting 4000 supporters, was held in January 1902 at
the People's Palace in the Mile End. It was preceded by simultaneous
demonstrations from Stepney, Hackney, Shoreditch and Bethnal Green,
each accompanied by the sound of drums.[34] A fictionalized, satirical
account of a Brothers meeting occurs in Robert Tressell's 1912 socialist
novel *The Ragged Trousered Philanthropists*:

> Some of you seem to think…that it was a great mistake on God's
> part to make so many foreigners. You ought to hold a mass
> meeting about it and pass a resolution something like this: 'This
> meeting of British Christians hereby protests against the action
> of the Supreme Being in having created so many foreigners, and
> calls upon Him to rain down fire, brimstone and mighty rocks
> forthwith upon the heads of all those Philistines, so that they
> may be utterly exterminated from the face of the earth, which
> rightly belongs to the British people'.[35]

SOCIALISTS AND FASCISTS

The Aliens Act 1905 was not simply a consequence of both fascist and
trade union agitation (abetted by a significant section of the ruling class).
Many of the early socialist groups (this being the era of the formation of
socialist organisations) were also deeply, if often ambiguously, implicated. For instance, Tom Mann, a famous rank-and-file dockers' leader
and member of the Independent Labour Party, spoke successfully at the
London Trades Council in favour of controls[36] and referred in the paper
Labour Leader to Jews as the distributors of 'blood-stained money'.[37]
Robert Blatchford in his socialist journal, *Clarion*, said controls against
Jews was a matter of 'legitimate self-preservation'.[38] H. D. Hyndman of
the Social Democratic Federation and its paper *Justice* polemicized
against 'the free admittance of aliens'.[39] There was one exception,
namely the Socialist League of William Morris. Its journal, *Commonweal*,
condemned the other Left groups, asking them: 'Are we to allow
the issues at stake in the struggle between the robbers and the robbed

to be obscured by anti-foreigner agitation?'.[40] The same article then offered solidarity to the Aborigines, Maoris, American Indians and black people everywhere. However, the Socialist League went into decline and became marginal to the debate, with little influence. It ceased to exist in 1901. Subsequently the rise of the Labour Party followed the Aliens Act 1905. As was seen in Chapter 1, Labour had a 'stateist' interpretation of socialism, *Ingsoc*, which (along with its pro-imperialism) leant itself to support for immigration controls as just another form of state economic planning. All this helps explain why today it is so hard to argue for a principled opposition to all controls even amongst those who regard themselves as progressive. Reactionary ideology and false consciousness survive and thrive unless challenged. Today the dominant tradition of the dead generations of a so-called socialism weighs like a nightmare on the brain of the living.

The wheel of reaction comes full circle when one of the few sources of memory retention of this history of early socialism is in fact fascist. The magazine *Spearhead*, owned by John Tyndall of the BNP, at the height of the National Front's notoriety carried an article in March 1980 saying: 'Modern socialists who support the so-called Anti-Nazi League and other anti-racialist organisations would be highly embarrassed to learn of the nationalist and racialist attitudes displayed by many early British socialists.'

It is this history of the hideous combination of bodies agitating for controls which helps define the whole of the twentieth century and the start of the twenty-first. However, it is not a history that can be ignored or avoided. In particular, the trade union and socialist movement has to face up to it in order to junk it completely. It can no longer be allowed to be forgotten. A classic way of ignoring the history, the way of liberal apologia, is to claim there can be 'fair' controls. But how can constructs such as immigration restrictions be sanitized or rendered fair when in their origins they are the consequence of fascist agitation supported directly or indirectly by significant sections of the organized labour movement? Arguing for anything less than complete abolition of controls is a travesty of rational thought and a rejection of the lessons of history.

LONG-TERM AND SHORT-TERM MEMORY LOSS

In *Nineteen Eighty Four*, falsification and destruction of memory could be contemporaneous with the obliterated event itself. In one vivid scene, a party member is making a warmongering speech in support of the conflict with Eurasia. In mid-sentence he is handed a slip of paper telling him the enemy has now changed. Nothing alters in the content of what he is saying: 'but suddenly the names were different. Without words said, a wave of understanding rippled through the crowd. Oceania was at war with Eastasia!'[41]

Likewise, it is not just the memory of agitation for immigration controls a century ago, or even forty years ago, that has been erased. In historic terms there can be virtually instant erasure of what was said or done yesterday. In the Asylum and Immigration Act 1996 the Tories established the notorious 'white list' of safe countries – from which any claim for asylum was to be deemed 'unfounded' and was put into an accelerated and abbreviated appeals system. This was heavily criticized in Labour's first immigration white paper *Fairer, Faster and Firmer*.[42] It was supposedly abolished by Labour in the Immigration and Asylum Act 1999. It was reintroduced (resurrected) by Labour in the Nationality, Immigration and Asylum Act 2002. The speed at which reality is changed and denied makes it virtually impossible to remember which politician said what and when. This is the reality control of *Nineteen Eighty-Four* – thought control through disorientation.[43] It wipes out memory.

THE LIBRARY OF JEWISH CATASTROPHE/ RINGELBLUM'S TIME CAPSULES[44]

Perhaps the people with the greatest consciousness of the need for memory preservation are the Jewish people. Because of the political catastrophes (expulsions/inquisitions/pogroms/genocides/holocausts) repeatedly inflicted on the Jews there is a real danger that the facts will be obliterated along with the people.

At the start of the First World War three Jewish intellectuals in Warsaw – J. L. Peretz, Jacob Dinezon and S. Ansky – issued an appeal to their fellow Jews, as quoted at the start of this chapter. The appeal is still of importance today.

Ansky (a Russian social-revolutionary and author of the play *The Dybbuk*) acted on his own manifesto. He collected material and produced a four-volume chronicle on pogroms unleashed by the war in Poland, Galicia and Bukovina. At the same time the Russian historian Elias Tcherikower documented in a circular the massacres of up to 250,000 Jews in the Ukraine:

> Jews, a terrible pogrom – *Tokhea* has befallen our cities and towns and the world does not know, we ourselves know nothing or very little about it. [Knowledge of this] must not be suppressed![45]

Tcherikower and his assistants had a premonition about the destruction of their archives, so copies of everything were made in triplicate, which was fortunate. The papers left in the Ukraine were destroyed in the civil war following the Russian revolution. When Hitler came to power, those deposited in Berlin were smuggled out to Vilna but burned by the Nazis in 1942. Those deposited in Paris were rescued by a French legionnaire in 1940. Perhaps the most significant and most vivid Jewish retention of memory, that is the memory of fatal experience, is the record of the Warsaw ghetto, including the Great Deportation (when 275,000 Jews were shipped off to Treblinka in cattle trucks) and the final uprising. This was compiled by Emanuel Ringelblum and his collaborators – a record in ten tin boxes and two milk canisters which were buried and then unbelievably unearthed after the war by the two surviving members of the archive, Rokhl Auerbach and Hirsh Wasser.[46]

THE MUSEUM OF ILLEGAL IMMIGRATION

Of course it is not simply history as history that is obliterated by immigration controls. Living contemporary human beings are pulverized and rendered literally non-existent, rendered unpersons, by being first defined as illegal and then being deported. Everyone removed in this way is effectively being dropped down their own memory hole. The rest of us remain in total ignorance of their fate.

Today the present campaigns against deportations and immigration controls may in themselves, by making public much of the private, help preserve the memory of the racism inflicted on the undocumented. But maybe campaigns in themselves are insufficient, as these also can be obliterated from history and therefore from memory. What is required is an archive of resistance, such as that in Haifa remembering the struggles by Jewish European refugees after 1945 to evade British gunboats that were then preventing entry to the British mandated (i.e. colonial) territory of Palestine This is the provocatively named Museum of Illegal Immigration. Can we hope that the *sans-papiers* and their supporters in this country (and in all other countries) will establish a Museum of Illegal Immigration, so that the memory of those detained and deported, of those who fought and resisted with success, will not be forgotten, will not be annihilated, will not be vaporized? This could be a living memory and part of the struggle against controls. It would live in the spirit of Bertold Brecht, the great German playwright, who in his 1930 play *Die Massnahme* (The Measures Taken) turned conventional reality on its head and proclaimed 'Hail to illegal labour'.

10. FROM INTERNATIONAL EXPLOITATION TO INTERNATIONAL RESISTANCE

HOW THE UNDOCUMENTED FIGHT BACK GLOBALLY

I am like a person who is drowning and is holding themselves up by one arm, but my arm is getting tired and it will soon be easier to just let go

— Fifteen-year-old Iraqi boy[1]

We need to scream. We need to speak loudly.

— Jaggi Singh[2]

The Immigration officials – they wanted us to provide the good respectful image: that we'd come in, and we'd go upstairs, and we'd sit down, and we'd wait, and we'd talk to them like things are normal. But things aren't normal! This was panic, and we acted in such a way. We occupied all the rooms to show that this was a serious situation. They didn't want the other people [i.e. other refugees] in the waiting room to see us because this would dirty up their image. This would take away from their image of their administrative life, of things being done normally. This would ruin that. So that's how we approached it.

— Nacera Kellou[3]

THE CHINA SYNDROME AND THE GLOBAL GLAZE

It is difficult to know which is more horrific, more morbid or more widely reported nationally and internationally: 58 Chinese people frozen to death in a refrigerated lorry bound for Dover in June 2000,[4] or 19 allegedly undocumented Chinese cockle pickers drowned in Morcambe Bay in February 2004.[5] These deaths are a leitmotiv for both the international exploitation of the Chinese and the international dimension of controls. All countries, particularly the most industrially advanced, have immigration restrictions and death/manslaughter is the global consequence of these restrictions. Often the victims are the same.

A recent book, *Forbidden Workers* by Peter Kwong,[6] is a political exposé of the mistreatment of migrant Chinese workers in the USA. It provides an account on its first pages of the running aground near Rockway Beach in New York on 6 June 1993 of a 42-year-old cargo steamer named (it would now seem ironically) the *Golden Venture*. The ship held 286 undocumented would-be migrants (i.e. workers) from mainland China who had been living in the ship's hold for four months. Ten of the undocumented drowned. Peter Kwong writes:

> Local media were called to witness the extraordinary sight of a high-walled, deep-sea freighter tilting in the sand off one of the most popular recreational beaches in New York City. The entire world soon saw images of soaked Chinese nationals huddling under blankets on the windy beach, staring in confusion at the television cameras.

This image is a *cinéma-vérité*, vox-pop echo of the film described by Winston in his diary at the start of *Nineteen Eighty-Four*, a film which won 'applause from the party seats', a film of the bombing and drowning of the refugees.[7] The very public, contemporaneous showing of this New York catastrophe, and the near-contemporaneous TV footage of the UK tragedies, is another global metaphor for Orwell's Big Brother and for the operation of immigration controls. Big Brother and immigration controls manage to function simultaneously both publicly and privately, overtly and covertly. In both there is public surveillance and arrest, then private interrogation and deportation. In Orwell's novel this dichotomy is contained on the one hand in the open scrutiny of everything and everyone (a helicopter skimmed down between the roofs: 'It was the police patrol snooping into people's windows'[8]), and on the other hand in the secret grilling of Winston.

In the world of immigration controls the snooping is now blatant – too many people and too many agencies are involved for it to remain a furtive national state, a local state or a privatized activity. In addition, the

Home Office is seen increasingly to be working in partnership with the media in conducting and publicizing raids on so-called 'illegal workers'. Sky's news for 25 October 2003, headed 'Raid on illegals in Sussex', not only contained a report of the arrest of undocumented workers but seems to have been issued simultaneously with the arrests, there being present and on the spot a Sky photographer. In this way the sphere of the public within immigration restrictions masquerades as 'news' but in reality this 'news' is indoctrination into acceptance (or fear) of controls through entertainment.

INTERNATIONAL CONTROLS

None of this is unique to the United Kingdom. The first quotation in this chapter starts to reveal the international dimension of controls, and this is vividly illustrated in scenes from two quite different books by two quite different authors.

The first is *Travels With Charley: In Search of America* by John Steinbeck. Steinbeck was refused admission to Canada from the USA because he was accompanied by his dog Charley. He was then being refused back into the USA because he was accompanied by his dog Charley. He says that 'nowhere is my natural anarchism more aroused than at national borders'.[9] Perhaps even more pertinent is a scene from Arthur Koestler's novel *Darkness at Noon*. Here the anti-hero escapes into France where he is arrested by the immigration authorities and told to keep walking – in half an hour he would be in Belgium and if he was ever caught again in France he would have his head knocked off. A few days later he is captured by the Belgium immigration authorities and was told to keep walking – in half an hour he would be in France and if he was ever caught in Belgium again he would have his head knocked off![10] This is a particularly apposite passage as Koestler's novel shares with *Nineteen Eighty-Four* a universally negative view of a future dominated by one-party totalitarian rule.

In much of his fictional and non-fictional writing, George Orwell had a precise vision of the world in his own time.[11] This was a vision where all political systems, all rival political empires (from fascism to Stalinism to capitalist liberal democracy) were converging into one identical form of rule and a new form of class society which was neither capitalist nor socialist – but instead was dictatorial rule through a collectivized bureaucratic managerial caste.[12] This was the essential theme of his 1945 classic novel *Animal Farm* where the revolution was subverted and a collective oligarchy of pigs dominated, walking on their hind legs and aping the humans they had replaced with the infamous slogans 'Four legs good, two legs better' and 'All animals are created equal, but some animals are more equal than others'.[13]

This world historic tendency towards bureaucratization as a new class system was repeated by Orwell in his political writings. In his 1940 essay 'Inside the Whale' he proclaimed with some justification (given the year of publication) that this was an entire 'epoch of fear, tyranny and regimentation',[14] – 'an age in which freedom of thought will be at first a deadly sin and later on a meaningless abstraction'.[15] In *Nineteen Eighty-Four* he says of Oceania, Eurasia and Eastasia that their philosophies and social systems are indistinguishable, that they all exist through totalitarian rule, that they all have the same permanent war economies, and that they would therefore gain no advantage by actually conquering one another because so long as they remain in conflict they prop one another up 'like three sheaves of corn'.[16]

Since the demise of the Soviet Union the political convergence of all systems has been realized, though it is a convergence not into a totalitarian, managerial dictatorship but into naked capitalism. It is these systems which compete with each other and which undertake this competition through exploitation of global labour via immigration controls. Exploitation, the search for the greatest extraction of labour and the greatest maximization of profit, has ultimately always been the lowest common denominator of immigration controls. Similarly, war itself is the product of the same quest for labour exploitation and profit maximization. So in *Nineteen Eighty-Four* Orwell says of the perpetual war between Oceania, Eurasia and Eastasia that, in so far as the war had any direct economic purpose, it is a war 'for labour power...All of the disputed territories... contain a bottomless reserve of cheap labour'.[17]

The oppression of the undocumented and/or the victims of war (the two often being synonymous) transcends time and space. The slave-like conditions endured by East European migrants in the Chicago cattle-slaughtering plants and described by Upton Sinclair in his 1906 novel, *The Jungle*, are directly comparable to the sweatshops and associated 'contempt for foreigners'[18] that today blight the globe. Remember the unknown worker in Sinclair's book who had 'been jammed against the wall (by a truck carrying dead carcasses) and crushed in a horrible and nameless manner'.[19] Remember Roman Kobitovich – already forgotten by the media – described on the BBC News as an 'illegal immigrant who worked in a top London restaurant'. He didn't just work there, he also lived secretly in the basement. After working double shifts and drowning his misery in drink, he slipped on the basement floor and broke his neck, his body being found only two days later.[20] It was Christmas. Remember the words of Jack Mapanje, Malawian poet, political activist and refugee in the UK, speaking for the undocumented of the world: 'What have you done to dub me economic migrant? What do you know about the economics migrants suffer?'[21]

INTERNATIONAL CO-OPERATION OF RIVALS: FORTRESS WORLD[22]

Paradoxically, rival exploiting states help prop one another up 'like sheaves of corn' through meeting regularly and formally, exchanging experiences on the most effective ways of controlling labour and developing controls. It is as though the biggest perceived threat is not rival capitalisms but the *sans-papiers* of the world. The 1988/89 Annual Report of the Immigration and Nationality Department[23] reveals:

> International liaison is not, however, confined to the European Community. The annual Four Country Immigration Conference which rotates between Australia, Canada, the USA and the United Kingdom took place in Canada in 1988 where the increasingly close liaison between countries experiencing similar problems was maintained…The Immigration Service also hosted the fifth International Immigration Fraud Conference at Shepperton in 1988. This was attended by 11 countries including Canada and the United States.

Membership of the annual International Fraud Conference has now increased to 19. In a letter from Fiona Mactaggart, a Home Office Minister, to Ivan Lewis MP it was said that the variety of inter-country conventions was deemed too many to enumerate: 'The number of meetings held make it impossible to list them all.'[24] It is not a question of Fortress UK, or Fortress Europe, but Fortress World.

This close transnational cooperation means inevitably that immigration controls are often globally identical or converging. Those we confront in the UK are by no means the worst, though often they appear *primus inter partes*. Nor is Newspeak and doublethink confined to the UK, rather they represent the global apologias for controls. In Canada, whereas some of the undocumented are categorized as 'illegals', others are defined as 'non-status refugees' – both groups having the same non-identity as Orwell's *unpersons*. One Algerian non-status refugee, Nacera Kellou (previously mentioned in the preface to the present book), describes their limbo situation in this way: 'Our sense of living, our sense of life, our sense of reflecting on things – this was all lost.'[25] Meanwhile, in the USA, political movements advocating even harsher, more racist, controls suggest strengthening of controls is somehow 'progressive' and a 'reform' – as in the Federation for American Immigration Reform (which also has the doublethink acronym FAIR). This is the same brand of doublethink that we saw in Chapter 5 used by British government ministers to justify the highly unprogressive, reactionary Asylum and Immigration (Treatment of Claimants, etc.) Act 2004.

DEPORTATION IS FREEDOM! – THROUGHOUT THE WORLD

It is possible to construct a political snapshot showing the commonality of controls internationally. Here is just a small segment of the picture.

- Employer sanctions, the transforming of bosses into immigration spies through penalizing them for the employment of undocumented labour, extends through most of the European Union and as far as New Zealand.

- Prison-like accommodation centres for asylum-seekers is becoming a global norm, as in Perth, Australia, where such a centre (a so-called 'residential housing project') will be surrounded by a double row of fencing and patrolled by guards 24 hours a day.[26] Australia leads the way in the establishment of 'offshore' detention of refugees, such as on the Pacific island of Nairu.[27]

- The encouragement of private whistleblowers and their transformation into vigilante organizations is rife, such as Ranch Rescue, based in Arizona, USA, which tracks down the undocumented under the slogan 'Private property first, foremost, and always.'[28]

- The USA is probably the world's leading player in linking welfare entitlement to immigration status, as shown by the notorious Proposition 187 – whereby in 1994 the voters of California agreed in a referendum to drive out undocumented aliens and to deter their entry by cutting them off from public provision, including medical services, and depriving their children of an education.

- Control through sexuality is internationally prevalent. Whatever the formal law, lesbians and gay men are universally unwelcome. The Immigration and Refugee Board in Canada has recently rejected the asylum case of a Mexican gay man on the grounds that he is not 'visibly effeminate' and therefore not vulnerable to persecution in his home land.[29]

These repressive mechanisms extend across time as well as space. Catherine Dolan, an unmarried, pregnant Irish woman tried to enter the USA in 1890 and was subject to the following interrogation:

> [Q] You have no friends or relatives in this country? [A] No Sir [Q] How much money have you? [A] Fourteen dollars. [Q] How long are you pregnant? [A] I don't know. [Q] When do you expect this child to be born? [A] I don't know. [Q] You don't know? [A] No Sir. [Q] Have you ever had a child? [A] No Sir. [Q] Never? [A] Never. [Q] You knew the man was a married man, didn't you? [A] I did Sir.

Catherine was refused entry.[30]

Fortress World has always been the historic trajectory of immigration controls, and doublethink has always been its mode of thought (or anti-thought). Alamdar and Montazar Bakhtiari, two asylum-seeking children from Afghanistan, were imprisoned in the notorious Woomera detention entre in Australia. After a mass breakout they applied for asylum at the British embassy in Melbourne. This was refused within hours and they were handed back to their captors. Within this interlocking web of intergovernmental cooperation, the Australian immigration minister said that the boys 'had the ability to stop detention arrangements by returning to their homeland' (which he claimed was Pakistan not Afghanistan).[31] So, once again, *Deportation is freedom!*. As the Roman poet Virgil wrote in another context, but one apposite to today's undocumented masses: 'What region of the earth is not full of our calamities?'[32]

THE RESISTANCE OF THE PROLES

Nineteen Eighty-Four can be interpreted as an essentially fatalistic and pessimistic book. Its final message can be seen as that of hopelessness in the face of apparently overwhelming political odds. Collective struggle against oppression is perceived as futile. O'Brien, in his role as agent provocateur, tells Winston and Julia that they cannot act collectively. They could only spread their knowledge 'outwards from individual to individual, generation after generation'.[33] In any event there will be no future knowledge even of any individual resistance, as all resistance is destined for the memory hole. So O'Brien tells Winston as part of his interrogation: 'And above all we do not allow the dead to rise up against us...You will never have existed.'[34]

Simultaneously with the obliteration of memory there exists a parallel, material, insane, reality, the one described by O'Brien to Winston and one previously quoted in Chapter 6: 'If you want a picture of the future, imagine a boot stamping on a human face – for ever.'[35] This is a reminder of the title and content of Jack London's prescient novel (it was published in 1907) of fascism – *The Iron Heel* – where the ruling oligarchy proclaims: 'We will grind you revolutionists down under our heel, and we shall walk upon your faces. The world is ours, we are its lords, and ours it shall remain.'[36] Ultimately Winston succumbs. The boot on the face turns him. It inverts his world view and he learns to love Big Brother.

It is this pessimism, this denial of the possibility of opposition to tyranny (unlike, for instance, in *The Iron Heel* where socialism ultimately triumphs), that has led left-wing reviewers to criticize Orwell's novel.[37] Isaac Deutscher, the eminent biographer of Trotsky, said it is a 'document of dark disillusionment not only with Stalinism but with every form and shade of socialism'.[38] In contrast, right-wingers embraced the novel and employed it as part of their cold war propaganda. Deutscher relates the following strange and vivid encounter from 1950:

> 'Have you read this book? You must read it, sir. Then you will know why we must drop the atom bomb on the Bolshies.' With these words, a blind, miserable news-vendor recommended to me *Nineteen Eighty-Four* in New York, a few weeks before Orwell's death. Poor Orwell, could he ever imagine that his own book would become so prominent an item in the programme of Hateweek?[39]

However, there is an alternative reading of *Nineteen Eighty-Four*. In this reading Orwell is by no means totally abstentionist on the issue of opposition to oppression. In some ways resistance is central to the book. There is Winston's personal resistance in keeping his diary, a struggle in the retention of memory. There is resistance in the very act of love-making between Winston and Julia. Orwell writes that it 'was a political act'.[40]

Under these circumstances of absolute totalitarianism personal protest may perhaps achieve a political dimension. But *Nineteen Eighty-Four* is also a primer for a hard political lesson – namely, that individual, non-collective struggle inevitably proves inadequate. It is ultimately apolitical or not sufficiently political. This does not deny its moral merit as struggle, and in any event victories can never be guaranteed under any circumstances and any configuration of forces. Orwell is here being neither positive nor negative but is simply presenting an objective commentary. As Spinoza said, 'neither laugh nor cry but understand'. However, there actually is a political optimism present in the book, even if it is usually hidden and buried beneath the weight of the cynicism: *there is hope of collective solidarity.*

This hope is reflected in another repeated mantra throughout the book, appearing first as an insight in Winston's secret diary: 'If there was hope it lay in the proles.'[41] The struggle of the proles represents an alternative future because they are not corrupted by nationalism (and therefore by racism): 'They were not loyal to…a country…The proles had stayed human.'[42] They were the future because 'The birds sang, the proles sang, the Party did not sing.'[43] The literary allusion is here reminiscent of the lyrics from the 1920s German anti-Nazi cabaret song 'Das Lila Lied' (The Lavender Music): 'They march in goosestep. We prefer to dance.'

THE RESISTANCE OF THE UNDOCUMENTED

It was Samuel Johnson who in the eighteenth century reputedly coined the phrase 'patriotism is the last refuge of the scoundrel'. Alongside war, immigration controls today represent the highest form of patriotism. But the scoundrels are being resisted. Resistance comes from the modern proles – the world's undocumented. Unlike in *Nineteen Eighty-Four*, where it is suggested that struggle may only emerge over generations and perhaps over a thousand years,[44] we live today in the midst of campaigns against restrictions on movement.

This resistance, like the controls, exists both temporally and spatially. It goes back in time and it goes round the globe. It has analogies with the struggle against the nineteenth-century Poor Law. During the Chartist-inspired general strike of 1842, the Stockport workhouse was attacked and its inmates liberated[45] – not unlike the destruction from within of Yarls Wood immigration detention centre in February 2002[46] and Harmondsworth detention centre in July 2004.[47] The fight-back against controls began simultaneously with the agitation for controls. This is clear from the UK context, which also illustrates the political point that the impetus for any struggle against controls always comes from the self-organization of the oppressed.

It has already been seen that the demand for restriction and exclusion was raised in the UK almost immediately on the arrival of Jewish refugees in the 1880s. This was met by a response from sections of the Jewish bourgeoisie (for instance the *Jewish Chronicle* was unremittingly hostile to the legislation). However, the main organized response came from Jewish workers, based mainly, but by no means exclusively, in London's East End. These workers orientated themselves to changing the position of the English labour movement and challenging the support of the latter for controls. In 1894 there was a rally of Jewish trade unionists in Whitechapel to protest against the TUC's resolution against immigration.[48] In December 1895 meetings were held in Leeds and Mile End, London, again against the TUC's latest restrictionist resolutions passed at its Cardiff conference. Eleanor Marx, the daughter of Karl Marx, and Prince Kropotkin, the Russian anarchist, spoke at the London rally.[49] Another meeting was convened in Whitechapel in 1901,[50] and the following year there was established an Aliens Defence League in Brick Lane.[51] In September 1902 the Federated Jewish Tailors Union of London organized a meeting of over 3000 people against controls; this attracted to its platform several individual English trade unionists.[52] In 1904 a Protest Committee was organized in Manchester which arranged at least one major outdoor meeting in Stevenson Square.[53]

All this agitation was significant. It turned back the tide of support for controls from English labour movement bodies.[54] For instance, after 1895 the TUC passed no further resolutions against immigration. Ultimately the agitation was not strong enough on its own to withstand the enactment of controls themselves. Nonetheless it established a feature that is a constant within controls – namely, resistance to controls.

CONTINUITY OF RESISTANCE

There is an unbroken continuity in the struggle against controls. This is clearly illustrated by two leaflets printed nearly one hundred years apart and included as appendices to the present book. One is *No One Is Illegal*, a manifesto against immigration controls published in 2003 and of which the present writer was a co-author. The other is *A Voice from the Aliens* published in 1895.[55] The latter was launched at the rallies in 1895 described above. It was written by Joseph Finn, secretary of the Mantle Makers Union, and was in the name of eleven (essentially Jewish) trade unions. It singled out particular English trade unionists for advocating controls, such as Charles Freak, Secretary of the National Union of Boot and Shoe Operatives. Its purpose was to confront the support for immigration controls first expressed by the TUC in its 1892 Congress.

Both these leaflets are subversive documents as they are opposed in principle to controls and thus help subvert what otherwise could be a consensus in support of controls. We know, of course, that controls were eventually introduced in 1905 with the Aliens Act, but *A Voice from the Aliens* still rings out as a call to the future and to future resistance, a call now taken up by *No One Is Illegal*. Both documents in their continuity of struggle can be seen publicly to vindicate the otherwise secret and personal diary of Winston Smith in *Nineteen Eighty-Four* – the diary in which Big Brother is denounced, the diary which Winston dedicates as follows: 'To the future or to the past…to a time when truth exists… From the age of uniformity…greetings!'[56]

INTERNATIONAL RESISTANCE

Resistance to controls is international. It is protean. It is a continuum. It takes many forms. It won't go away. Though often seeking the support of elected politicians, it does not seek to rely on such persons or on self-appointed so-called 'community leaders'. All this represents its strength. Here is another snapshot of struggle.

- There are individual campaigns against deportation or detention. These can range from simple letter-writing (such as the one that freed Suadh Abubakar from detention in Canada),[57] to occupying courtrooms (such as the solidarity action in Montreal for Parveen Kazmi in her fight against deportation to Pakistan),[58] to ones extending over many years, involving major local/national demonstrations and culminating in pitched battles with the police (such as that in the failed campaign of Viraj Mendis in Manchester against deportation to Sri Lanka).[59] Campaigns against detention or deportation have developed varied and innovative tactics. Viraj Mendis himself sought sanctuary in a local church. Within the USA there has at various times since the 1980s developed a sanctuary movement involving scores of churches and synagogues.[60]

- Campaigns can transcend the individual, can involve many people in the same situation and can become collectivized. In Canada there exists the Action Committee for Non Status Algerians. In the UK there has in the past existed the Divided Families Campaign (fighting to reunite Bangladeshi families) and the Manchester Wives and Fiancées Campaign (fighting both for the right of women to have their partners here and for the right of women to themselves remain here independent of any partner). Recently in Manachester women refugees have combined together in struggle through WAST (Women Asylum Seekers Together). In the last few years there has been established in several towns the Campaign In Defence of Asylum Seekers. In France there exists the most significant organization of the undocumented – the *sans-papiers*.

- Collective campaigns provide the strength for collective action in defence of the individual. Nacera Kellou, quoted above and a member of the Action Committee for Non Status Algerians, described the occupation of the Canadian immigration office in Montreal in solidarity with a family under threat of deportation (see the third quotation at the start of this chapter).

- Campaigns are unpredictable. They can appear anywhere, such as that in the Shetlands in defence of asylum-seekers.[61] They are often sustained by direct action, for instance by deportees or their supporters disrupting airline flights. In Germany an organization known as Deportation Class has campaigned against Lufthansa Airlines to prevent deportations. Trade unions, whilst still retaining support for the principle of controls and indulging in the doublethink of 'fair' controls,[62] nonetheless have been won over by the actions of the undocumented to support many individual campaigns against deportations. Sometimes this support has been more generalized. In September/October 2003 the AFL/CIO (the United State's equivalent to the British TUC) helped sponsor the Immigrant Workers Freedom Ride, whereby undocumented workers crossed the country with a programme for migrant rights, culminating in a major demonstration in New York.[63]

RESISTANCE FROM WITHIN

The ultimate strength of the struggle against controls resides in the self-organization of those most affected. Directly this means the self-organization of those subject to controls. Indirectly it means the collective decision not to collude in the relationship between immigration status and service provision by that new breed of immigration officers, workers within the welfare system. And these workers are beginning to stir.

This can be seen in the UK. Social workers in Leeds decided to disrupt plans under the Asylum and Immigration (Treatment of Claimants, etc.) Act 2004 to forcibly take into care children of failed asylum-seekers who refuse to leave the country.[64] The British Association of Social Workers has said it will 'support any members to challenge any direction by their employers to act unlawfully or unprofessionally in unjustifiably separating children from their parents'.[65] The Royal College of Midwives has passed a resolution agreeing not to 'inform' on the immigration status of mothers.[66] The Medical Practitioners Union (part of the union AMICUS) has launched a campaign to break the link generally between immigration status and health provision – and in particular to oppose recent proposals to extend this link to general practitioners.[67] If these threats were to transcend rhetoric and be activated and followed through, then pulling the plug in this way – resistance from within the belly of the beast – could destroy internal immigration controls.[68]

THE BATTLE FOR IDEAS

We saw in Chapter 5 how Leon Trotsky emphasized that central to all resistance is 'a battle of ideas', and how the very concept of a struggle against orthodoxy, of a fight for truth, is anathema to the society of *Nineteen Eighty-Four*. Likewise, if resistance to immigration controls is to have any validity it cannot remain just on the level of action, necessary though that is. It has to be combined with an ideological struggle, with the battle for ideas. It has to be based on fighting for the principle of no immigration controls. To be even more explicit: any action which contradicts this principle is highly problematic, should be avoided and can only be supported critically.

On this basis there is a weakness in much of the antagonism to controls. It is the weakness of the dead-end. This is because much of the opposition to controls is still based ideologically on the premise of the need for restrictions *in principle*. Two examples will be given here, both of which elaborate and develop points made in the manifesto *No One Is Illegal*. Both these examples raise very difficult political issues that can be resolved only through adopting an ethical political position of hostility to all controls.

The first example is the campaign to repeal the notorious section 55 of the Nationality, Immigration and Asylum Act 2002, under which asylum-seekers who make a 'late' (i.e. not on arrival) application for refugee status are denied welfare support. Such a campaign for the right to support might appear absolutely reasonable and unobjectionable. However, the nature of this so-called 'support' is the NASS-administered punitive poor law, against which all supporters of refugees battled when it was implemented by the 1999 legislation. So, fighting for the repeal of Section 55 effectively means fighting to *secure* poor law provision. The Victorian equivalent of such a bizarre position would have been for those excluded from the workhouse to fight to get into them – rather than close down these institutions which, as we have seen, was the prevalent position. In fact there was one group of people who did campaign, on the most reactionary basis, for the admission not of themselves but of others to these quasi-prisons. This was the Jewish Board of Guardians in Manchester who, to avoid their own communal welfare obligations, collaborated in placing deserted Jewish wives into the workhouse.[69] This is hardly a progressive example on which to model a campaign for the repeal of Section 55. Rather, the demand should be for the abolition of

NASS, for the abolition of all poor laws, and for the restoration of full benefits irrespective of immigration status.

The second example of the dead-end relates to deportations. Numerous deportations are resisted, but on 'compassionate grounds'. Given the balance of forces in the struggle against the Home Office, with the balance being manifestly on the side of the latter, it seems inevitable and correct that the legal and private presentation of a case be put on compassionate grounds. However, it is not at all inevitable, in fact it is wrong, that such arguments form the substance of a public, political campaign. Whatever the relationship between them, political campaigns are different from legal advocacy. Their purpose (or one of their purposes) is to make political points as part of the process of winning a victory. And the political point at issue here is the need to challenge at every step the legitimacy of controls themselves. Without challenging the very principle of controls then we are simply creating or reinforcing a vicious circle within which the undocumented remain trapped. The logic of basing any particular campaign against removal on compassionate grounds is that other campaigns are perceived as somehow neither valid nor acceptable because they lack these grounds. This is the politics (or anti-politics) of *exceptionalism*: particular cases are exceptional and therefore deserving of special ('generous') treatment by the state. It is the modern equivalent of the nineteenth-century distinction between the 'deserving' and 'undeserving' poor. It is the spurious argument for 'fair' controls seen on the level of the individual case.

The alternative – the politics of no controls as expressed in slogans such as SOLIDARITY NOT SYMPATHY and in actions such as collectivizing similar cases in struggle – is often denounced as too advanced or utopic, or even as premature. The reverse is the case. The idea that controls can be cleansed and turned into their opposite – that is, *fair* – is what is utopic. It is a modern form of miracle worship. Arguing against all controls, however difficult, however much it is swimming against the tide, presents the only way forward.

The British state understands the huge, unbridgeable gap between arguing a case on compassionate grounds and fighting for the abolition of all controls through the contesting of cases. Two unusual but sharp examples can be given of this understanding.

First, the National Lottery Board can be added to the list of those agencies that act as instruments of immigration controls. The Board is prepared to fund the National Coalition of Anti Deportation Campaigns, but (after Home Office intervention) only on the basis that it 'supports individual cases' and does not engage in 'doctrinaire' activities – that is, advocate the abolition of controls.[70]

The second example is truly Orwellian in its doctoring of photographs.[71] In the course of the May 2005 parliamentary general election, one of the Conservative Party candidates, Ed Matts, printed a photograph of a former Tory minister, Ann Widdecombe MP, carrying a banner saying 'Not Chaos and Inhumanity'. Matts himself carried a placard saying 'Controlled Immigration'. There is nothing exceptional in this – the Tories support controls, and Widdecombe is seen as being on the right wing of the party in this respect. However, it was revealed that the photographs were doctored. Previously Widdicombe and Matts had supported an asylum-seeking family under threat of deportation, and on that occasion Widdecombe's banner had read 'Let Them Stay'. It may or may not be surprising that they supported the couple. What the doctored photos show is that there is absolutely no distinction between supporting a case on compassionate grounds, on arguing for it as an exception, whilst championing the most extreme immigration controls. This is precisely the vicious circle which entraps the undocumented.

NO ONE IS ILLEGAL – BUT WHEN?

The view that it is too premature to argue for the abolition of immigration controls raises the question as to when exactly it will be correct or opportune to raise such an apparently heretical demand. Such a view echoes the accusation made by Senator Joe McCarthy and other cold-war anti-communists, that those calling for an alliance with the Soviet Union in opposing Nazism prior to the USA's entry into the Second World War were 'premature anti-fascists'. One is reminded of Primo Levi (anti-fascist and holocaust survivor) and the title of his novel *If Not Now When?* This novel describes the fight for survival by Jewish partisans behind the Nazi lines. Levi's title is a compressed version of what was reputedly said by Hillel, the Jewish rabbi and scholar born in Babylonian exile: 'If I am not for myself, then who else will be for me? And if I am only for myself, then what am I? And if not now, when?'

Or as Bobby Seale, founder member of the Black Panthers, famously wrote and entitled a book two thousand years later: *Seize the Time!*

The assertion that it is premature to raise the demand for no controls simply represents an ideological fear of confronting the deep-rooted state racism within controls. Imagine the same argument of untimely intervention used against racist attacks; it would have to be presented as something like: 'Don't challenge racist assaults. They are too popular. It's therefore too precipitate to criticize them. It will make us seem extremists. Let's just campaign against racist murders!'

Today's undocumented are at the moment living 'behind the lines' of racism and controls. If the demand for no controls is not going to be raised now, then when and by whom will it be raised? How long do we have to wait before the time is seized? Well, the demand is starting to be raised. For instance, a member of the Sans-Papiers National Coordinating Committee in France has said: 'It is now or never, for the democratic forces in the country to embrace this amazing movement of the most marginalized section of the working class and of society, the *sans-papiers*, who have no rights.'[72]

In particular, the demand for no controls it is being raised in the No One Is Illegal groups that are being established in various countries and various cities.[73] Quotations from the round-table dialogue between Canadian asylum-seekers and other political activists from the Montreal No One Is Illegal group (along with members of the Action Committee for Non-Status Algerians) on the politics of anti-deportation struggles appear at the start of this chapter. The manifesto *No One Is Illegal* has achieved a wide national and international circulation in the UK. The phrase 'No One Is Illegal' was devised by a holocaust survivor, Elie Weisel, in support of sanctuary for asylum-seekers.[74] It needs to be emphasized again that immigration controls are not genocide – yet. However, the assertion that no one is illegal challenges both the *Nineteen Eighty-Four* reduction of humanity to 'unpersons' and their Nazi reduction to *Untermenschen*, as well as the contemporary reduction of the undocumented to 'exceptions'. It is a rallying call to collective struggle, solidarity, self-organization and self-assertion – 'If I am not for myself, then who else will be for me?' Or as Orwell puts it in *Nineteen Eighty-Four*, 'if there was hope it lay with the proles.'[75]

11. THE PLANET WITHOUT A VISA

> When Mekabou Fofana (an asylum-seeker) was in Pennsylvania's Lehigh County Prison, an inmate serving time for murder asked the Liberian teenager how many people he had killed. 'I said I didn't kill anyone' Fofana recalled. 'I just got arrested at the airport'
>
> — *News item*[1]

WHILE THERE IS LIGHT

In July 1981, at the height of a generalized urban insurrection throughout the major cities of the UK, twelve Asian youths were arrested in Bradford and subsequently charged with conspiracy to make bombs. The manufacture of the latter was never denied. What was argued was that they were only to be used in a case of racist or fascist attack. In what otherwise might seem a fantastic outcome – but was in fact the consequence of a national political campaign – all were acquitted on the grounds of 'self-defence is no offence'. Many of the defendants had previously been actively involved in immigration campaigns, particularly that of Anwar Ditta in her struggle to be reunited with her children. Anwar subsequently spoke in court for them.

One of the defendants, Tariq Mehmood, later published a semi-autobiographical novel, *While There is Light*. In this he encounters a religious asylum-seeker (an *Ahmadi*) being deported on a flight to Pakistan, and the following conversation takes place,[2] a conversation which succinctly describes immigration controls:

'Didn't the Home Office believe your story?' I ask.

'I wouldn't be with you if they did,' Lahori says letting out a false laugh. 'They came for me one morning and didn't even give me

171

enough time to pack. I don't even have presents for my children. Just one little bag with a few clothes is all I could manage.'

'English are clever bastards you know,' the old man says breaking an icy silence.

'J'ACCUSE'

In January 1898 there appeared what was probably the greatest newspaper article ever. It was by the French novelist Emile Zola, and took the form of an open letter to the French President. The substance of the letter was proof that the conviction for treason of Captain Alfred Dreyfus, a Jewish artillery officer in the French army, had been the result of an anti-semitic frame-up. Probably no other article has ever provoked such international controversy nor had such an impact on a nation's body politic. It eventually resulted in Dreyfus's freedom. The article was entitled 'J'Accuse' – I Accuse.

Now is the time for another Zola, as well as another Orwell. A modern Zola could shout and argue 'I accuse' against every single aspect of immigration controls, for instance: *I accuse* immigration controls of being premised on the destruction if language; *I accuse* immigration controls of being based on a Big Lie, the Big Lie of an historic freedom of entry for refugees; *I accuse* immigration controls of corrupting and drawing into collusion local-authority and voluntary-sector workers, and just about everyone else; *I accuse* immigration controls of creating simultaneously both rule by racist law and a state of racist lawlessness; *I accuse* immigration controls and their flip-side, so-called anti-terrorist legislation, of paving the way, softening us up, for the strong, totalitarian state; *I accuse* immigration controls of being insane in their proclamation 'Deportation is Freedom!'; *I accuse* the English of being 'clever bastards'.

What Zola (like Trotsky) understood is that there is no way out of anywhere without the revelation of the truth. The truth is that there can be no apologia, no justification, no excuse, no sanitization of controls. The truth is there can be no 'fair' controls or 'just' controls' or 'compassionate' controls or 'non-racist' controls. There can be no compromise, no conciliation. There can only be an exposé and destruction of controls. Anything aiming short of this is again premised on collusion, complicity and co-option.

RECLAIMING LANGUAGE

In immigration controls and in *Nineteen Eighty-Four*, all language as mediated through Newspeak and doublethink becomes a Babel of nonsense. The Old Testament biblical image of the Tower of Babel is here apposite, because when God allegedly destroyed the tower he 'confounded the language of all the earth'.[3] All subsequent language was to become not a form of communication but a source of confusion.[4] In the context of immigration controls this is seen at its most vivid in the token discourse between politicians claiming to be in conflict but in fact being in agreement. It is all a charade, which is part of the maddening process of immigration controls.

A classic but typical example was the 'debates' (this itself being Newspeak vocabulary for lack of debate) in respect of the enactment of the Conservative government's Asylum and Immigration Act 1996. Labour MPs consistently voted against the Act whilst agreeing in principle with all its assumptions. Jack Straw, Labour's chief spokesperson at the time, persistently made remarks such as: 'No-one doubts the need to tackle the problem of bogus asylum-seekers'[5] and 'There is no need for this measure to be controversial. There is agreement across the Floor'.[6] Some opposition! Some doublethink! Perhaps Orwell could have called this phenomenon *samespeak*.

RETRIEVING HISTORY

It is clear that Orwell's model for totalitarianism, for the mode of rule in Oceania and seemingly also Eurasia and Eastasia, was the Soviet Union at the height of its internal tyranny (*Nineteen Eighty-Four* was written in 1948). For example, the anti-mathematics of $2+2=5$ that Winston was finally forced to accept as a token of his defeat[7] was taken from an actual Soviet poster 'proving' that an announced Five Year Plan had been completed in four,[8] whereas in truth none of the announced plans were ever completed (or, to put it another way, all are still awaiting completion). It is also quite transparent that the two main protagonists in Oceania represent what were, in the manner of a classic Greek tragedy, perhaps the two major personal and political foes of the twentieth century. In the right corner is Big Brother ('black-haired, black-moustachio'd'[9]) playing Joseph Stalin. In the left corner is Emmanuel Goldstein ('a lean Jewish face'[10]) with white hair and a goatee beard, playing Leon Trotsky. From early in the book it is clear where Winston's and Orwell's sympathies reside. Goldstein is 'the sole guardian of truth and sanity in a world of lies'.[11] The lesson of *Nineteen Eighty-Four* and of immigration controls is that dishonesty leads to madness. Only the truth is sane. And the truth is that immigration controls have been, are and always will be inherently racist.

Paradoxically, Trotsky's own life represented a refutation of the deceitful mantra as to freedom of entry for refugees. He was in danger of his life from 1928, when he was expelled from the (Newspeak-inspired) Soviet Politburo, and was eventually assassinated by a Stalinist agent in Mexico in 1940. Isaac Deutscher refers to him in the title to the third volume of his biography as the *Prophet Outcast*, and this lyrically describes the refusal to grant him asylum by any country in Europe – including Britain with its then Labour government under Ramsey Macdonald.[12] There is a specific myth that 'liberal' Britain has welcomed revolutionaries fleeing the 'tyrannies' of Europe. The example of Karl Marx is often paraded. However, this was before the Aliens Act 1905 imposed controls, and there was no need for asylum rights in the absence of controls. In any event, though Marx was allowed entry he was not welcome here and was denied British citizenship.[13] Trotsky, writing in his autobiography *My Life*, described his own search for asylum in this way: 'At times, it seemed as if I were attending a "pan-European" performance of a one-act comedy on the theme of principles of democracy.'

The comedy, if such it ever was, has now turned to tragedy for the undocumented of the world. Trotsky provided an apt summary to this tragedy in the title to the relevant chapter of his autobiography – 'The Planet Without a Visa'.

THE 'MEMORY HOLE' OF MAGNA CARTA

Immigration controls are not the only political sphere in which operates the memory hole. In a sense most recorded history contains a distortion of the past as most recorded history is written by the victors, or their successors, anxious to vindicate their role. What distinguishes immigration control is that, at each and every stage, the rewriting of history is a central, essentially institutionalized, feature. So there often arises the paradoxical situation whereby most sides in the political argument over controls incorporate falsehoods that have been accepted from other areas of historiography. The most recent examples were the parliamentary debates over the Anti-Terrorism Act 2001 and the Prevention of

Terrorism Act 2005. The former allowed for detention without trial of non-British citizens and the latter of both British and non-British citizens. Both pieces of legislation were criticized as being in breach of habeas corpus in general and the ancient Magna Carta in particular. For instance, Crispin Blunt MP said in parliament:

> I turn first to the *Magna Carta*, 790 years ago. Chapter 29 stated that no freeman shall be taken or imprisoned or seized of his freehold or liberties or free customs, or be outlawed, or exiled, or any other wise destroyed; nor will we not pass upon him, nor condemn him but by lawful judgment of his peers, or by the law of the land. We will sell to no man, we will not deny or defer to any man either justice or right.'[14]

Magna Carta (drawn up in 1215) is a popular icon of supposed freedoms won by the baronial class against the Big Brother of his day, King John, and which still retains the same nationalistic status as 'Rule Brittania', 'There'll Always Be An England' and 'God Save The Queen'. In reality the charter contained many quite reactionary and racist provisions. It was a reflection of both its own age and of the dominant class (the nobility) that enforced it. However, these racists provisions have been lost to history. Now is the time to rediscover and expose them. In particular there was the stigmatizing of Jews as a group to whom debts need not be repaid. Chapters 10 and 11 of the charter read:

> If one who has borrowed from the Jews any sum, great or small, die before that loan be repaid, the debt shall not bear interest while the heir is under age, of whomsoever he may hold; and if the debt fall into our hands, we will not take anything except the principal sum contained in the bond. And if anyone die indebted to the Jews, his wife shall have her dower and pay nothing of that debt; and if any children of the deceased are left under age, necessaries shall be provided for them in keeping with the holding of the deceased; and out of the residue the debt shall be paid, reserving, however, service due to feudal lords; in like manner let it be done touching debts due to others than Jews.

Though non-Jews are included right at the end of these paragraphs, yet the emphasis on Jewish usury is plainly problematic and needs to be thought about. It is remarkable how this stereotyping of Jews, this anti-semitism, has been so obliterated from history. It is a devastating example of the memory hole.

SHOPPING YOUR (DEAD) GRANDFATHER

We have seen how, in *Nineteen Eighty-Four*, children spied on and denounced their parents, and how this eventually led to the interrogation and imprisonment of Parsons. As usual when it comes to immigration controls, life goes one better than fiction. In January 2005, the *Sunday Telegraph* carried an advert by Michael Howard MP as leader of the Conservative Party.[15] In near-biblical tones it was headed 'I believe we must limit immigration'. The advert itself was reminiscent of the party posters of Oceania which were in the name of Big Brother and which 'were plastered everywhere'.[16] Howard's advert represented a xenophobic attack on the undocumented, proclaiming:

> There are literally millions of people in other countries who want to come and live here. Britain cannot take them all. A Conservative government will set an annual limit on immigration and a quota for asylum-seekers'.

Having attacked *sans-papiers* and asylum-seekers in general, Howard subsequently in the *Daily Telegraph* of February 2005 went even further and denounced his own grandfather as having entered the country 'unlawfully'.[17] It transpired that Howard's family was Jewish and came from Romania. The *Telegraph* reported that his grandmother died at Auschwitz (itself a sanitised description of her being murdered) but his grandfather escaped and came to the UK, in breach of immigration controls. Furthermore, Howard's own father fled here in the 1930s as a refugee. His father subsequently applied for British citizenship and lied about the grandfather's history (presumably to protect him), saying he had perished in Romania. So in fact two generations of the Howard family were in breach of immigration and nationality laws, respectively. The *Telegraph* article throughout referred to the grandfather in that most Newspeak of all vocabulary – as an *illegal immigrant*.

This really does reach a post-Orwellian scenario of Big Brother spying on and denouncing himself! Why did Howard do this? Perhaps it would require a psychologist to understand. However, there would appear to be three interlocking reasons.

First, Howard had absorbed the basic philosophy of *Nineteen Eighty-Four*, namely that there is an absolute duty to condemn 'outlaws', 'foreigners' and 'traitors' and an absolute prohibition on questioning why the human objects of moral panic are defined in this way. Second, it would seem that as a career politician he was anxious to pre-empt the revelation by anyone else of his family history. Third, he was willing to take on the role of the victim of anti-semitism without being prepared, or having the insight, to acknowledge this. Anti-semites have always demanded that Jews grovel before them and grovel in public – witness the humiliation of religious Jews in Nazi Berlin being forced to scrub the pavements (pavements on which, incidentally, they were not allowed to walk). Howard can here be seen grovelling, to accept that where Jews are concerned we are all responsible for the sins of not just our parents but also our grandparents – grovelling for some sort of forgiveness.

Of course it is only a profound refusal to reflect on the real (i.e. racist) politics of immigration controls that would lead anyone to regard entering the UK in flight from Nazism as a sin. As is said in *Nineteen Eighty-Four*, and as we have already seen, 'orthodoxy means not thinking'.[18]

EXPOSING COLLUSION

The Home Office, like Big Brother, can operate only through collusion – through its agents. Outside of its own organization (where NASS now dominates) its number-one agent is the local state (number two is rapidly becoming components of the voluntary sector). This collaboration has now gone well beyond any formal, juridical, level. It is no longer based on any legal sanction. Rather it has reached a point where local authorities, their managers and workers *instinctively* refuse services to those they deem to be without the correct immigration status.

This is the unspoken reality behind the otherwise well-publicized deaths of two black children, denied adequate social services care. The two children were Victoria Climbié, murdered by her foster mother and boyfriend in 2000, and Toni-Ann Byfield, caught in the crossfire and shot dead with her father in a drugs war in 2003. Both children had been in the country only a short time. Both were known to be at risk. Both cases received much media attention. And in both cases evidence as to the role and responsibility of immigration controls and their relationship to local authority social services was effectively suppressed in the publicity. But there was such evidence. An official report by Birmingham City Council into Toni-Ann's murder said: 'There were delays in producing assessments and reports and in establishing Toni-Ann's immigration status, which affected the quality of decision making.'[19] And in the second phase of the Climbié inquiry, the Family Rights Group's chief executive said: 'There appears to be a culture within many social services departments that such applicants are not eligible for any support because of their immigration status. They appear to be treated as a group apart from other families seeking help for children in need.'[20] This is a culture of professional corruption through political collusion.

The Orwellian nexus between social services and the Home Office was clinched with the arrest, detention and threatened deportation to Jamaica of Roselyn Richards, the mother of Toni-Ann Byfield. Roselyn had come to the UK to attend the inquest into the murder of her daughter. A government spokesperson said the expulsion of Roselyn was necessary so "the public can have confidence" in immigration controls.[21] This is no different than the confidence in Big Brother continually indoctrinated into the Oceanic public.

RESISTING RACIST LAWS AND LAWLESSNESS

Just as local authorities and their workers operate immigration controls through culture and instinct and no longer through statute or law, so also in *Nineteen Eighty-Four* a party member is required to have not only the right opinions but 'the right instincts...If a person is naturally orthodox [in Newspeak, a *goodthinker*], he will know...what is the true belief'.[22] Such a robotic relationship to immigration controls, such *goodthinking*, is central to the administration of welfare and just about everything else in our contemporary society.

There is a contradiction within *Nineteen Eighty-Four* between law and discretion (or 'instinct'). On the one hand, every personal activity (that is, activity not in the service of Big Brother) is rendered illegal, rendered a crime – to the point where there is the ultimately intrusive madness of *thoughtcrime*. On the other hand, Orwell also writes that Winston's secret diary was not illegal because 'nothing was illegal since there were no longer any laws'[23] – which, as we have seen,[24] was repeated later in the novel as 'In Oceania there is no law'.[25] This contradiction within the novel between law and non-law, between legalism and anti-legalism, is a contradiction within totalitarianism, and it is more apparent than real. Once law is absolute, once it covers every conceivable situation, then that is the end of the rule of law. The state has absolute power; and absolute power means absolute, unfettered *discretion* by the state, by the rulers of the state and by the agents of the rulers.

This is a situation analogous to the all-pervading, all-embracing, all-intrusive nature of immigration controls. The real lesson from history is that every law since 1905 – the Aliens Act – has provided a stage in this development of the ending of the rule of law. The development has been exponential, manufactured at an ever-increasing rate. From 1905 until 1962 there were just three major pieces of primary legislation.[26] From 1962 until 1993 there were six.[27] From 1993 until 2004 there have been another four.[28] As in *Nineteen Eighty-Four*, 'war had been literally continuous',[29] so the attack on the undocumented is unbounded in all dimensions and transcends law. This is why legal fetishism – servile, subservient, obeisance towards the law, towards immigration controls – is not just a nonsense but a dangerous nonsense.

RESISTING THE REMORSELESS MARCH OF CONTROLS

It is frightening to examine how comprehensive have become immigration restrictions. A recent book which reprints the main texts of UK immigration law as at September 2003 consists of 1006 pages, including 12 statutes, the immigration rules, 4 procedure rules, 21 other statutory instruments, 13 pieces of European legislation and 9 international conventions, alongside other documents.[30] In *Nineteen Eighty-Four* Orwell writes that 'the search for new weapons continues unceasingly,'[31] and this was one of the very few remaining activities in which the inventive or speculative mind could find any outlet.

In today's world these weapons consist of the production and reproduction of immigration laws, documents that are the equivalent of pieces of military/judicial ordinance. This jurisprudence has developed in a short time span. The first UK control, the Aliens Act 1905, contained just eight pages. This is also a world to which there is devoted a significant proportion of the national economy.[32] If all this enthusiasm and money for controls went into something productive or creative – from building schools to relieving global poverty to writing poetry – the world would be immeasurably better for us all.

THE ALTERNATIVE TERROR

Today's world is undoubtedly a perilous place, and it is arguable who has the responsibility for this. What is incontrovertible is that the 'terrorism' of so-called 'rogue' states and organizations has been used as yet another excuse for the strengthening of the terror of immigration controls,

themselves part of the construction of the modern, strong, anti-demo-
cratic state. The enactment of anti-terrorist legislation in the UK[33] is
reflected globally. Just 45 days after the bombing of the Twin Towers the
USA unleashed the (Orwellian-entitled) Patriot Act 2001, which effectively ensured the all-seeing gaze of Big Brother by authorizing the FBI
to intercept phone calls, faxes and emails without a warrant. Canada has
witnessed the Immigration and Refugee Protection Act 2001, the
Anti-Terrorism Act 2001, and the Public Safety Act 2002. These
measures have done more to extend the power to detain, sentence and
monitor the undocumented than to apprehend those engaged in
violence, whilst at the same time they have strengthened in the popular
imagination the association between terrorism and immigration.

In spite of the unique trauma of the Twin Towers, there is absolutely
nothing new historically in this association. Once again we are seeing
the unacknowledged and tragico-farcical repetition of a suppressed
history.[33] One excuse given for the Aliens Act 1905 was that all Jewish
refugees were anarchists in disguise. W. H. Wilkins, the ardent immigration restrictionist, declared in his 1892 book *The Alien Invasion* that he
knew of 'secret' Jewish revolutionary societies whose existence 'cannot
be doubted', and that:

> They are formed of the class of man who marched to Hyde Park
> the other day with a banner inscribed 'Down with the Czar'.
> These societies have papers of their own circulated amongst
> themselves, written in Yiddish, breathing the vilest political
> sentiments – Nihilism of the most outrageous description.[35]

Queen Victoria, in a letter of 13 July 1894, wrote to the then Prime
Minister, Lord Rosebery, at a time when parliament was discussing immigration controls, that she felt strongly about 'allowing those monstrous
anarchists and assassins to live here and hatch their horrible plots in our
country'.[36] Interestingly, Edgar Wallace in his otherwise pulp thriller
novel *The Four Just Men* (published in 1905, the year of the Aliens Act)
depicted in a positive fashion, almost as freedom fighters, a group of
anarchists intent on assassinating a Home Secretary supporting legislation against refugees: 'We allow you until tomorrow evening to consider
your position in the matter of the Aliens Extradition Bill…[otherwise]
you will die at eight in the evening.'[37] The assassination was eventually
successful. However, though a bestseller, this novel had no long-term
ideological significance in gaining support for refugees. The fantasy

nature of the plot eventually overrode and diminished the politics contained within the book.

Historical analogies do not end here. In December 1910 there occurred the so-called Siege of Sydney Street, in which a group of purported alien anarchists shot a Special Branch officer and were trapped in a house in Sydney Street, Stepney, London. This led to demands for 'anti-terrorist' legislation.[38] Legislation was not enacted then – it took another ninety years. On 14 January 2003, Detective Constable Steven Oakes was shot and killed in Crumpsall Lane, Manchester, whilst raiding a house under immigration and 'anti-terrorist' legislation. The following Monday the *Sun* newspaper claimed that 'Britain is now a Trojan horse for terrorists.' On Tuesday, the *Daily Mail* alleged in an editorial that the UK was 'a haven for Albanian gangsters, Kosovan people and Algerian terrorists'. On Wednesday, the *Daily Express* said that 'the nightmare scenario [of terrorism] of which we warned is here'. The fascist British National Party then posted on its website a front-page *Express* article linking asylum-seekers with terrorism, stating 'British press is helping to spread BNP message.' Immigration controls, 'anti-terrorism', totalitarianism – this is the intertwined message not just of moral panic but also of fascism.

RACISM REPACKAGED

The manuscript for the present book went to the printers in the immediate aftermath of the bombings of London of July 7 2005 – bombings which have convulsed both civil society and the body politic.

Once again this has lead to a generalised stereotyping of the *foreigner*, the *alien*, the *other*. And this stereotyping has gone on within the context of an invocation of the 'war time spirit'. Britain or England or at least London is now literally engaged in its own 'perpetual war' against the stranger – the same perpetual war fought by Oceania. It is a war where the enemy is everywhere but is never actually seen.

In spite of the horrific consequence of the action – mangled bodies on mangled trains and buses – this convulsion is in essence no different than that which has been politically and repeatedly constructed by advocates of immigration control at all times since the arrival of Jewish immigration at the end of the nineteenth century. So it is not surprising that the immediate reaction to the bombing was not an analysis as to the reasons for their occurrence but a demand for further controls – as though there was some inherent connection between migration and suicide attacks.

Behind this demand was another one, an Orwellian one couched in Orwellian terms: a cry for yet more conformity and uniformity. It took the form of an attack on 'multiculturism' and so far has reached its depths with the call by Hazel Blears, a Home Office Minister, for Britain to 'rebrand ethnic minorities'. In this world of PR and packaging – of which 'New' Labour is a clear example – it is being suggested that 'minorities (should) be described as, for example 'Asian-British' rather than simply as 'Asian'.[39]

In the past slaves were branded, literally and with fire, as proof of ownership – as though they were cattle. In 1440 the Portuguese started branding slaves by burning a mark on their skin to show who they belonged to. This subsequently became the way all European slave owners controlled information about their African slaves. Some even branded their slaves with a cross once they had forcibly baptised them as Christians.

Under the modern market economy it has hitherto been commodities (including political parties), not people, that have been 'rebranded'. However the commoditisation of the alien reduces her or him to a piece of capital, to an object, to a new form of enslavement – the enslavement of a forced identity within a hostile society ever ready to deport and expel.

DOUBLE-CROSS, DEPORTATION AND DIGNITY

Collusion with immigration controls leads to the deception of those subject to the controls. Central to the politics of *Deportation is freedom!* is not just doublethink but double-cross. And, as has been stressed throughout this book, nowhere is double-cross and collusion more evident than in the construct of 'voluntary departure' and those organizations employed to implement such hidden deportation. The further removed from the awful, brutal reality of the situation then the more euphemistic become the descriptions of expulsion. Barbara Roche, the then Minister for Immigration, said in connection with deportation: 'The most important thing is that it's done with dignity.'[40]

Deportation? Dignity? The forced removal of human beings? All this is the reduction of our language to Newspeak. It is the destruction of language. It is deportation posing as freedom. It is, as shown by this chapter's initial quotation, one refugee being wrongfully arrested for murder on arrival at an airport. It is another refugee screaming out 'every asylum-seeker is dead already'.[41] It is Orwellian. It is *Amtssprache*. It is *Nineteen Eighty-Four*. It is immigration controls. It is insane.

APPENDIX 1: A VOICE FROM THE ALIENS[1]

ABOUT THE ANTI-ALIEN RESOLUTION OF THE CARDIFF TRADE UNION CONGRESS, 1905

We, the organized Jewish workers of England, taking into consideration the Anti-Alien Resolution, and the uncomplimentary remarks of certain delegates about the Jewish workers specially, issue this leaflet, wherewith we hope to convince our English fellow workers of the untruthfulness, unreasonableness, and want of logic contained in the cry against the foreign worker in general, and against the Jewish worker in particular.

It is, and always has been, the policy of the ruling classes to attribute the sufferings and miseries of the masses (which are natural consequences of class rule and class exploitation) to all sorts of causes except the real ones. The cry against the foreigner is not merely peculiar to England; it is international. Everywhere he is the scapegoat for other's sins. Every class finds in him an enemy. So long as the Anti-Alien sentiment in this country was confined to politicians, wire-pullers, and to individual working men, we, the organized aliens, took no heed; but when this ill-founded sentiment has been officially expressed by the organized working men of England, then we believe that it is time to lift our voices and argue the matter out.

It has been proved by great political economists that a working man in a country where machinery is greatly developed produces in a day twice as many commodities as his daily wage enables him to consume.

For one half, he himself is the market; for the rest (the surplus), a market must be found elsewhere. Until the market is found, and the surplus sold off, the worker must remain idle – unemployed.

The greater the producing power, the larger the surplus. The larger the surplus is, the longer is the period of unemployment. The larger the number of the unemployed, the keener and fiercer is the competition for work. Consequently, the harder are the times and the greater the sufferings of the worker. Who, then, is to be blamed? Surely we cannot blame the foreign working man, who is as much a victim of the industrial system as is the English working man. Neither can we blame the machine which displaces human labour. The only party at fault is the English working class itself, which has the power, but neither the sense nor courage, to make the machines serve and benefit the whole nation, instead of leaving them as a source of profit for one class. To punish the alien worker for the sin of the native capitalist is like the man who struck the boy because he was not strong enough to strike his father.

We will assume, for the sake of argument, that the foreign worker *is* injurious to the English worker, and that the Government will prohibit him from coming here. What then? England as a Free Trade country would thereby suffer severely; because the same commodities which the foreign worker used to produce here (being at the same time a source of income to the country), he will then produce abroad – much cheaper, too, because the cost of living is lower there. Those commodities will then be imported here. Will this benefit the English worker? Let Mr Freak and Mr Inskip answer.

The Freakians and Inskipians claim that the immigration of workers from other countries over-gluts the labour market, displaces English labour, and reduces the wages of the native workmen. From this it would logically follow that the emigration of workers from the country would have the contrary effect, i.e. would relieve the market, and thus bring on good times. In short, the more the immigration, the worse for a country; the more the emigration, the better for a country. If this is so, then how will they account for the following facts and figures?

The average annual immigration of aliens in England according to the report of the Board of Trade for 1891–92–93 has been 24,688,[2] whilst the average annual emigration is put down by the Dictionary of Statistics at 164,000.[3] In face of these figures, we repeat our argument. If immigration over-gluts the market then emigration must logically relieve it. And, seeing that the emigration is more than six times the immigration, we cannot see why England should cry out so loudly about the foreigner. We will carry the question further, and we will prove to our English fellow workers that immigration or emigration in no way affects the condition of the working men or the state of the labour market.

In Germany the immigration is one-tenth of the emigration. In the United States it is vice versa. Still, the wages of a tailor in Germany is 15s., whilst in the United States it is 58s. What will our opponents say to this? Again, in 1831–40 the immigration in the United States was 699,000. In 1881–89 it was 4,792,000; still, in the former period the daily wage of a tailor was 4s. 6d., whilst in the latter period it was 8s. 4d.[4] With these statistics in view we can safely say, that if the English worker has reason to be dissatisfied with his lot, let him not blame his foreign fellow working man; let him rather study the social and labour question – he will then find out where the shoe pinches.

Leaving the foreign worker in general, we will now deal with the Jewish worker in particular.

We, the Jewish workers, have been spoken of as a blighting blister upon the English trades and workers, as men to whose hearts it is impossible to appeal, and were it not for us, the condition of the native worker would be much improved, he would have plenty of work, good wages, and what not. Well, let us look into facts; let us examine the condition of such workers with whom the Jew never comes in contact, such as the agricultural labourer, the docker, the miner, the weaver, the chain maker, ship builder, bricklayer and many others. Examine their condition, dear reader, and answer: Is there any truth in the remark that we are a ' blighting blister ' upon the English worker?

It is alleged that we are cutting down the wages of the English worker, and no proof is given in support of such an allegation. We on the other hand claim that English workers are reducing our wages and we will prove our claim.

That the ready-made clothing trade, the second-class made-to-order tailoring trade, the mantle, waterproof clothing, cap, slipper, and cheap shoe trades have been created by the Jewish workers in this country – no one who knows anything about it will deny. Mr Booth in his book *Life and Labour of the People*[5] declares that 'The ready-made clothing trade is not an invasion on the employment of the English tailor, but an industrial discovery'.

In the report of the Board of Trade on the effects of immigration, speaking of the boot and shoe trade we find the following: 'The foreign Jews are, to a large extent, engaged on a common class of boots and shoes, some of which probably could not profitably be made by English labour under the existing statement, and might hence cease to be produced, or at least leave London (either for the provinces or abroad) were it not for the presence of Jewish labour.'[5] The reader should not fall into the mistake that the Jewish worker can produce the cheap class of boots because he will work for lower wages – far from it. In fact, the Jewish workers earn better wages in this cheap class than the English do in the better class. This is due to their great abilities in turning out large quantities. In a circular issued by the Mantle Makers' Union to the mantle manufacturers we read the following:

> Germany and France, though behind England in the evolution of other trades, were ahead of her in the mantle trade. They have created a new branch of the trade in question. They have combined the quality, style, and workmanship of the bespoke tailor-made, with nearly the cheapness of the cheap ready-made. How did they do it? By applying the present mode of capitalistic manufacture – that is, production on a large scale, use of machinery and the division of labour, to the bespoke tailor-made garment. Thus England has been a market for Germany and France. Some years ago, certain English manufacturers realized that the same class of garments could be made in this country. Circumstances brought to England the class of workers, experts in that work, and the trade is now rapidly growing.

This is again corroborated by an article on the mantle trade, which appeared in a German periodical, the *Neue Zeit*, No. 39, of the year 1893, where the writer points out to his countrymen the cause of the diminution of the mantle trade in Germany. 'The cause is,' he says, 'the transference of the trade to England by the Russian and Polish Jews.' We could fill a book with quotations, statements and figures, in favour of our claim. From what has been said, the truth-seeking reader will see how groundless is the accusation that we displace English labour.

Not only are we engaged in trades which we have introduced, but we have to a very great extent provided work for the English workers. According to the report mentioned above, the Jewish workers that are employed in the boot and shoe trade are less than one and a half per cent of the total number of workers employed in that trade. The export of boots and shoes from the United Kingdom from the year 1873 till 1893 increased about 25 per cent. Taking into consideration that the Jewish products are mostly exported, and that their influx into the boot and shoe trade took place during that period, is it not reasonable to assume that the great increase in trade is to some extent due to them?

But that is nothing to what has been accomplished in the clothing trades. The trousers and vests are made entirely by English women; the weaving, cutting, book-keeping, and all work connected with the counting house is performed only by English men and women. We will also remind our English friends of the fact that when the Jewish tailors of Leeds struck in 1888, the English workers in the cloth mills were put on half time.

When you, our English fellow workers, cry out so loud against our competition, while you fail to prove that it exists at all, when you call us a blighting blister, then what ought we to say to our English sister-slaves who are actually taking the bread out of our mouths by working for half the price, and are driving us out of the workshops which we have built up? Can they deny that they are making a mantle for a shilling, for which we have received two shillings? We feel their throat-cutting competition in every trade which we have created, and which they have stepped into. Those who investigate the subject readily admit it. Thus we read in the report of the Board of Trade the following statements: 'At present the Jews need only fear the competition with the English female labour.' Again: 'In the machining department, where foreign men compete with English women, the latter are gaining ground on the former.'[7]

In view of the foregoing facts, we ask the impartial reader: Who is competing with whom, who is displacing whom – the Jew the English, or the English the Jew!

We have been branded by the Freakians and Inskipians as a class of people who are behind in the labour movement, who will not be organized, and to whose hearts it is impossible to appeal. We beg leave to ask these gentlemen whether their appeals to our hearts during the boot makers struggle with their masters did or did not find a response? If their memories fail them, we will recommend them to the Strike Committee. Did it require much appealing to our hearts in the time of the great miners' struggle to induce us to organise a committee which raised £38 16s. 4d., besides what our unions donated from their funds? We could enumerate many instances which would illustrate the deep sympathy with which the hearts of the Jewish working men are filled in response to every appeal made to them by their English fellow workers. But we must refrain, lest it be said that we are 'boasting'.

The gentlemen named above would have the world believe that we are blacklegs, and that we will not be organized. True, some of us are hard to be convinced of the benefits of organization, but when we can point to an army of 3,000 union men in London alone, out of a total of about 10,000 Jewish working men, then we believe that we can hold up our heads against either English, Scots, Irish, or Welsh.

That there are some blacklegs amongst us is nothing more than natural, you will find them among all nations. But one thing must be admitted. It is this: That we have not amongst us an official organized army of blacklegs, such as the English can boast of, viz. 'a free labour party'.

We are behind the English working men in the labour movement, but were we not in front of them in the last 1st of May demonstration?

Just as we were about to write our concluding remarks in this leaflet, we have been informed by the Press that a deputation of the organized English working men met the Government and laid before them many resolutions that were passed at the Cardiff Congress. Of all that was asked, only one thing was granted. It is this: That all alien exploiters, swindlers, blacklegs, drunkards, idlers of all sorts who *have* money are welcomed here; but that skilful, industrious, honest working men, who have either been out of work for a long time, or have been locked out by their masters for taking part in strikes and boycotts, and therefore have no money, shall be prohibited from coming here.

We cannot congratulate the English working-class on this achievement. We believe that with all its influence with its great organizations and enormous funds, with its millions of votes, and, above all, with its great intelligence it ought to have achieved something better and nobler. In conclusion, we appeal to all right-thinking working men of England not to be misled by some leaders who have made it their cause to engender a bitter feeling amongst the British workers against the workers of other countries. Rather hearken to the voices of such leaders as will foster a feeling of international solidarity among the working people.

In conclusion, we appeal to our fellow-workers to consider whether there is any justification whatever for regarding as the enemies of the English workers the foreign workers, who, so far from injuring them, actually bring trade here and develop new industries; whether, so far from being the enemies of the

English workers, it is not rather the capitalist class (which is constantly engaged in taking trade abroad, in opening factories in China, Japan, and other countries) who is the enemy, and whether it is not rather their duty to combine against the common enemy than fight against us whose interests are identical with theirs.

Independent Tailors, Machinists, and Pressers' Union
United Ladies' Tailors and Mantle-Makers' Union
United Cap Makers' Union
International Bakers' Union
Independent Cabinet Makers' Association
East London Branch of the National Union of Boot and Shoe Operatives
Amalgamated Society of Tailors, Jewish Branch
Slipper Makers' Union
International Sew-Round and Operative Union
Upper Machiners' Union
Cabinet Makers' Alliance, Hebrew Branch

APPENDIX 2: NO ONE IS ILLEGAL![1]

MANIFESTO OF THE NO ONE IS ILLEGAL GROUP (UK), 6 SEPTEMBER 2003

DEFEND THE OUTLAW!

Immigration controls should be abolished. People should not be deemed 'illegal' because they have fallen foul of an increasingly brutal and repressive system of controls. Why is immigration law different from all other law? Under all other laws it is the *act* that is illegal, but under immigration law it is the *person* who is illegal. Those subject to immigration control are dehumanized, are reduced to non-persons, are nobodies. They are the modern outlaw. Like their medieval counterpart they exist outside of the law and outside of the law's protection. Opposition to immigration controls requires defending all immigration outlaws.

BEWARE THE FASCIST! UNDERSTAND THE ENEMY!

Immigration controls are not fascism. Detention centres are not extermination camps. However, immigration laws are different from other laws in one other significant way. They are the result, at least in part, of organized fascist activity. This country's first controls were contained in the 1905 Aliens Act and were directed at Jewish refugees fleeing anti-semitism in Eastern Europe and Russia. A major, perhaps *the* major, reason for the implementation of this legislation was the agitation of the British Brothers League. This was a proto-fascist organization which was formed in 1901 specifically around the demand for controls, which organized major demonstrations in London's East End and which can legitimately be viewed as the main force behind the legislation. The first controls directed against black people – the 1962 Commonwealth Immigrants Act – quickly followed events in Notting Hill and Nottingham in 1958. These were the so-called 'race riots' – so-called to give a spurious impression of both spontaneity and non-political street fighting. The reality was that these physical and political attacks on black people were engineered by explicitly fascist organizations such as Oswald Mosley's Union Movement and Colin Jordan's White Defence League. And these organizations had a specific demand – immigration controls. Fascist front organizations such as the British Immigration Control Association subsequently continued the agitation until legislation was enacted.

Oswald Mosley himself was quoted in the left-wing *Reynolds News* (5/11/61) as claiming the Bill leading to the 1962 Act was the 'first success' for fascist activity in this country.

Immigration laws are inherently racist, since their purpose is to exclude outsiders. And they feed and legitimize racism. Far from being a natural feature of the political landscape, they are a relatively recent and disastrous distortion of it, explicable only by racism. This, together with the fascist origins of such laws, renders problematic the notion of 'reform', as opposed to abolition, of immigration controls.

IMMIGRATION CONTROLS ARE MORE THAN THEY SEEM

Immigration controls deny people's right to freedom of movement and the right to decide for themselves where they wish to live and to work. They also deny people access to rights such as the right to work and the right to social and legal protections enjoyed by some of the current inhabitants of the place to which they migrate. In the process they cause intolerable suffering to many people. The sole purpose of this suffering is to deter others who might come to this country to claim asylum, to work or to join family here. People are thus punished not for anything they have themselves done, but for what others might do in the future.

Controls are not simply about exclusion and deportation. They are a total system. A system of extremes of pain and misery. They are international in the sense that virtually all countries, particularly all industrial countries, use controls. They are also international in the way the old British Empire was international. British Embassies, British High Commissions, British Consulates encircle the globe denying visas or entry clearance to the unchosen. A vast edifice of repression is built to prevent the movement of people. Those who attempt to flee wars and repression, or to improve their situation through migration, are forced to resort to buying false papers from agents or, worse, to travel clandestinely, again usually with the help of often unscrupulous agents. In the process many of them suffer great hardship, and thousands die. The answer is not to abolish agents, unscrupulous or otherwise. It is to abolish the controls on which the agents, the pain and the misery breed.

Controls are also internal to the modern state and in particular to the modern British state. They require the expansion of repressive and violent activities such as surveillance, security, prisons and policing, changes which threaten to permeate society as a whole. The deaths of Joy Gardner and others at the hands of immigration officers are a portent for the future.

Immigration officers have become part of what Karl Marx's colleague Friedrich Engels described as 'the armed bodies of men' who constitute the state. Under immigration laws around 2000 immigrants and asylum-seekers who have not been charged with any crime, including children, babies and pregnant women, are locked up without trial, without time limit, and with minimal access to bail. Asylum-seekers who are not detained are no longer allowed to work. Since 1996 employers have become an extension of the immigration service, responsible for the immigration status of their workers and liable to criminal sanction for employing undocumented workers. Over the last two decades entitlement to most welfare state benefits and provision has to some extent or another become linked to immigration status. Those without the required status go without. They are excluded from virtually all non-contributory benefits, child benefit, social housing and homelessness accommodation, in-patient hospital treatment, significant areas of community care legislation relating to the destitute, the sick, the elderly and the otherwise vulnerable, protection under child care legislation, state education provision in prisons and detention centres and in the proposed new accommodation centres. So much for the idea that those coming from overseas obtain priority treatment! Instead since 1999 asylum-seekers from overseas have been deliberately transformed into an under-class subject to a regime that is the direct copy of the nineteenth century poor law. Like the poor law there is maintenance below subsistence level (70 per cent of income support). Like the poor law there is forced dispersal into accommodation over which those dispersed have no choice. Under legislation introduced in 2002 many asylum-seekers are no longer to have even this miserable entitlement, neither supported by the state nor allowed to work.

Immigration controls are not only about refugees. This is just the latest government myth. Migrants and immigrants – those coming to work and those wanting to join family here – along with visitors and students are all equally subject to controls along with refugees. Except unlike refugees they are not even entitled to the fake safety net of the poor law. History is important. It is the immigrant communities, especially of the Indian subcontinent and the Caribbean, who from the 1970s launched a direct attack on immigration control by organizing around campaigns against deportations and for family reunion. It is these campaigns which laid the foundations for the present movement in defence of refugees.

CAN THERE BE NON-RACIST OR FAIR CONTROLS?

Immigration controls are racist. The first post-war controls, contained in the 1962 Commonwealth Immigrants Act, were directed at black people. However, all those subject to immigration control are not black. Within the last decade there has emerged or re-emerged a racism against those from Eastern Europe often combined with an anti-Islamic racism which ensures controls are directed against all those from Bosnians to Serbs to the Roma to the nationalities of the new Russian empire. There is nothing new about this. The first immigration controls, contained in the 1905 Aliens Act, were imposed against refugees – Jewish refugees fleeing persecution in Eastern Europe and Tsarist Russia. Controls were again imposed on Jews attempting to escape Nazism. In short, the first half of the twentieth century was about controls against Jews, the second half about controls against black people and the last decade has been about controls against anyone fleeing war, poverty or mayhem or anyone wanting to join family here.

Today there exists, however fragmented, a movement against immigration control – a movement which challenges deportations, which opposes detention centres, which offers solidarity to refugees. The great strength of this movement is that it has united and formed a coalition between liberals and socialists, between reformists who don't challenge controls on principle and socialists who are opposed to all controls – and who argue no-one is illegal. The greatest weakness of this movement is that on the level of ideas liberalism dominates. Many of those critical of controls believe that such controls can somehow be sanitized, be rendered fair, be made non-racist. Even socialists are sometimes reluctant to raise the demand for the abolition of all immigration controls or to take this demand to its logical conclusions, in case this alienates potential allies against the abuses that follow from them. The result is that the argument against controls is simply not presented. Many people, perhaps most fair-minded people, if they are presented with the case, do agree that in principle immigration controls are wrong, but many also believe that to argue for their abolition is unrealistic.

But ideas matter and so too does the struggle for ideas. Wrong ideas can at best lead to confusion and dead-ends and at worst collusion with the present system. It is our position – a position which denies anyone is illegal, a position that is for a world without borders – that immigration restrictions can never be rendered fair or non-racist. This is for the following reasons. First, controls are inherently racist in that they are based on the crudest of all nationalisms – namely the assertion that the British have a franchise on Britain. Second, they are only explicable by racism. Their imposition is a result of and is a victory for racist, proto-fascist and actual fascist organizations. It is impossible to see how legislation brought into being by such means, legislation accompanied by the most vile racist imagery and assumptions, can ever be reconfigured and rendered 'fair'. Third, the demand for 'fair' controls simply ignores the link between immigration controls and welfare entitlements. This link is itself intrinsically unfair – and racist. Finally, controls can never be 'fair' to those who remain subject to them.

The demand for no controls – based on the assertion that no one is illegal – is frequently derided as utopian and is compared adversely to the 'realism' of arguing for fair controls. However this stands political reality on its head. The struggle against the totality of controls is certainly uphill – it may well require a revolution. However the achievement of fair immigration restrictions – that is, the transformation of immigration controls into their opposite – would require a miracle.

MORE PROBLEMS WITH ARGUMENTS FOR REFORMS

The proclamation, our proclamation, that *No One Is Illegal* means what it says – it does not mean some people are not illegal or only some people are legal. The demand for no controls means no collusion with either the arguments for controls or with controls themselves. However, controls have become so politically legitimized over the relatively short period of their existence that it has become all too easy to accept their existence whilst simultaneously opposing them. Here are some examples of what we are arguing against – deliberately difficult and we hope provocative examples:

First, we are absolutely and unconditionally in favour of campaigns against deportation. However, we are critical of the emphasis given to so-called 'compassionate' grounds – in particular the recurring themes of sickness, age, vulnerability of children, violence towards women and destruction of family relationships. Of course we accept that these issues have to be presented, and presented forcibly, to the Home Office in private as part of any legal argument. The present balance of power – with the Home Office having most of the power – requires this presentation. However this does not require campaigns against deportation to construct themselves politically and publicly around such compassionate grounds. What this does is make a distinction between the 'worthy' and the 'unworthy' – between those with compassionate grounds and those without. It legitimizes the racist-inspired obligation that people feel to justify their presence here. In doing this it transforms what is normally undesirable – for instance ill health – into something highly desirable in order to try to remain here. Under the guise of gaining support on humanitarian grounds it actually dehumanizes individuals, and denies them their dignity, by reducing them to the sum total of their disabilities and vulnerabilities. It creates a competition between those subject to immigration controls as to who has the more 'compassionate' grounds. Ultimately it makes it virtually impossible for young, fit, childless, single people without an asylum claim to fight to stay. This is why we support the slogan 'Solidarity not Pity'. We support unconditionally the right of all people to stay here if they wish to, and irrespective of their personal circumstances.

Second, we are absolutely in favour of exposing the lies and hypocrisies of those advocating immigration controls – such as the lie that people coming here are a 'burden' on welfare or are 'flooding' the country. It is important to reject the notion that if immigration controls were abolished this country would be invaded by the populations of entire continents; the reality is that the vast majority of people prefer to stay where they are if this is at all possible. However we are opposed to building a case against immigration controls on the grounds that immigration is in the economic self-interest of the current inhabitants of this country, both because such an argument is wrong in principle and because the situation can change. For example although it was true until recently that more people left this country than came here, this is no longer the case. And while migrants, immigrants and refugees are currently net contributors to the welfare system, supposing it could be shown that new arrivals are somehow accessing a 'disproportionate' percentage of welfare, would that mean we now have to support controls? Statistics are useful to refute distortions and lies, but cannot be the bedrock of our opposition to controls. Statistics can be a hostage to political fortune. Principles cannot. This is why we support the principle of *No One Is Illegal*.

Third, we recognize the many contributions made to British society by migrants, immigrants and refugees stretching back centuries. Britain has been constructed out of waves of migration – the very idea of there being an 'indigenous' population is both politically racist and historically nonsensical. However, we are opposed to all arguments that seek to justify the presence of anyone on the grounds of the economic or cultural or any other contributions they may make. It is not up to the British state to decide where people should or should not live, or anyone else but migrants and refugees themselves. We support the unfettered right of entry of the feckless, the unemployable and the uncultured. We assert *No One Is Illegal*.

GAINS FOR SOME MEAN EXCLUSION OF OTHERS. NO 'EQUAL-OPPORTUNITIES' IMMIGRATION CONTROLS!

An obvious, if often overlooked, feature of immigration control and the struggle against it, is that defining who may be excluded from it by necessity entails defining who is included in it. *No One Is Illegal* means that reform of immigration control, in whatever way such reform is presented, is at best problematic, at worst unacceptable because it would leave some people subject to control. It would still leave immigration outlaws. The degree to which any demand falling short of total abolition of controls is acceptable can only be measured by the degree in which it takes up the fight for all outlaws. All specific demands against controls need to be put in the context of and worked out through a position of opposition to all controls. Again we present some deliberately controversial examples:

First, we are critical of the demand for a government 'amnesty' against immigration outlaws. The level of our criticism will depend on the level at which the amnesty is pitched. Who is to be included in this demand? More important, who is to be excluded? What gives anyone opposed to controls the right to define who is to be excluded? *No One Is Illegal* means what it says – anyone in the entire world who wishes to come or remain should have the right to do so. On a pragmatic basis amnesties have to be criticized as they will be used by the Home Office to entrap those not included in the amnesty. This is precisely what happened when in 1974 a Labour government declared a tightly defined amnesty – deporting many of those who applied under the mistaken belief they fell within the definition.

Second we are critical of demands which, however well meant, leave even more vulnerable and exposed to immigration controls those not contained within the demand. An example is the demand that women coming here for marriage who are subsequently subject to domestic violence should not be subject to the requirement that they remain living with their partner for twelve months in order to acquire full immigration status. After years of campaigning this demand has now been met in part. As such it is clearly a tremendous gain for those women who otherwise would have the impossible choice of remaining in a violent relationship or being deported. However, where does this leave all those women not subject to violence who wish for whatever reason to leave the relationship? For them not being battered by their partner has now become a positive disadvantage for immigration purposes. This is yet another example of how something morally outrageous – abuse of women – has become something highly desirable in immigration law. It is simply not a tenable position to argue. The only tenable position is to fight for the right of all, men or women, to remain irrespective of their personal situation.

Third, immigration controls are not just racist. In their nationalism they encompass virtually all reactionary ideology. So unsurprisingly they are homophobic. Until recently there has been no provision for a gay partner to come or remain. However, we are critical of the campaign for 'equality' with heterosexual relationships for gay relationships within immigration control. There cannot be equal-opportunities immigration controls – unless one is in favour of the equality of the damned. For the last forty years immigration control has systematically attacked, undermined and wrecked tens of thousands of mainly black extended families from the Indian subcontinent, the Caribbean and Africa. Demanding equality with heterosexual couples simply ignores the inherent racism of controls and therefore the relationship between racism, sexism and homophobia. An additional problem is that the demand for the rights of gay couples elevates romance into a political goal – what about the single gay person, the celibate, the lonely, those of no sexual orientation or the promiscuous of any sexual orientation? Including gay couples within immigration law and its spurious 'rights' means that all these other people are by definition excluded. Their status as outlaws is intensified. The way forward is to fight for the rights of all gay women and men along with everyone else to be able to come and remain irrespective of personal circumstances or relationships. The only equal-opportunities immigration controls are no immigration controls.

Fourth, demanding to be 'included' within controls – in the sense of demanding specific provision for gay couples – seems itself quite strange in that everyone else is fighting to be excluded from the tentacles of controls. However, this contradiction only exists because, given the existence of controls, then absolutely everyone is already 'included' in them to a greater or a lesser extent – in that everyone remains liable to investigation as to whether or not they are subject to them. In this sense women experiencing domestic violence still very much remain subject to controls – as they are obliged to undergo the humiliation of reliving the violence by having to prove its existence. The only political answer to these issues is to fight for no controls.

Fifth, each piece of immigration legislation going back to 1905 (and dramatically intensified in the last decade) can be seen as another brick in the wall – the wall preventing entry of the undesirable, the unchosen. It is therefore not sufficient to demand the repeal of the latest piece of legislation, to remove the latest brick – the whole wall has to go. Otherwise all those excluded by previous legislation remain outlaws and, what is worse, forgotten outlaws. Simply demanding the repeal of the most recent, and only the most recent, laws only serves to legitimize those preceding them. An example is the agitation against that part of the Nationality, Immigration and Asylum Act 2002 (the latest legislation) which denies support to asylum-seekers who make 'late' asylum applications – thus rendering these refugees destitute. However, in 1999 there was a campaign against the then latest legislation – the Immigration and Asylum Act. This was the legislation which created the poor law of forced dispersal and below-subsistence support. But now the agitation is to include late asylum applicants within the poor law! Again this is not a tenable political position. At the same time there is being forgotten all those undocumented non-asylum-seekers, migrants and immigrants, who have effectively been without any support due to provisions in various pieces of legislation prior to 1999. These statutes were themselves once new, were once campaigned against and are now forgotten – along with those subject to them.

No One Is Illegal means fighting to destroy immigration controls in their entirety and at the same time fighting to break the link between welfare entitlement and immigration status.

SOCIALISM

Many if not all of the arguments used to justify immigration controls are simply ludicrous and are more the result of racist-inspired moral panic than of any connection with reality. Such is the notion that the entire world population would come to this country if there were no controls: even if such an absurd notion were true, it should prompt concern for their reasons for coming rather than fear. Nonetheless these objections to open borders need to be answered and they require a socialist and anti-imperialist analysis. The objections about 'overcrowding' can only be answered by discussing socialist use of resources – use based on needs not profits. The objection, the surreal objection, that migrants, immigrants and refugees obtain luxury housing and endless welfare compared to British workers needs to be answered both by pointing out the truth (namely that just the opposite is the case) but also by a recognition that benefits and welfare are woefully inadequate for everyone – both for the documented and the undocumented – and that both have a shared interest in fighting for better welfare. The objection that those fleeing the devastation of the Third World have no right to come here can be met by pointing out the imperial responsibility for this devastation, both in the past and currently. As the Asian Youth Movement used to say: 'We are here because you were there.' The objection that a state has the right to control its own borders can only ultimately be answered by questioning the nature of the nation state and borders. We agree and sing along with John Lennon – 'Imagine There's No Countries'.

THE WAY FORWARD - BREAK THE LINKS, PULL THE PLUG!

- To build the widest possible alliance in all struggles against immigration controls amongst those of differing political views. But to do this without collusion with controls and without compromising with the principle of no controls. To do this on the basis of challenging and winning over those involved to a position of opposition to all controls. *No One Is Illegal – no exceptions, no concessions, no conciliation.*

- To raise the demand for no immigration controls within all actions and campaigns in support of migrants and refugees. A no-controls position should not be a necessary precondition of support for any particular campaign, but we should argue constantly within all campaigns for such a position. We should argue for campaign slogans to reflect a position of opposition to controls, not *refugees are our friends* or *refugees are welcome here* but slogans which recognize that we are in favour of freedom for all as a right, not a charity: *No One Is Illegal – Free movement…no immigration controls.*

- To support and build every single campaign against deportation. To do this on the basis of solidarity not compassion. *No One Is Illegal – No need for justification of presence!*

- To support and build every campaign against detention/removal centres, since these are one of the clearest and most outrageously brutal and unjust consequences of immigration controls. No refugees or migrants should be detained simply because they want to be in this country. All detention/removal centres, and also all accommodation, induction and any other repressive 'centres' designed to enforce the unenforceable, should be closed. *No One Is Illegal – No detentions!*

- To fight against all forms of collusion with immigration control and with the Home Office. In particular this means local authorities and voluntary sector organizations refusing to implement the new poor law. Local authorities should refuse to act as sub-contracted agents providing accommodation (often otherwise unlettable) for the forced dispersal scheme. Voluntary sector agencies should likewise refuse Home Office monies to enforce the poor law either through the provision of accommodation or advice. *No One Is Illegal – Break the links between welfare entitlement and immigration status!*

- For workers within the welfare system to refuse to comply with the denial of benefits or provisions based on immigration status. Most workers within the welfare state, at either local or national level, entered their jobs in the belief they would be providing some form of socially useful service. Instead they now find they are denying services and have become part of the apparatus of immigration control. *No One Is Illegal – No compliance, be in and against the state!*

- Of course non-compliance by individual workers would leave them absolutely vulnerable to victimization and dismissal. Non-compliance requires major trade union support. It is manifestly important to try to win trade unions to a position of no immigration controls. To do this it is equally important to form rank and file groupings within unions of welfare workers who are being obliged to enforce internal immigration controls. *No One Is Illegal – Workers' control not immigration controls!*

- For a massive trade union campaign of recruitment of undocumented workers – of immigration outlaws. Such a recruitment campaign would help break the division between the documented and the undocumented. It would enable a campaign to develop against sweated labour and for the protection of migrant rights – rights to a fair wage, right to proper work conditions and, most of all, the right to work itself – as now it is unlawful to work without the correct immigration documentation. It would also provide another base for the undocumented to resist deportation and to fight for the regularization of their status. *No One Is Illegal – Everyone has the right to work, the right to be in a union, and the right to have proper working conditions!*

WE ARE NOT ALONE!

No One Is Illegal is a phrase first used by Elie Weisel, a Jewish survivor from Nazi Germany, a refugee and a Nobel prize winner. He was speaking in 1985 in Tucson, Arizona, at a national sanctuary conference in the USA in defence of the rights of refugees to live in the USA. The sanctuary movement undertaken by religious communities in the USA (and to a far lesser extent in the UK) in support of those threatened by immigration controls is one of many pieces of resistance to controls. Over the last few years *No One Is Illegal* groups have been formed throughout Europe and North America – for instance in Germany (*Kein Mensch Ist Illegal*), Spain (*Ninguna Persona Es Ilegal*), Sweden (*Ingen Manniska Ar Illegal*), Poland (*Zaden Czlowiek Nie Jest Nielegalny*) and Holland (*Geen Mens Is Illegaal*). In August 1999 anarchists organized a demonstration in Lvov, Poland, against the deportation of Ukranian workers under the banner of *No One Is Illegal*. In France the *sans-papiers* campaign under the slogan *personne n'est illégalle*. There have been *No One Is Illegal/No Border* camps at the joint borders of Germany, Czech Republic and Poland, and *No Border* camps at Frankfurt, southern Spain and Salzburg. In June 2002 there was a demonstration against war, globalization and in defence of refugees under the same slogan in Ottawa, Canada. In England, groups are emerging calling themselves *No Borders*. The demand for no controls, rather than being seen as extreme, operates as a rallying call to the undocumented and their supporters. Our aim in producing this, our initial manifesto, is to encourage the formation of *No One Is Illegal/No Border* groups throughout this country – groups specifically and unreservedly committed to the destruction of all immigration controls.

Steve Cohen (Manchester)
Harriet Grimsditch (Bolton)
Teresa Hayter (Oxford)
Bob Hughes (Bristol)
Dave Landau (London)

CONTACTING US

Please contact us if you wish to add your or your organisation's name as a supporter of this manifesto, or if you would like a speaker at one of your meetings. If you would like to help us financially in the production of campaign material, please make cheques out, in sterling, to 'The No One Is Illegal Group'. Our postal address is: No One Is Illegal, Bolton Socialist Club, 16 Wood Street, Bolton BL1 1DY. Email: info@noii.org.uk. Website: www.noii.org.uk.

NOTES

NOTES - PREFACE

1. Nacera Kellou from the Action Committee for Non-Status Algerians, quoted in Michelle Lowry and Peter Nyers (2003) 'Roundtable Report, No One Is Illegal: The Fight for Refugee and Migrant Rights in Canada,' *Refuge: Canada's Periodical on Refugees 21*, 3, May.
2. See House of Lords parliamentary debate of 4 March 2004; and House of Lords judgment in A (FC) and others (FC) (Appellants) *v.* Secretary of State for the Home Department (Respondent) – for example paragraph 37 of the judgment.
3. Amrit Wilson and Sushma Lal (1985) *But My Cows Aren't Going to England*, South Manchester Law Centre, p.6.
4. *Where Do You Keep Your String Beds?* is the title of a 1974 Runnymede Trust pamphlet by Mohammed Akram and Sarah Leigh on entry clearance from Pakistan.

CHAPTER 1

1. *Voices From Detention* (2002), Barbed Wire Britain, p.9. www.barbedwirebritain.org.uk
2. George Orwell: *Nineteen Eighty-Four*, Penguin Books, 1990 edition, p.39. All future references from *Nineteen Eighty-Four* are from this edition and are indicated thus: 'Orwell: p.-' .
3. Orwell: p.37.
4. Ibid.: p.223.
5. Cm 6472.
6. Orwell: p.56.
7. Ibid.: p.122.
8. Ibid.: p.216–217.
9. *The Times*, 17 November 1961.
10. For the history of Labour's support for immigration controls, see Steve Cohen (1987) *It's the Same Old Story*, Manchester City Council, p.31.
11. Orwell: p.38.
12. Ibid.: p.225.
13. Likewise, the Labour Party always confusingly identified nationalization of resources (such as steel) and welfare (such as health) with socialism – the word 'nationalization' being itself somewhat strange when used by those supposedly opposed to nationalism. The real issue here for socialists is the distinction between workers' control and state control.
14. Paul Foot (1965) *Immigration and Race in British Politics*, Penguin, p.191. Foot also says that the *Tribune* journal took a similar position.
15. See Steve Cohen (2003) '*Never Mind the Racism Feel the Quality*', in *No One Is Illegal*, Trentham Books.
16. *Morning Star*, 12 February 2005.
17. Orwell: p.316.
18. Ibid.: p.79.
19. Ibid.: p.26
20. IND press release on 31 March 2004 (145/2004) publicising proposed new European Union directives on immigration control.
21. Stanley Cohen (2002) *Folk Devils and Moral Panics*, 3rd edn., Routledge, p.1.
22. Ibid.: p.xviii.

23.   As pointed out in the preface, in this book the terms *refugee* and *asylum-seeker* are usually used interchangeably, though *refugee* technically denotes a person granted asylum and this will be indicated where appropriate.

24.   Steve Cohen and Nadia Siddiqui (1986) *What Would You Do If Your Fiancée Lived on the Moon?* South Manchester Law Centre.

25.   Amrit Wilson and Sushma Lal, *But My Cows Aren't Going to England,* supra.

26.   Hence the Commonwealth Immigrants Act 1968.

27.   Hence the Commonwealth Immigrants Act 1962.

28.   Louise London (1999) *Whitehall and the Jews, 1933–1948: British Immigration Policy and the Holocaust,* Cambridge University Press.

29.   Steve Cohen (2003) 'Anti-Communism in the Construction of Immigration Controls' in *No One Is Illegal,* Trentham Books.

30.   Bernard Gainer (1972) *The Alien Invasion: Origins of the Aliens Act of 1905,* Heinemann.

31.   p.9.

32.   Orwell: p.189.

33.   Ibid: p.240.

34.   Stanley Cohen (2002) *Folk Devils and Moral Panics,* 3rd edn.., Routledge, p.xviii.

35.   Otis Graham (2004) *Unguarded Gates,* Rowman and Littlefield, pp.4–5.

CHAPTER 2

1.   Zimbabwean refugee, quoted in Andrew Bradstock and Arlington Trotman (2003) *Asylum Voices,* Churches Together in Britain and Ireland, p.6.

2.   See http://news.bbc.co.uk/1/hi/programmes/asylum_day/3055809.stm.

3.   *The Australian,* 14 June 2004.

4.   'Solidarity' (paper on Alliance for Workers Liberty) 3/53, 2004.

5.   T. W. E. Roche (1969) *The Key in the Lock: Immigration Control in England from 1066 to the Present Day,* John Murray, p.4.

6.   Ann Dummett and Andrew Nicol (1990) *Subjects, Citizens, Aliens and Others,* Weidenfeld & Nicolson, p.11.

7.   Peter Fryer (1984) *Staying Power: The History of Black People in Britain,* Pluto Press, p.12.

8.   Dummett and Nicol, supra, pp.40–41.

9.   Ibid., p.43.

10.   Roche, supra, pp.47–55.

11.   Dummett and Nicol, supra, p.84.

12.   Catherine Jones (1977) *Immigration and Social Policy in Britain,* Tavistock, pp.48–49 and 56.

13.   On White, see Bernard Gainer (1972) *The Alien Invasion: Origins of the Aliens Act of 1905,* Heinemann. Also Edward Pearce, 'The Scum of Europe', *History Today,* November 2000. Also G. R. Searle in his introduction to White's *Empire and Efficiency,* 1974, Harvester Press.

14.   Arnold White (1899) *The Modern Jew,* Heinemann, p.15.

15.   *Hansard,* 15 February 1983, col.230.

16.   Ibid., 15 February 1983, col.224.

17.   For more detailed analysis, see Steve Cohen (1988) *A Hard Act To Follow: The Immigration Act 1988,* South Manchester Law Centre, pp.14–19.

18.   See Marek Kohn (1995) *The Race Gallery,* Jonathan Cape. Also Stephen Jay Gould (1996) *The Mismeasure of Man,* Norton and Co.

19.   Arnold White (1901) *Empire and Efficiency,* Heinemann, p.120.

20.   For a comprehensive look at the cases, see M. J. Landa (1911) *The Alien Problem and Its Remedy,* London. Landa was the reporter for the *Jewish Chronicle.*

21.   *Jewish Chronicle,* 9 March 1906, p.11.

22.   Ibid., 14 June 1907, p.22.

23.   Ibid., 9 March 1906, p.11.

24.   Sir Edward Troup (1926) *The Home Office,* 2nd edn., Putnam's Ltd, p.144.

25.   On the relationship between eugenics and immigration controls, see Steve Cohen and Debra Hayes (1998) *They Make You Sick,* Greater Manchester Immigration Aid Unit, pp.3–8. Also Steve Cohen (2001) *Immigration Controls, the Family and the Welfare State,* Jessica Kingsley, p.263 and 316.

Also Steve Cohen (2003) 'The Mighty State of Immigration Controls' in *No One Is Illegal*, Trentham Books.

26. *The Standard*, 1 January 1905.
27. *Hansard*, 2 May 1905.
28. See *They Make You Sick*, supra (note 25).
29. G. Wolsenholme in his book *Immigration, Medical and Social Aspects*, quoted in *They Make You Sick*, supra.
30. *Empire and Efficiency*, supra (note 19), p.83.
31. *Jewish Chronicle*, 11 October 1907.
32. *Hansard*, 16 November 1987.
33. Hyde v. Hyde 1866.
34. *The Modern Jew*, supra (note 14), p.16.
35. Quoted in Steve Cohen (1988) *A Hard Act To Follow*, supra (note 17), p.18.
36. Quoted in *They Make You Sick*, supra (note 25), p.19.
37. Ibid., p.21.
38. *Voices From Detention* (2002) Barbed Wire Britain, p.13.
39. Orwell: p.83.
40. Ibid.
41. *They Make You Sick*, supra, p.19.
42. Harold Pinter (1993) *The Caretaker*, Faber & Faber, p.52.
43. Orwell: p.271.
44. Thomas Szasz (1988) 'The Moral Physician' in *The Theology of Medicine*, Syracuse University Press.
45. Thomas Szasz (1973) *The Manufacture of Madness*, Paladin, Ch.13.
46. R. D. Laing (1967) *The Politics of Experience*, Penguin (1990 edition), p.55.
47. Ibid., Introduction.
48. Ibid., p.49.
49. Orwell: p.272.
50. Ibid., p.44.
51. *Immigration Controls, the Family and the Welfare State*, supra (note 25), p.126.
52. Appeal no. 00TH00945/HX-79282-95.
53. *Immigration Controls, The Family and the Welfare State*, supra (note 25), p107.
54. Orwell: p.68.
55. See Steve Cohen (1982) *From Ill Treatment to No Treatment*, South Manchester Law Centre, ch.6.
56. Orwell: p.37.
57. Ex parte Zamir (1980) A.C. 930.
58. Ex parte Mughal. Widgery LCJ in the Divisional Court [1973] 1 WLR 1133. The detainee appealed to the CA, which dismissed the appeal, but on other grounds – [1974] QB 313.
59. See, for instance, *Voices From Detention* (2002), Barbed Wire Britain. Also Andrew Bradstock and Arlington Trotman (2003) *Asylum Voices*, Churches Together in Britain and Ireland.
60. Orwell: p.220.
61. Ibid.: p.204.
62. Ibid.: p.29.
63. Ibid.: p.10.
64. See World Socialist website, 25 July 2003: www.wsws.org/articles/2003/jul2003/ital-j25.shtml
65. *Daily Star*, 6 December 2002.
66. Paul Simon, 'Call Me Al', from the album *Graceland*.
67. Quoted in *Socialist Worker*, 8 July 2000.
68. Orwell: p.15.
69. Ibid.: p.193.
70. *Jewish Chronicle*, 30 May 1919, with reference to the Alien Restriction (Amendment) Act 1919.
71. Aliens Order 1920.
72. T. Aleinikoff and D. Martin (1995) *Immigration Process and Policy*, West Publishing Co., p.617; quoted in Steve Cohen (1992) *Imagine There's No Countries*, Greater Manchester Immigration Aid Unit, p.35.

73.   *Sunday Express,* 25 January 2004.
74.   *The Guardian,* 23 May 2002.
75.   Liz Fekete (2003) *Canary Island Tragedy,* Institute of Race Relations.
76.   Orwell: p.296.
77.   Ibid.: p.254.
78.   Amrit Wilson and Sushma Lal (1986) *But My Cows Aren't Going to England,* South Manchester Law Centre, p.14.
79.   Ibid., p.56.
80.   *Immigration controls, the Family and the Welfare State,* supra (note 25), p.141.
81.   Immigration and Asylum Act 1999.
82.   BBC news, 5 August 2003.
83.   NCADC news service, 28 November 2003
84.   *Dover Express* 1 October 1998, quoted in Vaughan Robinson *et al.* (2003) *Spreading the Burden?,* Policy Press, p.16.
85.   *East London Observer,* 18 January 1902, reporting Henry Norman MP.
86.   Robinson, supra (note 84), p.21.
87.   *Daily Telegraph,* 17 August 1998, quoted in Robinson, supra, p 17.
88.   Ibid.
89.   Robinson, supra (note 84), p.170.

CHAPTER 3

1.   Frank Mossfield, *Hansard,* House of Representatives (Australia), 26 June 2003.
2.   Orwell: p.54.
3.   Ibid.: p.55.
4.   Ibid.: p.48.
5.   *The Sun,* 16 May 2002; 29 July 2002; 16 January 2004, respectively.
6.   *The Scotsman,* 13 November 2003.
7.   *Washington Times,* 11 May 2002.
8.   Orwell: p.21.
9.   *Hansard,* 17 December 2003, col.1592.
10.   Orwell: p.314.
11.   Ibid.: e.g. p.290.
12.   These tracks were withdrawn (censored) on the DVD version.
13.   Orwell: p.65.
14.   Home Office, 11 November 2003.
15.   Orwell: p.21.
16.   Ibid.: p.319.
17.   Ibid.: p.139.
18.   W. H. Wilkins (1892) *The Alien Invasion,* London.
19.   D. Thomas (2003) *An Underworld At War,* John Murray.
20.   Steve Cohen and Debra Hayes (1998) *Immigration Controls: They Make You Sick,* Greater Manchester Immigration Aid Unit, p.39.
21.   *The Times,* 3 September 1958.
22.   Ibid., 27 August 1958.
23.   *The Guardian,* 3 September 1958.
24.   Ibid., 21 September 1979.
25.   *Hansard,* Standing Committee on the 1981 British Nationality Act, 19 March 1981.
26.   *The Guardian,* 1 February 1978.
27.   Compulsory HIV testing for asylum-seekers was rejected by the All-Party Parliamentary Group on AIDS in its July 2003 report *Migration and HIV: Improving Lives in Britain (an inquiry into the impact of the UK nationality and immigration system on people living with HIV),* p.76.
28.   Joshua Trachtenberg (1995) *The Devil and the Jews,* Jewish Publication Society, pp.102–106.
29.   Ibid., p.106.
30.   Ibid., p.102.
31.   BBC news, 28 August 2003.

32. *Ananova*, 17 August 2003.
33. *Daily Telegraph*, 16 January 2004.
34. Ibid., 25 October 2003.
35. *The Sun*, 18 February 2002.
36. BBC news, 18 July 2003.
37. Ibid.
38. World de Deutsche Welle, 2 December 2003 '*Euro-Med talks focus on immigration and economic ties*'.
39. Helen O'Nions (1999) 'Bonafide or Bogus? Roma Asylum seekers from the Czech Republic', *Web Journal of Current Legal Issues*, p.1.
40. *The Observer*, 11 October 2004. See also Humfrey Malins MP, *Hansard*, 17 December 2003, col. 1604.
41. Orwell: p.313.
42. Ibid.
43. Taken from the *Sylhet Tax Pattern*, produced in 1976 by the British High Commission in Dhaka, Bangladesh, to 'prove' that Bangladeshi men in the UK were committing tax fraud by claiming allowances for non-existent children and then years later attempting to bring these or other 'bogus' children to the UK as dependants. See also Ranjit Sondhi (1997) *Divided Families: British Immigration Control in the Indian Subcontinent*, Runnymede Trust, pp.53–55.
44. *Daily Telegraph*, 18 February 2002.
45. Paragraphs 4.5.14, 4.5.15 and 4.3.2.
46. *Genetic Privacy: The National Interest*, on Australian Radio National, 1 June 2003.
47. *The Sun*, 29 November 2003.
48. *Straits Times*, Singapore, 4 March 2004.
49. BBC: *EU Business*, 18 February 2004. Benefit entitlements were subsequently limited (such as by redefining the habitual residence test).
50. *Guardian Online*, 10 June 2002.
51. Section 54 of the Nationality, Immigration and Asylum Act 2002.
52. *Daily Mirror*, 25 February 2004 (article by Sue Carroll).
53. *The Independent*, 30 December 2003.
54. See www.britainonline.org.pk/highcomm/downloads/15oct.pdf, 15 October 2003.
55. Orwell: p.55.
56. Ibid.: p.60.
57. Parekh (1994) in Sarah Spencer (ed.) *Strangers and Citizens*, IPPR and Rivers Oram Press, p.91.
58. Orwell: p.214.
59. Ibid.: p.77.
60. *Hansard*, 24 May 1976.
61. See House of Lords judgment in A (FC) and others (FC) (Appellants) *v.* Secretary of State for the Home Department (Respondent).
62. Cm 5387.
63. Orwell: p.123.
64. Jack London (1990) *The Iron Heel*, Journeyman Press, p.155.
65. Damien Schaible (2004) 'Life in Russia's Closed City', *New York University Law Review 76*. Also see the Moscow No One Is Illegal group website at www.nelegal.net/.
66. *The Observer*, 11 July 2004.
67. See http://democracysmells.tripod.com/Newspeak.html
68. *Hansard*, 17 December 2003, col. 1592.
69. See the website for the Noborder Network and its anti-IOM campaign, at www.noborder.org. See also the (undated) pamphlet *Stop IOM* produced by AntirassismusBuro Bremen. (www.antirassismus-buero.de; email iom-watch@web.de).
70. See www.iomlondon.org/
71. Home Office, *The Voluntary Assisted Returns Programme: An Evaluation* (Findings 175) 2002.

CHAPTER 4

1. Quoted in Hanneh Arendt (1964) *Eichmann in Jerusalem*, Penguin, p.48.
2. BBC press release of 15 January 2002 advertising the movie *Conspiracy* based on the Wannsee Conference.

3. T. W. E. Roche (1969) *The Key in the Lock*, John Murray, p.127.
4. *The Guardian*, 13 January 2004.
5. Orwell: p.319.
6. Ibid.: pp.6 and 225.
7. Ibid.: p.79.
8. Ibid.: p.24.
9. Ibid.: p.245.
10. Ibid.
11. Ibid.: p.69.
12. *The Independent*, 15 October 1986.
13. HC. 654-1 and HC. 654-11.
14. Appendix 44.
15. Press release of the Institute of Race Relations, 26 July 2004.
16. Orwell: p.175.
17. Quoted in David Roskies (1999) *The Jewish Search for a Usable Past*, Indiana University Press, p.18.
18. Metropolitan Books, New York, 2002.
19. Orwell: p.6.
20. Ibid.: p.7.
21. 8 May 2003.
22. George Orwell (1946) 'Politics and the English Language' in *Inside the Whale and Other Essays*, Penguin (1967), p153.
23. Paragraph 281 of minutes of evidence.
24. Ibid.
25. Appendix 25.
26. Paragraph 301 of minutes of evidence.
27. Paragraph 175 of minutes of evidence.
28. Paragraph 305 of minutes of evidence.
29. Paragraph 309 of minutes of evidence.
30. Paragraph 280 of minutes of evidence.
31. Paragraph 256 of minutes of evidence.
32. Paragraph 358 of minutes of evidence.
33. Arendt, supra (note 1), p.48.
34. Orwell: p.321.
35. Arendt, supra, p.114.
36. Letter of 4 March 2004, circulated in the March 2004 Immigration Legal Practitioners Association (ILPA) mailing.
37. Orwell: p.315 – any word – this again applied in principle to every word in the language – could be negatived by adding the affix *un-*, or could be strengthened by the affix *plus-* or for greater emphasis, *doubleplus.*

CHAPTER 5

1. A. Bradstock and Arlington Trotman (eds) (2003) *Asylum Voices*, Churches Together In Britain and Ireland, p.33.
2. *The Guardian*, 8 July 2004.
3. For example, *Permanent Revolution and Results and Prospects*: www.marxists.org/archive/trotsky/works/1931-tpv/rppr.htm.
4. Trotsky (1933) *The Soviet Economy in Danger*, Pioneer Publishers. Also see Trotsky's *Trotskyism and the PSOP* – 'Revolutionary ardour in the struggle for socialism is inseparable from intellectual ardour in the struggle for truth.'
5. Orwell: p.223.
6. Ibid.: p.322.
7. Ibid.: p.6.
8. Ibid.: p.26.
9. George Orwell (1946) 'The Prevention of Literature', in *Shooting an Elephant and other Essays* (1950), Secker and Warburg, p.126.

10. At the time of writing even the Home Office has now been forced to drop this doublethink and postpone Iraqi removals (*The Observer*, 18 April 2004).

11. Home Office press release, 16 June 2003 (ref. 160/2003).

12. Pasadena Star-News, 6 April 2004.

13. Orwell: p.37.

14. The words of a refugee hunger striker, quoted in *Race and Class 39*, 2 (1992).

15. Quoted in Marta Hinestroza (2003) *Listen To The Refugee's Story*, Illisu Dam Campaign Refugees Project/The Corner House/Peace in Kurdistan.

16. *The Independent*, 16 April 2004.

17. 'I Feel Like I'm Fixing To Die Rag' by Country Joe and the Fish.

18. Orwell: p.79.

19. Quoted in *Levine, the Life of a Revolutionary*, by R.Levine-Meyer (Eugen Levine's widow).

20. Steve Cohen (2001) *Immigration Controls, the Family and the Welfare State*, Jessica Kingsley Publishers, p.86.

21. Ibid., p.40.

22. Sushma Lal and Amrit Wilson (1986) *But My Cows Aren't Going to England*, South Manchester Law Centre, p.21.

23. For more on these Newspeak constructions, see *Nineteen Eighty-Four*, p.315.

24. Mengele was the notorious doctor who conducted genetic 'experiments' on twins in Auschwitz concentration camp.

25. 'The Great DNA Swindle', in Steve Cohen (1991) *A World Without Borders*, Greater Manchester Immigration Aid Unit.

26. Information from leaflet of October 2003 from Black Women's Rape Action Project.

27. Lal and Wilson, supra (note 22), p55.

28. Franz Kafka (1999, first published 1925) *The Trial*, Vintage. All future references are to this 1999 edition.

29. Ibid., p.7.

30. Ibid., p.9.

31. Ibid., p.34.

32. Ibid., p.54.

33. In particular see Christina Pougourides (1995) *A Second Exile*, North Birmingham Mental Health NHS Trust.

34. Steve Cohen and Debra Hayes (1998) *They Make You Sick: Immigration Controls and Health*, Greater Manchester Immigration Aid Unit/Manchester Metropolitan University (quoting from Pougourides), p.21.

35. Orwell: p.220.

CHAPTER 6

1. Paragraphs 1.14, 2.2 and 5.4.

2. Executive Summary, paragraph 13, and Executive Summary paragraph 3, paragraphs 1.1, 1.2.

3. On Marx, Malthus and Ireland, see e.g. John Bellamy Foster, *Malthus's Essay on Population at Age 200, A Marxian View, Monthly Review 50*, 7, December 1998.

4. Quoted at p.13 in *Workers Control Not Immigration Controls*, Steve Cohen, Greater Manchester Immigration Aid Unit (undated).

5. Quoted in Suzanne Rickard (1998) *Malthus and His Legacy: 200 Years of the Population Debate*, National Library of Australia, Canberra (www.naf.org.au/rickard.rtf).

6. *Manchester City News*, 12 May 1988 (editorial headed 'Invasion of England by foreign paupers').

7. Section 26.

8. Section 2.

9. Article 31 of Convention.

10. Section 14.

11. Section 15.

12. Section 36.

13. Section 33 and Schedule 3.

14.   Thanks in formulating this point are due to Peter Nyers, 'Abject Cosmopolitanism: the Politics of Protection in the Anti-deportation Movement', *Third World Quarters 24*, 6, pp.1069–1093, 20-03.

15.   Section 35.

16.   *Hansard*, 1 December 2003, col. 1674.

17.   Ref. 326/2003.

18.   Orwell: p.37.

19.   Ibid.: p.280.

20.   David Blunkett MP, *Hansard*, 17 December 2003, col. 1603.

21.   *Hansard*, 16 November 1987. For similar quotes see Steve Cohen (undated) *A Hard Act to Follow*, South Manchester Law Centre, pp.29–30.

22.   See www.labour.org.uk/ac2003qandaarchive/?chatid=46

23.   Orwell: p.42.

24.   Ibid.: p.40.

25.   Ibid.

26.   Paragraph 5.15.

27.   Paragraph 1.3.

28.   *The Guardian*, 1 November 2003.

29.   *Hansard*, 17 November 2003, col. 1670.

30.   For more on the contradictions between economic racism and social racism, see Steve Cohen (2003) 'Never Mind The Racism' in *No One Is Illegal*, Trentham Books.

31.   *The Times*, 1 November 1961.

32.   This information is taken from a leaflet produced by Barbed Wire Britain and the Network to End Migrant and Refugee Detention.

33.   Paragraph 2 of the 1994 Immigration Rules.

34.   Sarah Spencer (ed.) (1994) *Strangers and Citizens: A Positive Approach to Migrants and Refugees*, IPPR and Rivers Oram Press. For an extended and critical book review, see Steve Cohen, *Immigration and Nationality Law and Practice 8*, 4, 1994.

35.   Ibid., p.333.

36.   Ibid., p.346.

37.   Ibid., p.345.

38.   Ibid., p.342.

39.   Ibid., p.12.

40.   Ibid., p.315.

41.   Amanda Sebestyen, February 2004 letter in *Red Pepper*.

42.   Orwell: p.214.

43.   Ibid.: pp.13–14.

44.   Ibid.: p.156.

45.   Ibid.: p.156.

46.   Quoted by Anne Karpf in 'We've Been Here Before', *Guardian Weekend*, 8 June 2002.

47.   *Guardian Online*, 24 January 2003: 'Press whips up asylum hysteria'.

48.   *The Sun*, 4 July 2003.

49.   Ibid., 21 January 2003.

50.   *Daily Express*, 24 March 1938.

51.   *Guardian Online*, 24 January 2003: 'Press whips up asylum hysteria'.

52.   *Guardian Online*, 19 August 2001.

53.   *Guardian Unlimited*, 15 December 2001.

54.   Arthur Miller (1952) *The Crucible*, Penguin edition (2003), p.77 (spoken by Judge Hathorne).

55.   Ibid., p.17 (spoken by Mary Warren).

56.   Lillian Hellman (1976) *Scoundrel Times*, Little, Brown and Co.

57.   M. Dummett (2001) *On Immigration and Refugees*, Routledge, p.72.

58.   V. Robinson, R. Andersson and S. Musterd (2003) *Spreading the 'Burden': A review of Policies to Disperse Asylum Seekers and Refugees*, Policy Press, p.177.

59.   Ibid., p.173.

60.   Nigel Rose (2004) 'Taking the Asylum War to Blunkett', *Red Pepper*, January. See the reply by No One Is Illegal Group in *Red Pepper*, April 2004.

61.   Orwell: p.140.

CHAPTER 7

1. Found written on a leaflet advertising an asylum meeting in Leicester in April 2004.
2. *A Crying Shame: Pregnant Asylum Seekers and their Babies in Detention*, published by the Maternity Alliance, Bail for Immigration Detainees and London Detainee Support Group, September 2002, p.11.
3. Orwell: p.56.
4. Ibid.: p.75.
5. Income support, income-based jobseekers' allowance, housing benefit, Council Tax benefit, a social fund payment, child benefit, working families tax credit, attendance allowance, severe disablement allowance, invalid care allowance, disabled persons' tax credit, disability living allowance.
6. Section 21 of National Assistance Act 1948 (adult residential care), Section 45 of Health Services and Public Health Act 1968 (promotion by local authorities of welfare of old people), and paragraph 2 of schedule 8 of the National Health Services Act 1977 (arrangements by local authorities for the prevention of illness and for care and aftercare). Scottish and North Irish legislation is likewise limited.
7. For full analysis of legislation, see Steve Cohen (2001) *Immigration Controls, the Family and the Welfare State*, Jessica Kingsley Publishers.
8. The benefits are listed in the rules. They are generally the same benefits, access to which is anyhow dependent upon immigration status.
9. The start of the end of the poor law as such (though arguably it just continued under a new name) can perhaps be dated from the Poor Law Act 1930 when Public Assistance started. Only the aged found their way into the workhouses and outdoor relief was restored.
10. For an analysis of the 2002 Act, see Steve Cohen (2003) 'Secure Removal Centres Safe Votes' in *No One Is Illegal*, Trentham Books.
11. For a comprehensive examination of all the relevant legislation where entitlement is linked to immigration status, see Steve Cohen (2001) *Immigration Controls, the Family and the Welfare State*, Jessica Kingsley Publishers.
12. Orwell: p.272.
13. National Health Services (Charges to Overseas Visitors) Regulations 1982. For the history of this, see Steve Cohen (1981) *From Ill Treatment to No Treatment*, South Manchester Law Centre. Also Steve Cohen and Debra Hayes (1998) *Immigration Controls: They Make You Sick*, Greater Manchester Immigration Aid Unit.
14. National Health Service (Charges to Overseas Visitors) (Amendment) Regulations 2004.
15. *Guardian Unlimited*, 15 May 2004. See Department of Health Consultation Paper *Proposals to Exclude Overseas Visitors from Eligibility to Free NHS Primary Medical Services*, May 2004.
16. *Guardian Unlimited*, 22 April 2003.
17. *Times Online*, 10 December 2003.
18. Ibid.
19. *Guardian 2*, November 1981, quoted in *From Ill Treatment to No Treatment*, supra (note 14), p.49.
20. Orwell: p.74.
21. Gareth Stedman Jones (1971) 'Introduction', in *Outcast London*, p.1.
22. Ibid.: p.108.
23. Charles Dickens (first published 1857–8) *Oliver Twist*, Penguin Books (2003), p.15.
24. Ibid.: p.13.
25. Ibid.
26. HC. 654-1 and HC. 654-11.
27. Paragraph 327 of minutes of evidence.
28. Paragraph 335 of minutes of evidence.
29. Paragraph 337 of minutes of evidence.
30. Orwell: pp.41–42.
31. Ibid.: p.62.
32. *Guardian Unlimited*, 21 July 2004.
33. *A Crying Shame*, supra (note 1), p.4.
34. Quoted from Castles and Davidson – *Citizenship and Migration* – (who took the terminology from Mariniello) in 'And Now it has Started to Rain – support and advocacy with adult asylum seekers in the voluntary sector', Peter Fell in *Social Work Immigration and Asylum* (ed. Debra Hayes and Beth Humphries), Routledge, 2004, p.115.

35.   Steve Cohen (1985) 'Antisemitism, Immigration Control and the Welfare State', *Critical Social Policy,* no.13. Reprinted in *Critical Social Policy: A Reader,* Sage Publications (1996), and in Steve Cohen (2003), *No One Is Illegal,* Trentham Books.

36.   Ibid., and Steve Cohen (2001) *Immigration Controls, the Family and the Welfare State,* Jessica Kingsley Publishers.

37.   Surprisingly, Anaura Bevan, the first Minister of Health and architect of the NHS, did not see it in this way. Bevan said in a parliamentary debate of 19/9/1949, 'It amazes me that there is something wrong in treating a foreign if he or she falls ill. The assumption is one of the curses of modern nationalism.' In his autobiography, *In Place of Fear* (1952), he wrote 'One of the consequences of the universality of the British health system is the free treatment of overseas visitors'.

38.   T *v.* Secretary of State for the Home Department (2003 EWCA Civ 1285). See also the judgment of Justice Newman in Zardasht *v.* Secretary of State (2004 EWHC 91 Admin).

39.   Orwell: p.268.

40.   M. O'Brien (2000) 'Class Struggle and the English Poor Laws', in M. Lavalette and G. Mooney (eds.) *Class Struggle and Social Welfare,* Routledge.

41.   Bob Dylan, 'Like A Rolling Stone'.

42.   Janis Joplin, 'Me and Bobby McGee', written by Kris Kristofferson.

43.   Edwin Chadwick, one of the Poor Law Commissioners, quoted in O'Brien, supra, p.27.

44.   Ibid. (Sir George Nicholls was the Commissioner).

45.   As a result of pressure and protest, vouchers were withdrawn in April 2002.

46.   Section 4 of the Immigration and Asylum Act 1999. On hard cases support, see Steve Cohen, *Immigration Controls, the Family and The Welfare State,* supra, p.102.

47.   R *v.* Inhabitants of Eastbourne (1803) 4 East 103, quoted in London Borough of Hammersmith and Fulham Ex Parte 'M' [1996] EWHC.

48.   See minutes of evidence and appendix, 30 August 1889.

49.   Regulation 20 in Asylum Support Regulations 2000.

50.   David Englander (1998) *Poverty and Poor Law: Reform in 19th Century Britain,* Longman, pp.12 and 15.

51.   Al-Ameri *v.* Royal Borough of Kensington & Chelsea; Osmani *v.* Harrow LBC and Glasgow City Council (intervener) (2004) HL (2004) 1 All ER 1104.

52.   Section 11 of the Asylum and Immigration (Treatment of Claimants etc.) Act 2004.

53.   Sir J. P. B. Kay-Shuttleworth, quoted in Tony Novak (1998) *Poverty and the State,* Open University Press, p.36.

54.   Section 54 and Schedule 3.

55.   Section 9.

56.   Standing Committee B on Asylum and Immigration (Treatment of Claimants, etc.) Bill 2004, 15 January 2004, col. 199.

57.   Beverley Hughes MP, Standing Committee B, Asylum and Immigration (Treatment of Claimants, etc.) Bill, 13 January 2004, col. 154.

58.   Excerpt from a speech given to SS leaders on 4 October 1943 at Posen, Poland. Source: J. Noakes and G. Pridham (1984) *Nazism: A Documentary Reader,* vol. 3, University of Exeter Press, pp. 1199–1200.

CHAPTER 8

1.   Tony Saint, 'They Shall Not Pass', *Sunday Observer,* 1 June 2003.

2.   Steve Cohen (2003), 'The Local State of Immigration Controls', in *No One Is Illegal,* Trentham Books.

3.   Frederick Engels (1978) *The Origin of the Family, Private Property and the State,* Foreign Languages Press (Peking).

4.   Immigration (Carriers Liability) Act 1987 (replaced by Part 2 of the Immigration and Asylum Act 1999 and amended by Schedule 8 of the Nationality, Immigration and Asylum Act 2002)

5.   Section 8 of the Asylum and Immigration Act 1996 as amended by Section 22 of the Immigration and Asylum Act 1999 and section 147 of the Nationality, Immigration and Asylum Act 2002. Employers have a statutory defence if they can show they have checked specified documents. From 1 May 2004, the documents that are acceptable have been amended by NIAA

2002, s147. A national insurance number is no longer sufficient evidence of the right to work. The Home Office has published *Changes to the Law on Preventing Illegal Working: Short Guidance for UK* (April 2004) outlining the acceptable documents.

6. Section 24 of the Immigration and Asylum Act 1999. For history, see Steve Cohen (2001) 'Do You Take this Man to be Your Lawful Wedded Immigration Officer?', *Immigration, Nationality and Asylum Law 15*, 3; reprinted in *No One Is Illegal*, supra.

7. Section 19 of the Asylum and Immigration (Treatment of Claimants, etc.) Act 2004.

8. See *Campaign Against the Proposed Changes to Legal Aid Funding* (report by National Coalition of Anti Deportation Campaigns news services, 13 October 2003).

9. Letter from Legal Services Commission, 4 November 2004, to Bury Law Centre.

10. *Home Office Group Corporate Plan 2004–5*, published by the Home Office Communication Directorate 2004, p.25.

11. Quoted by Peter Sedgwick in his Introduction to Victor Serge (1972) *Year One of the Russian Revolution*, Penguin; reprinted Bookmarks (1992).

12. Orwell: p.20.

13. Ibid.: p.311. Though this is the last page of the novel itself there follows an Appendix on *The Principles of Newspeak*.

14. Ibid.: p.18.

15. Ibid.: p.272.

16. Interestingly the post of Home Secretary (though of course not controls themselves) can in some sense be traced back to as far as the twelfth century, the word *secretarius* in this period retaining its Latin meaning of a person admitted to the secrets of another – a not inappropriate modern usage given the secrecy within which controls and immigration law frequently operate (see Edward Troup, *The Home Office*, Putnams, 1926, p.7).

17. Orwell: pp. 216–217.

18. Ibid.: p.4.

19. Sections 129–133 of the Nationality, Immigration and Asylum Act 2002.

20. Orwell: p.60.

21. Sections 134–139.

22. Channel 4 news, 1 April 2004.

23. Arthur Miller (1955) *A View From The Bridge*, Heinemann Plays (1995), p.50.

24. *The Sun*, 17 March 2004.

25. Section 12 of the Asylum and Immigration (Treatment of Claimants, etc.) Act 2004.

26. Paragraph 4.73.

27. James Fergusson (2004) *Kandahar Cockney: A Tale of Two Worlds*, HarperCollins, p.338.

28. T. W. E. Roche (1969) *The Key in the Lock: Immigration Control in England from 1066 to the Present Day*, John Murray.

29. Ibid.: p.xii.

30. Ibid.: p.100.

31. Ibid.: p.247.

32. *Evening Standard*, 24 April 1968, quoted in Roche, supra, p.245.

33. Roche, supra, p.13.

34. Orwell: p36.

35. Herbert Marcuse (1964) *One Dimensional Man*, Routledge Classics (2002).

36. Ibid.: pp.92–94.

37. Ibid.

38. Roche, supra, p.207.

39. Ibid.: p.110.

40. Ibid.: p.211.

41. *Sunday Observer*, 1 June 2003.

42. Tony Saint (2003) *Refusal Shoes*, Serpent's Tail.

43. Ibid.: p.179.

44. Ibid.: p.102.

45. Sir Edward Troup (1926) *The Home Office*, Putnam's, p.145.

46. See www.pcsunion.com/index.htm.

47. Appendix 31, PCS Memorandum, House of Commons Home Affairs Committee report on Asylum Removals, Fourth Report of Session 2002–03, Vol. 2, HC654-2.

48.   Steve Cohen (1991) 'The Immigration Service Union – A Scab Union', in *For a World Without Borders*, Greater Manchester Immigration Aid Unit.
49.   ISU membership circular 56.
50.   *The Sun*, 16 October 1986.
51.   *Daily Express*, 18 July 1986.
52.   15 October 1986.
53.   During a 1952 tour of the United States a concert was organized on 18 May at the International Peace Arch on the border between Washington State and British Columbia. This was done as an act of defiance against the authorities who refused to allow him to cross the border. Paul Robeson stood on the back of a flatbed truck on the American side of the Canada–US border and performed for a large crowd on the Canadian side, variously estimated at between 20,000 and 40,000.
54.   Asylum Support Regulations 2000, paragraph 15.
55.   Steve Cohen (2003) 'The Local State of Immigration Controls', in *No One Is Illegal*, Trentham Books.
56.   *Jewish Chronicle*, 20 March 1925.
57.   Ibid.: 16 July 1920.
58.   Steve Cohen (2001) *Immigration Controls, the Family and the Welfare State*, Jessica Kingsley Publishers, p.21.
59.   IND ref. IMG/96 1176/1193/23.
60.   Steve Cohen, *Immigration Controls, the Family and the Welfare State*, supra, chs. 12 and 13.
61.   R *v.* Hammersmith and Fulham LBC exp M (1997) I CCLR 85 CA. See also Steve Cohen (2003) *The Local State of Immigration Controls* (supra) and the table of cases in Willman/Knafler/Pierce, *Support for Asylum Seekers*, LAG 2001, for the large number of cases in which local authorities contested liability.
62.   18 March 1999. See Cohen, *The Local State of Immigration Controls*, supra, p.25.
63.   Ibid.
64.   Supra, Appendix 35.
65.   Minutes of Bury Multi-Agency Asylum meeting, 21 January 2004.
66.   Bury Asylum Seekers Team, Bury Council, *Bury Welcomes Asylum Seekers and Refugees*, final draft May 2004.
67.   Rosemary Sales and Rachel Hek (2004) 'Dilemmas of Care and Control: The Work of an Asylum Team in a London Borough', in D. Hayes and B. Humphries (eds.) *Social Work, Immigration and Asylum*, Jessica Kingsley Publishers.
68.   *Manchester City Council's dedicated asylum and refugee services – background information* (undated but sent to author in May 2004).
69.   Dated 15 December 2003.
70.   John Collett (2004) 'Immigration is a Social Work Issue' in Hayes and Humphries, supra (note 67).
71.   Immigration and Asylum Act 1999, Schedule 14, clause 73.
72.   Letter from Fiona Mactaggart MP, on behalf of the Home Office, to Ivan Lewis MP, 27 April 2004.
73.   Camcorder Guerillas at www.camcorderguerillas.net/
74.   *Indymedia Scotland*, 23 June 2004.
75.   Orwell: p. 323.
76.   Email to author, 20 January 2004.
77.   Letter from Fiona Mactaggart MP to Ivan Lewis MP, 19 April 2004. According to this the BNP has never contacted the Home Office regarding immigration.
78.   The Withholding and Withdrawal of Support (Travel Assistance and Temporary Accommodation) Regulations 2002.
79.   M *v.* Islington, CA [2004] EWCA Civ 235, Lord Justice Buxton, paragraphs 20–21.
80.   Asylum and Immigration (Treatment of Claimants, etc.) Act, Sections 10(7)(b)(ii) and 10(9).
81.   Asylum and Immigration (Treatment of Claimants, etc.) Bill, Committee (on Recommitment), House of Lords, 15 June 2004.
82.   15 April 2003.
83.   11 April 2003.
84.   Orwell: p.319.

85. NASS eventually resigned from the group under pressure of the group's members, though some voluntary-sector agencies (not including asylum-seekers themselves) wanted NASS to remain.

86. Letter to author, undated.

87. For further reading on the information presented in this section (pp.139–141) see Steve Cohen (2002) 'Dining With the Devil' in Steve Cohen, Beth Humphries and Ed Mynott (eds.) *From Immigration Controls to Welfare Controls*, Routledge. Reprinted in *No One Is Illegal*, supra.

88. Letter from Fiona Mactaggart MP, on behalf of the Home Office, to Ivan Lewis MP, 26 March 2004.

89. Letter from Wendy Coello of the Home Office RANS Unit to Millie Barratt of the (Voluntary Sector) Inter-Agency Team, 1 April 2003.

90. Under Section 98 of the Immigration and Asylum Act 1999.

91. The Court of Appeal has recently ruled in the case of Limbuela and others that Section 55, where it results in homelessness, can be a breach of human rights by resulting in inhuman and degrading treatment. The case went to the House of Lords (*Guardian Unlimited*, 21 May 2004).

92. Explained in a letter from Fiona Mactaggart MP to Ivan Lewis MP on 22 January 2004. Agencies with funding (2002/3) are Migrant Helpline (£6,300,000), Refugee Action (£3,800,000), Refugee Arrivals Project (£2,150,000), Refugee Council (£11,000,000), Scottish Refugee Council (£1,100,000), Welsh Refugee Council (£445,000).

93. Email correspondence circulated by NCADC, 25 April 2004.

94. Letter in *Red Pepper*, April 2004.

95. Supra, note 81.

96. See article by Steve Cohen in *Solidarity*, 2 June 2005.

97. Email from Nigel Rose of Refugee Action of 19 November 2004.

98. Orwell: p.14.

99. BBC news, 20 December 2004.

100. Mario Savio, Berkeley University sit-in, 1964, quoted in Mark Kurlansky (2004) *1968: The Year that Rocked the World*, Jonathan Cape, quotes at start of book.

101. Edmund Burke (1770) 'Thoughts on the Cause of the Present Discontents,' in Henry Froude (ed.) *The Works of the Right Honourable Edmund Burke*, vol. 2, Oxford University Press (1909), p.83.

CHAPTER 9

1.   David Roskies (1999) *The Jewish Search for a Usable Past*, Indiana University Press, p.18.

2.   Orwell: p.37.

3.   Ibid.: p.36.

4.   Ibid.: p.81.

5.   Ibid.: p.259.

6.   Ibid.: p.37.

7.   Ibid.: p.43.

8.   *Daily Telegraph*, 7 April 2004.

9.   Orwell: p.227.

10. Ibid.: p.9.

11. Ibid.: p.29.

12. In *Fahrenheit 451*, Montag declares that he burns books to ashes and then burns the ashes – 'That's our official motto'.

13. For further reading on the information in this section (pp.144–145) see Steve Cohen (1988) *From the Jews to the Tamils*, South Manchester Law Centre; reprinted in part in Steve Cohen (2003) 'All In The Same Boat', in *No One Is Illegal*, Trentham Books.

14. Orwell: p.312.

15. *Hansard*, 3 June 1985.

16. Ibid.: 18 February 1987.

17. Ibid.: 16 March 1987.

18. Paragraph 8.1. Cm 4018.

19. *Hansard*, 17 December 2003.

20. *Jewish Chronicle*, 25 October 1907.

21. Ibid.: 1 November 1907.

22.   Ibid.: 25 October 1907.
23.   Louise London (2000) *Whitehall and the Jews 1933–1948: British Immigration Policy and the Holocaust*, Cambridge University Press.
24.   September 2003.
25.   For further reading on the information presented in this section (pp.147–149) see Steve Cohen (1987) *It's the Same Old Story*, Manchester City Council. Also Steve Cohen (2003) 'Anti-Semitism, Immigration Controls and the Welfare State', in *No One Is Illegal*, Trentham Books.
26.   Both quotes from *The Eighteenth Brumaire of Louis Bonaparte* 1852, p.1.
27.   Steve Cohen, *Workers Control Not Immigration Controls*, Greater Manchester Immigration Aid Unit, undated.
28.   In particular Bill Morris who, when General secretary of the Transport and General Workers Union, was constantly critical of that aspect of the immigration poor law whereby NASS 'supported' asylum-seekers by giving them vouchers, not money (*Guardian Unlimited*, 29 September 2000).
29.   Pp. 186–7.
30.   *Manchester Evening News*, 11 July 1895.
31.   See generally on the TUC: Miles and Phizacklea (1977) *The TUC, Black Workers and New Commonwealth Immigration 1954–1973*, Research Unit on Ethnic Relations Working Papers no. 6, University of Aston.
32.   *The Guardian*, 11 July 1957.
33.   Ibid.: 2 September 1958.
34.   *Jewish Chronicle*, 17 January 1902, and *East London Observer*, 18 January 1902.
35.   Robert Tressell (1912) *The Ragged Trousered Philanthropists*, Lawrence & Wishart (1955), p.22.
36.   *London Evening News*, 27 May 1891 and 19 June 1891.
37.   *Labour Leader*, 19 December 1894.
38.   *The Clarion*, 12 October 1895.
39.   *Jewish Chronicle*, 1 April 1904.
40.   *Commonwealth*, 28 April 1888. See also *It's the Same Old Story*, supra (note 25), p14.
41.   Orwell: p.188.
42.   *Fairer, Faster and Firmer*, paragraphs 9.9 and 9.10, 1998 Cm 4018.
43.   Orwell: p.37.
44.   These are the titles of Chapters 2 and 3 of David Roskies' *The Jewish Search for a Usable Past*, Indiana University Press, 1999. These chapters provide the information detailed in the section below (pp.151–152).
45.   Ibid.: p.20.
46.   Ibid.: pp.23 and 26.

CHAPTER 10

1.   A fifteen-year-old Iraqi boy, detained by Australia for over two years while his family sought asylum, described his desperation that he had not been allowed to go to a normal school for the duration of his detention. He had already attempted suicide on more than one occasion. From *By Invitation Only, Australian Asylum Policy* (2002) Human Rights Watch, New York, p.80.
2.   Quoted in Michelle Lowry and Peter Nyers (2003) 'Roundtable Report. No One Is Illegal – The Fight for Refugee and Migrant Rights in Canada', in *Refuge: Canada's Periodical on Refugees 21*, 3, May.
3.   Ibid.: describing the occupation of the Canadian immigration office in Montreal in solidarity with a family under threat of deportation.
4.   BBC news, 19 June 2000.
5.   *Guardian Unlimited*, 9 February 2004.
6.   Peter Kwong (1997) *Forbidden Workers: Illegal Chinese Immigrants and American Labor*, New Press.
7.   Orwell: p.11.
8.   Ibid.: p.4.
9.   John Steinbeck (2002) *Travels With Charley: In search of America*, Penguin Books.
10.   Arthur Koestler (1940) *Darkness at Noon*, Vintage (1994), p.27.

11. For an overview of Orwell's politics, see Paul Flewers (2000) *I Know How, But I don't Know Why – George Orwell's Conception of Totalitarianism*, New Interventions. For a study of contradictions within *Nineteen Eighty-Four* and within Orwell's socialism generally, see Paul Flewers (ed.) (2005) *George Orwell, Enigmatic Socialist*, Socialist Platform.

12. However, also see Orwell's 1945 essay 'Second Thoughts on James Burnham' in *Shooting an Elephant and Other Essays*, Secker and Warburg (1950). Orwell here agrees with Burnham's description in *The Managerial Revolution* of the convergence towards managerialism but denies this is historically inevitable.

13. George Orwell, *Animal Farm*, Penguin (1989), pp.89 and 90.

14. George Orwell, 'Inside the Whale', reprinted in *Inside the Whale and Other Essays*, Penguin (1967), pp.17.

15. Ibid.: p.48.

16. Orwell: p.205.

17. Ibid.: p.195.

18. Upton Sinclair (1986) *The Jungle*, Penguin, p.189.

19. Ibid.: p.77.

20. BBC news (UK edition), 28 April 2004.

21. Jack Mapanje (2004) 'Fleeting Child of the 3-Day Week', in *The Last of the Sweet Bananas*, Bloodaxe Books, p.202.

22. For further reading on the information presented in this section (pp.158–159) see Steve Cohen (1992) *Imagine There's No Countries*, Greater Manchester Immigration Aid Unit, ch. 2.

23. Now renamed the (Orwellian) Immigration and Nationality Directorate.

24. 2 July 2004.

25. Nacera Kellou from the Action Committee for Non-Status Algerians, quoted in 'Roundtable Report', supra (note 2).

26. *Post*, Western Australia, 6 December 2003.

27. *Guardian Unlimited*, 17 December 2003.

28. See www.ranchrescue.com/

29. Email of 4 May 2004 on the smartgroup ccrlist@yorku.ca

30. Eithne Luibhéid (2002) *Entry Denied: Controlling Sexuality at the Border*, University of Minnesota Press, p.4.

31. *The Guardian*, 19 July 2004.

32. Virgil, *The Aeneid*, 1–46 (Quae regio in terris nostri non plena laboris).

33. Orwell: p.184.

34. Ibid.: pp.266–267.

35. Ibid.: p.280.

36. Jack London (1990) *The Iron Heel*, Journeyman Press, p.63.

37. See Flewers (2000), supra (note 11).

38. I. Deutscher (1969) 'Nineteen Eighty-Four: The Mysticism of Cruelty', in *Heretics and Renegades*, p.35; quoted in Flewers (2000), supra, p.21.

39. Deutscher, supra; quoted in Flewers (2000), p.1.

40. Orwell: pp.132–133.

41. Ibid.: pp.72, 89, 229.

42. Ibid.: p.172.

43. Ibid.: p.230.

44. Ibid.: pp.163, 184.

45. Mark O'Brien (2000) 'Class Struggle and the English Poor Laws', in Lavalette and Mooney (eds.) *Class Struggle and Social Welfare*, Routledge, p.32.

46. *Guardian Unlimited*, 13 August 2003.

47. See Chapter 7.

48. *Jewish Chronicle*, 21 September 1894. On Jewish resistance generally, see Steve Cohen (1987) *It's the Same Old Story*, Manchester City Council, pp.18–19.

49. *Jewish Chronicle*, 13 December 1895.

50. Ibid.: 7 June 1901.

51. Ibid.: 24 January 1902.

52. *London Eastern Post and Chronicle*, 20 August 1902.

53. *Jewish Chronicle*, 17 June 1904, and *Manchester Guardian* 20 June 1904.

54.   Steve Cohen (1997) *It's the Same Old Story,* Manchester City Council, p.15.
55.   An original copy can be found in the Rollin Collection at the Modern Records Centre, University of Warwick library.
56.   Orwell: .p30.
57.   Email of 16 January 2004 on the smartgroup ccrlist@yorku.ca
58.   Ibid.: 28 November 2003.
59.   For more on the campaign, see Janet Batsleer (1988) 'The Viraj Mendis Defence Campaign: Struggles and Experience of Sanctuary', *Critical Social Policy* no. 22. Also Eddie Abrahams (1989) *Citizenship and Rights: The Deportation of Viraj Mendis, Critical Social Policy.*
60.   For more on the sanctuary movement in the USA, see Steve Cohen (1988) 'Sanctuary in the USA', *Legal Action,* September 1988; also a review of the literature by Steve Cohen in *Immigration and Nationality Law and Practice,* October 1988.
61.   *Sunday Herald,* 11 April 2004.
62.   Steve Cohen, *Workers Control Not Immigration Controls,* Greater Manchester Immigration Aid Unit, undated.
63.   See AlterNet at www.alternet.org/story/16835
64.   *Leeds Today (Yorkshire Evening Post),* 19 December 2003.
65.   BASW circular to members on the 2004 Act, 24 March 2004.
66.   *Society Guardian,* 16 May 2004.
67.   For details see www.mpunion.org.uk.
68.   Steve Cohen (2004) 'Breaking the Links: Pulling the Plug' in Hayes and Humphries (eds.) *Social Work, Immigration and Asylum,* Jessica Kingsley Publishers 2004.
69.   Bill Williams (1976) *The Making of Manchester Jewry 1740–1875,* Manchester University Press, pp.288–289.
70.   *The Guardian,* 23 October 2002.
71.   BBC, 12 April 2005.
72.   Quoted in Teresa Hayter (2004) *Open Borders: The Case Against Immigration Controls,* 2nd edn., Pluto Press p.151.
73.   Steve Cohen (2003) 'Preface' in *No One Is Illegal,* Trentham Books, p.17.
74.   See Weisel's essay in Gary MacEoin (ed.) (1985) *Sanctuary: A Resource Guide for Participating in the Central American Refugee Struggle,* Harper & Row.
75.   See note 41.

CHAPTER 11

1.   See *America: A Freedom Country,* published by the Lutheran Immigration and Refugee Service, Baltimore, 2004.
2.   Tariq Mehmood (2003) *While There is Light,* Comma Press, p.28.
3.   Genesis 11, pp.1–9.
4.   Paul Chilton suggests that the language theme in Orwell's novel has its roots in the story of the Tower of Babel; see Chilton (1988) *Orwellian Language and the Media,* Pluto Press.
5.   *Hansard,* 22 February 1996.
6.   Ibid.: 11 December 1995.
7.   Orwell: p.303.
8.   Paul Flewers (2000) *I Know How, But I don't Know Why: George Orwell's Conception of Totalitarianism,* New Interventions, p.22.
9.   Orwell: p.18.
10.   Ibid.: p.14.
11.   Ibid.: pp.16–17.
12.   See: Isaac Deutscher (1970) *The Prophet Outcast,* Oxford University Press, pp.16–19; Colin Holmes (1979) *Trotsky and Britain, The Closed File,* Study in Labour History, Bulletin 39; Leon Trotsky (1930) 'The Planet Without a Visa', in *My Life,* first published 1930, available online at www.marxists.org/archive/trotsky/works/ 1930-lif/index.htm.
13.   Francis Wheen (1999) *Karl Marx,* Fourth Estate, p.356.
14.   *Hansard,* 23 February 2005.
15.   *Sunday Telegraph,* 21 January 2005.

16. Orwell: p.4.
17. *Daily Telegraph*, 12 February 2005.
18. Orwell: p.60.
19. BBC news (world edition), 29 April 2004.
20. *Society Guardian*, 5 April 2002.
21. ic www.birmingham.gov.uk 4 August 2005
22. Orwell: p.220.
23. Ibid.: p.8.
24. Chapter 5.
25. Orwell: p. 220.
26. The Aliens Act 1905, the Aliens Restrictions Act 1914, and the Aliens Restrictions (Amendment) Act 1919.
27. The Commonwealth Immigrants Act 1962, the Commonwealth Immigrants Act 1968, the Immigration Act 1971, the British Nationality Act 1981, the Carriers Liability Act 1986, and the Immigration Act 1988.
28. The Asylum and Immigration Appeals Act 1993, the Asylum and Immigration Act 1996, the Immigration and Asylum Act 1999, the Nationality, Immigration and Asylum Act 2002, and the Asylum and Immigration (Treatment of Claimants, etc.) Act 2004.
29. Orwell: p.36.
30. Margaret Phelan and James Gillespie (2003) *Immigration Law Handbook* 3rd edn., Oxford University Press.
31. Orwell: p.201.
32. See series of written answers to David Crausby MP: *Hansard*, 15 January and 2 February 2004.
33. See the preface and Chapter 5.
34. Steve Cohen (2003) 'We're Still in the Same State', *Jewish Socialist*, no. 48, summer.
35. W. H. Wilkins (1892), *The Alien Invasion*, London, p.47.
36. Quoted in Bernard Gainer (1972) *The Alien Invasion*, Heinemann, p.156.
37. Edgar Wallace (1950) *The Four Just Men*, Pan Books, p.119.
38. See Gainer, supra (note 35); pp.206–207.
39. *Times*, 8 August 2005
40. *Guardian Unlimited*, 23 May 2001.
41. Words of one of the refugees acquitted after being charged with arson to Yarl's Wood detention centre.

APPENDIX 1

1. See p.164 in this book for information on the publication of this leaflet.
2. Report of the Board of Trade, 1891-92-93, p.9.
3. *Dictionary of Statistics* p. 247.
4. Ibid.: pp.579, 583, 251.
5. Booth's *Life and Labour of the People*, p.213.
6. Report of the Board of Trade, 1891-92-93, pp.93, 94.
7. Report of the Board of Trade, 1891-92-93, pp.93, 94.

APPENDIX 2

1. See p.164 in this book for information on the publication of this manifesto.

INDEX

Endnotes are denoted by the letter n after the page number followed by the note number; for example, 204n72 refers to note 72 on page 204